MANGA MUSCLES

AN ARTIST'S GUIDE TO DRAWING POWERFUL MALE BODIES

Syu Itadori | Kishi Ueno | KiKi | GomTang

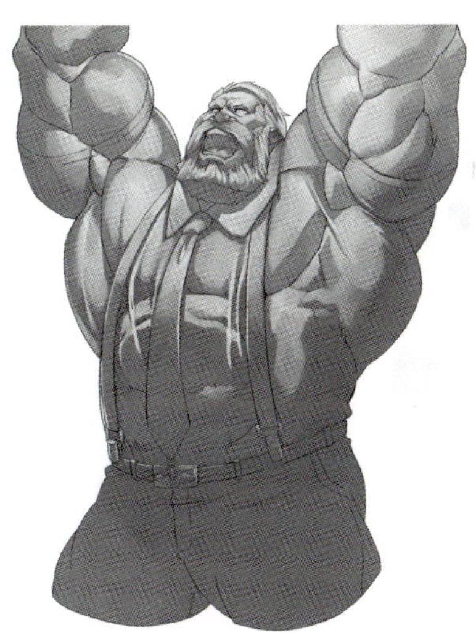

TUTTLE Publishing

Tokyo | Rutland, Vermont | Singapore

Table of Contents

Basic Concepts

CHAPTER 1:

How to Draw Muscles—The Basics

CHAPTER 2:

Various Ways to Draw Muscles

CHAPTER 3:

Differentiating Characters

Basic Concepts

What Are Strong Muscles?

About the Muscles Covered in This Book

The muscles and their explanations covered in this book, including the basics, are all intentionally hyper-fictionalized muscles, essentially forming a fantasy anatomical framework.

This book is a specialized study focused on illustrations of the strong muscles that appear in fighting games, comics, manga and movies. Therefore, it greatly differs from real anatomy and structure.

These are muscles that cannot exist in reality, but do exist in illustrations. You may have seen them but cannot draw them because they differ from reality. This book explains such fictional muscles.

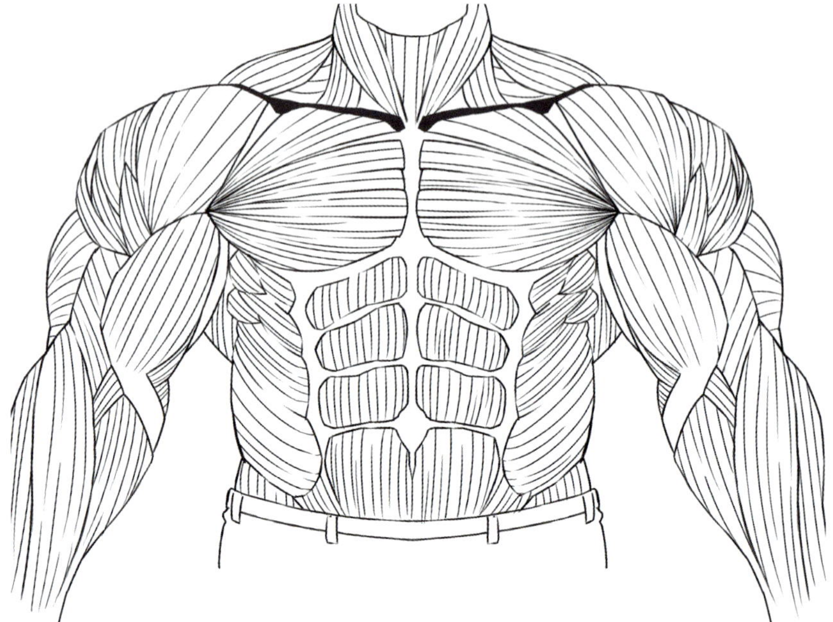

What is Skeletal Muscle?

Additionally, muscles have common names, anatomical names, artistic names, and bodybuilding names, and the names may change depending on the genre. This book primarily uses names based on artistic anatomy but may use terms or names from other genres in some explanations.

Muscles are tissues with the property of contraction that constitute an animal's organs of movement. There are three types of muscles: *visceral muscles* (muscles that operate in internal organs), *cardiac muscles* (muscles that make up the walls of the heart), and *skeletal muscles*. Among these, this book deals with skeletal muscles. Skeletal muscles primarily attach to the skeleton and support or move it. When animals move their limbs, it is these muscles that move the body.

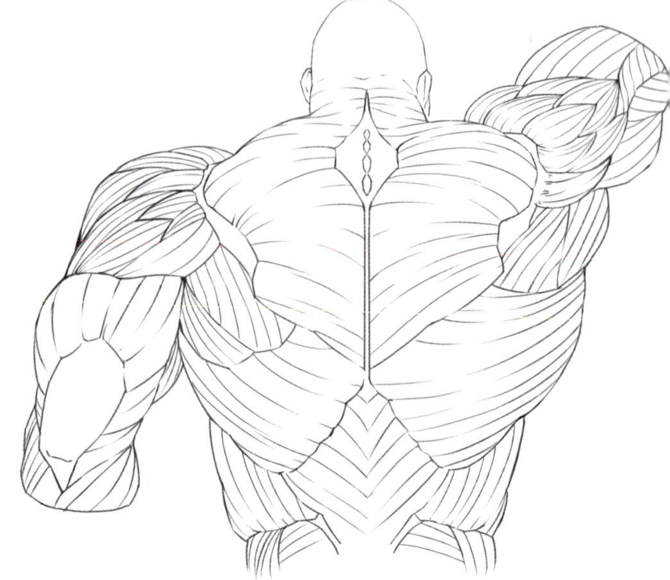

Mechanism and Basics of Muscles

Muscle Contraction

Each skeletal muscle is not a single tissue but a bundle of long tubes called *muscle fibers*. Animals can move their limbs because their muscles contract during movement.

Muscle movement involves both contraction and relaxation. By contracting, muscles bulge and change shape. For this reason, the muscles used to move the body, called "agonist muscles," often come in pairs.

Thus, the structure of muscles is very important for animals and humans. Before drawing muscular characters, let's first look into what kinds of muscles exist.

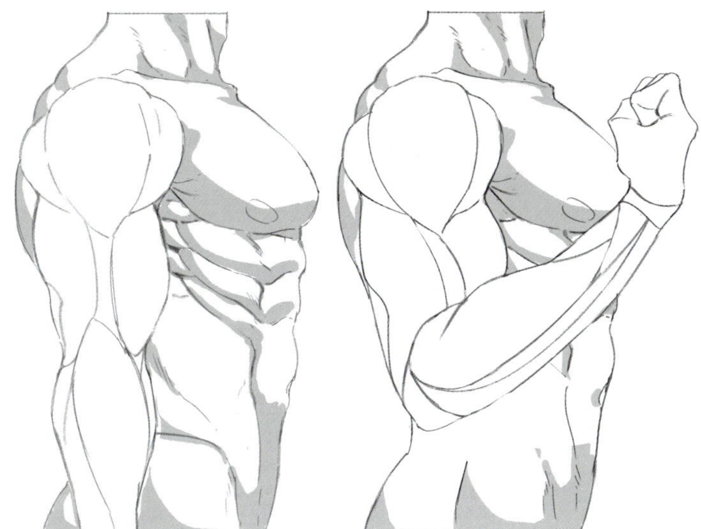

Main Muscle Shapes

Refer to page 12 for the names of each muscle.

Convergent Muscles

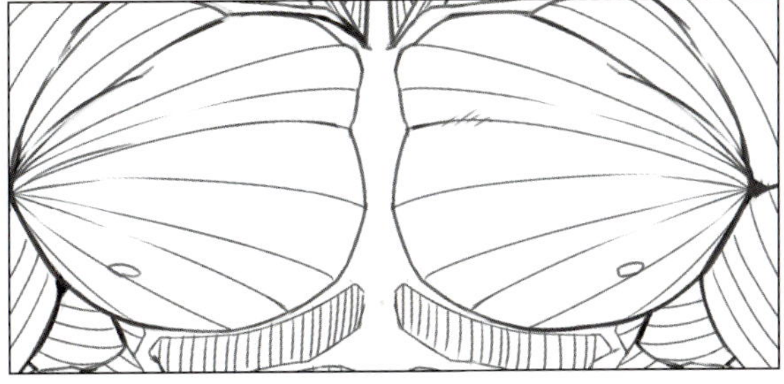

These muscles spread out from the base in multiple directions. The pectoral muscles are a typical example.

Pennate Muscles

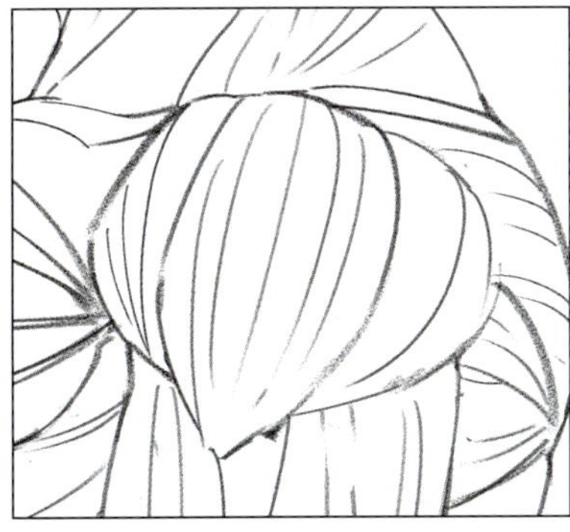

The deltoid muscles are representative examples of these muscles, which split into multiple sections from the base.

Fusiform Muscles

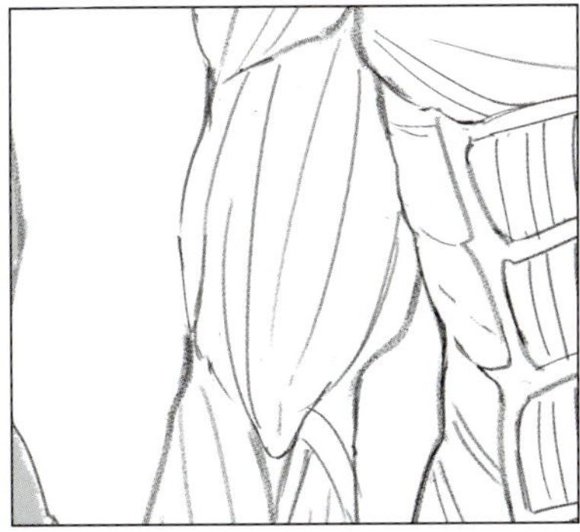

As the name suggests, these muscles are shaped like a spindle (a spoke of a spinning wheel). The biceps brachii is a typical example.

Rectus Abdominis

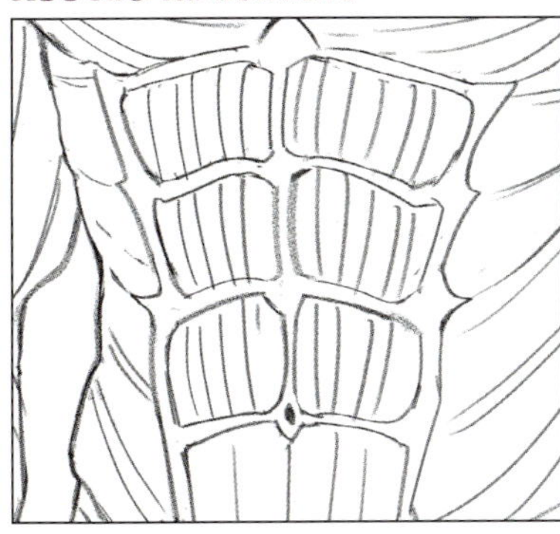

Commonly known as the abdominal muscles, or "abs," these muscles run straight and vertically from the ribs to the pubic bone.

Actual Muscles and Manga Muscles

Exaggerated Body Types

The muscular body types that appear in fighting games, manga, etc. are drawn with strong exaggeration compared to actual muscles. It becomes clear when you compare them with a more realistic human body type (light blue in the drawing to the right). The differences are not only in size and muscle mass but also at the skeletal level.

For example, the skeleton on the right side of the drawing has an exaggeratedly large rib cage and wide shoulders that would not be so broad without larger, thicker clavicles and arm bones.

When drawing strongly exaggerated muscles, it is necessary to intentionally deviate from the structure of real skeletons and muscles. The character on the right side of the drawing has arms and legs drawn much larger in proportion to their height. Normally, they would be smaller, but they are drawn larger to maintain the sense of proportion in the drawing.

The body types and muscles covered in this book, throughout both the basic and differentiated drawing sections, are these hyper-fictionalized muscles. In other words, they are fantasy anatomical diagrams.

Of course, there are parts that align with actual anatomy, but they are also significantly modified in specific ways for the purpose of illustration. Please use this book with the understanding that the forms portrayed here are rather different from real anatomy.

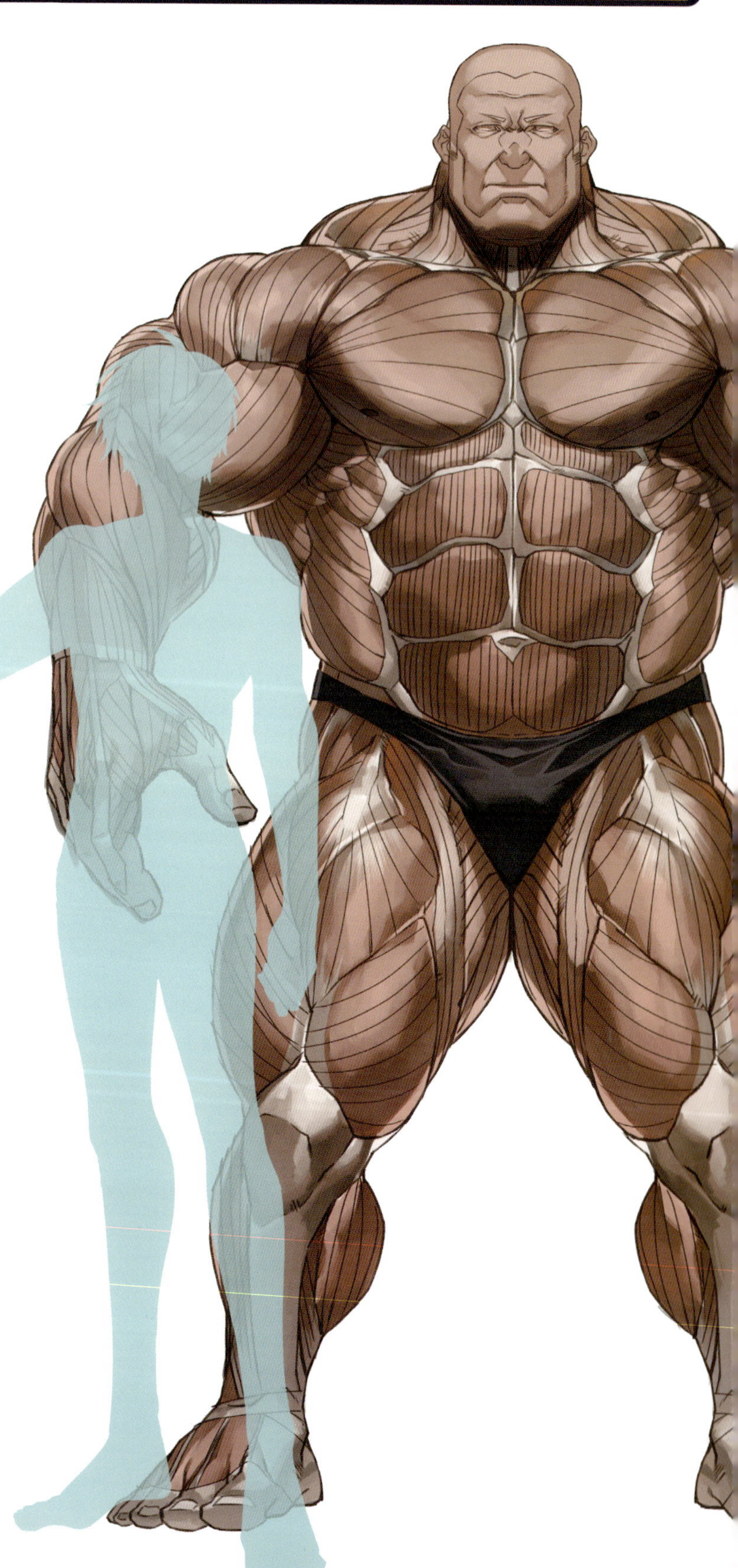

Knowing the Basics for Fiction

This book covers imaginary anatomical diagrams starting with the basics. If you understand the basics of actual human muscles, it becomes easier to draw convincing fictional muscles.

Knowing the muscles that exist in the human body allows you to draw exaggerated muscles more naturally and in a cool style.

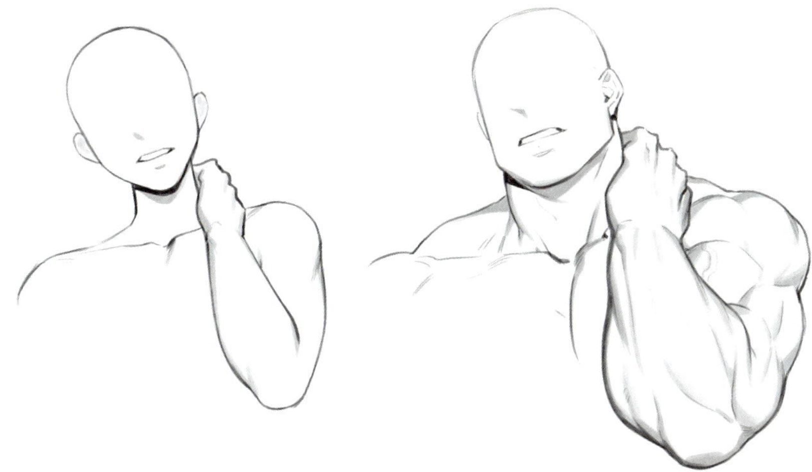

Varying Levels of Exaggeration According to the Character

When drawing exaggerated muscles, it is also important to adjust the level of exaggeration to fit the character you want to depict.

For example, for a lean type of character, you would draw them closer to a realistic skeleton and with muscles that fit a realistically athletic person. The further the muscle mass and skeleton deviate from the realistic human form, the more the character takes on a superhuman appearance. This enhances the impression of the character as a "power type" (as shown in the lower pair of the illustrations to the right).

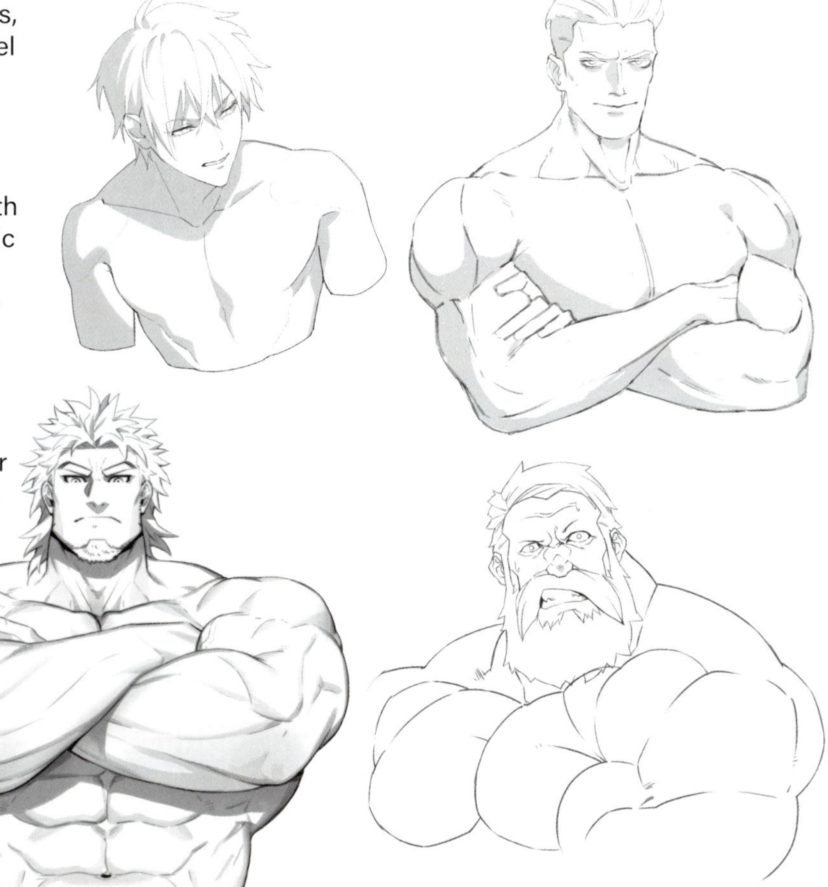

Body Type Comparison

In this book, muscles are primarily divided into four types for explanation: lean body type, muscular body type, heavyweight bodybuilder body type and fantasy titan body type. While all of these are more muscular and defined than the average physique, each has its own distinct characteristics in how they are drawn.

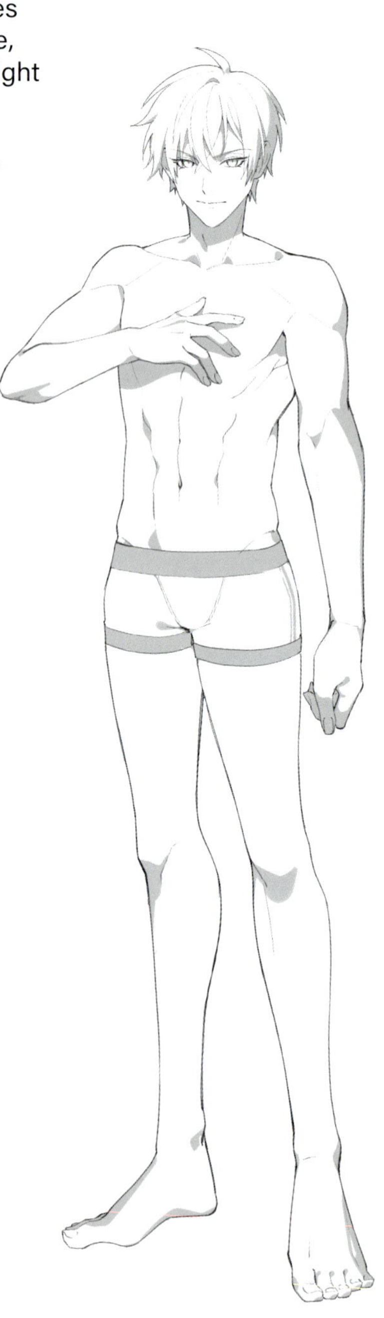

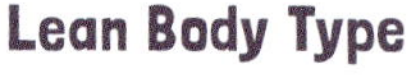

Lean Body Type

In this book, this is considered a relatively slim body type. Generally, it still falls into the category of "very fit." It gives a well-proportioned impression and is suitable for young or handsome characters.

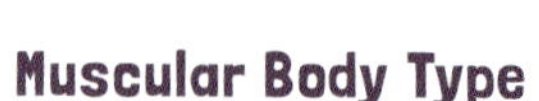

Muscular Body Type

A well-trained athlete's body type. These muscles give the impression of being consciously developed through sports or work. They provide a masculine and powerful impression.

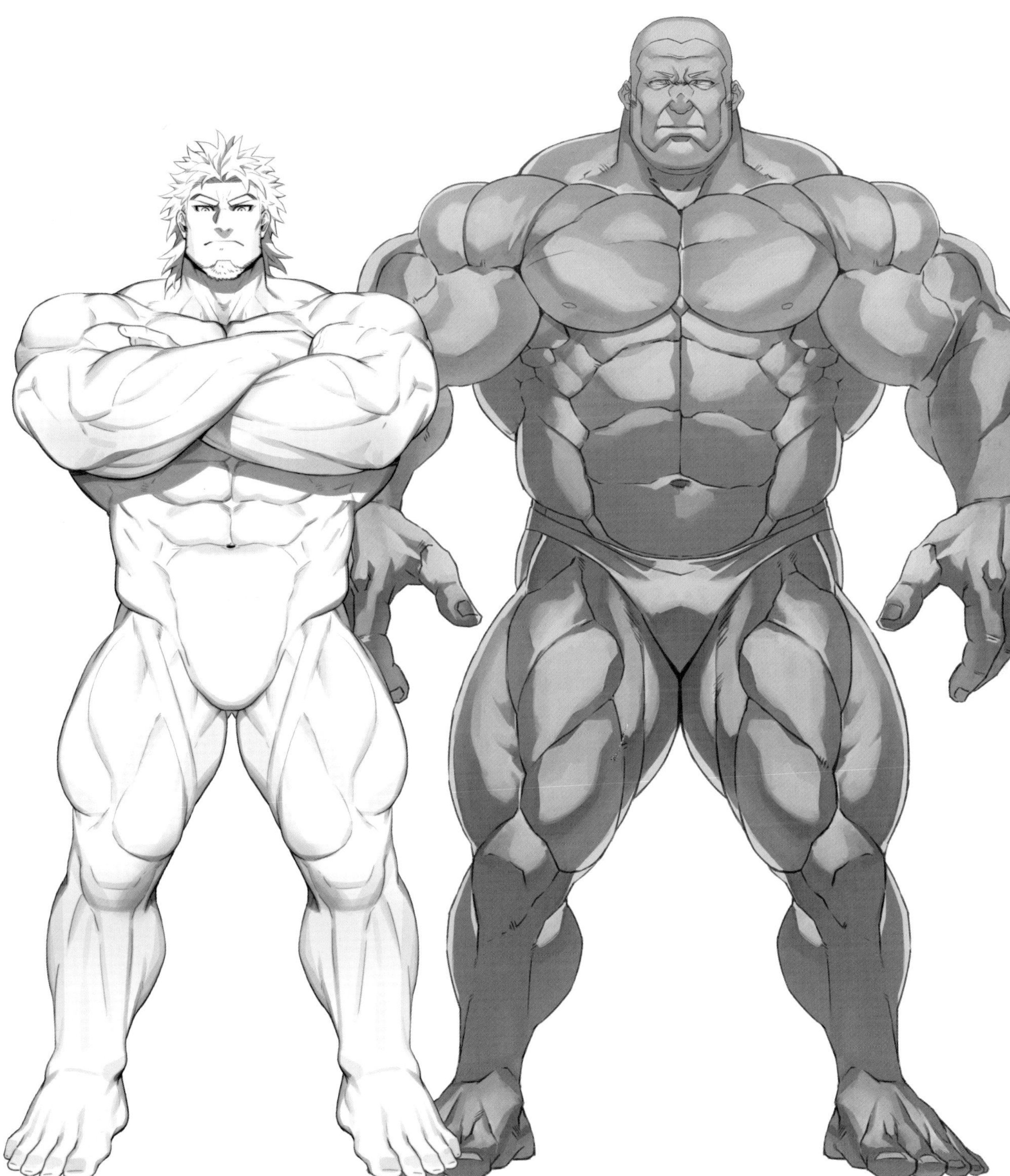

Heavyweight Bodybuilder Body Type

A bodybuilding physique with extremely developed muscles. Each muscle is significantly enlarged, and the contours are greatly altered from the average body type. It is immediately recognizable as a "power type" physique.

Fantasy Titan Body Type

Muscles that go beyond reality. In addition to the muscles, the shoulders and limbs are also larger. The skeleton itself differs from the average build and is commonly seen in fighting game characters.

The Appeal and Contrast of Giant Characters

Exaggerating Size

One method to showcase the impact and sense of threat of muscular characters is through "size exaggeration." Let's look at an example where a muscular protagonist character (bottom right of the illustration) is contrasted with another character.

When depicted at a normal height (for example, around 2 meters), the muscular protagonist will appear puny compared to the massive antagonist, and this contrast is further emphasized due to the depth perspective. In the illustration below, the inconceivably muscular antagonist is sized over 3 meters. By drawing the character much larger than the protagonist, their impact is enhanced. Juxtaposing contrasting-size characters will better express each characters' strength and size.

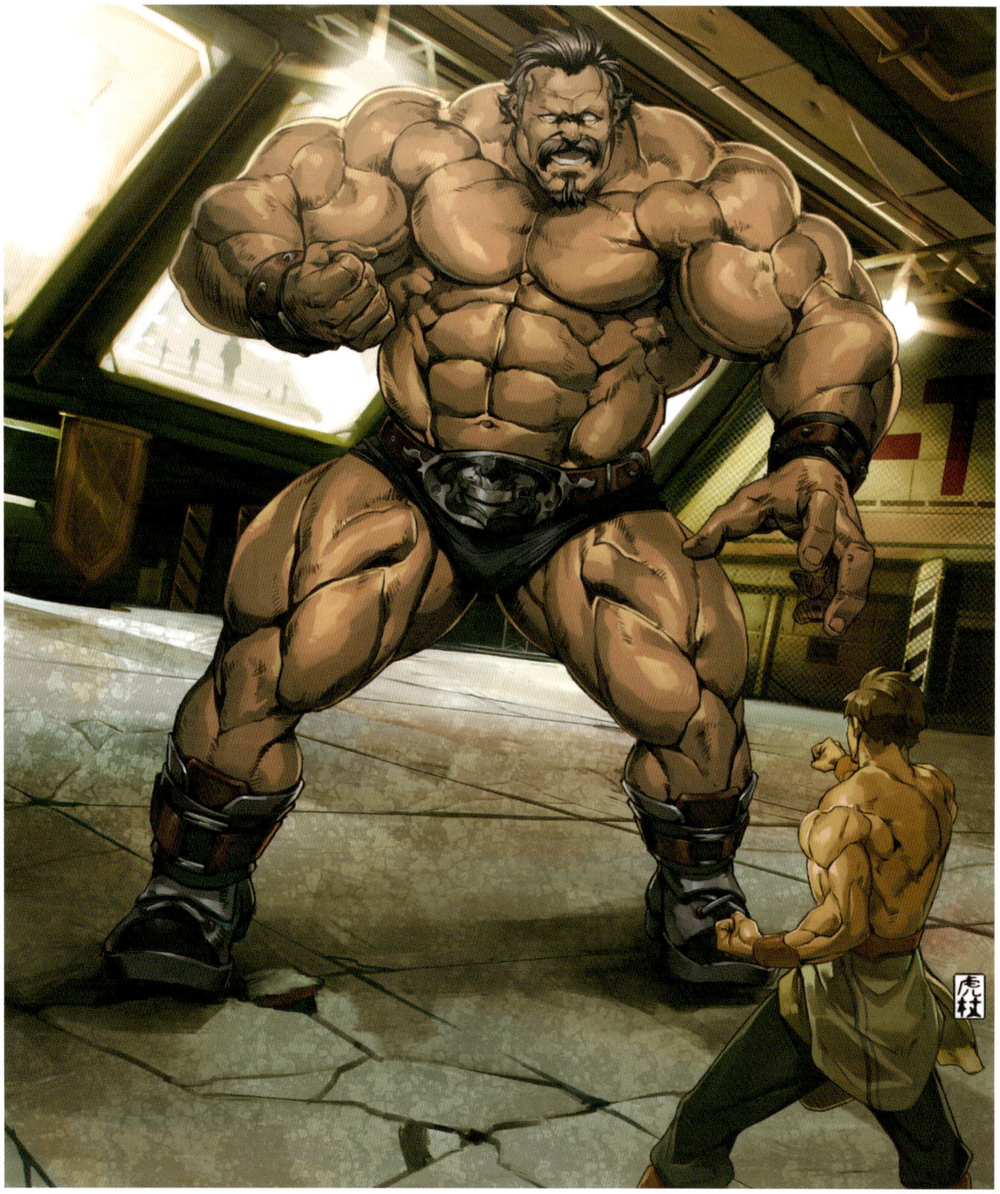

CHAPTER 1

How to Draw Muscles —The Basics

Full-Body Muscle Diagram—Front View

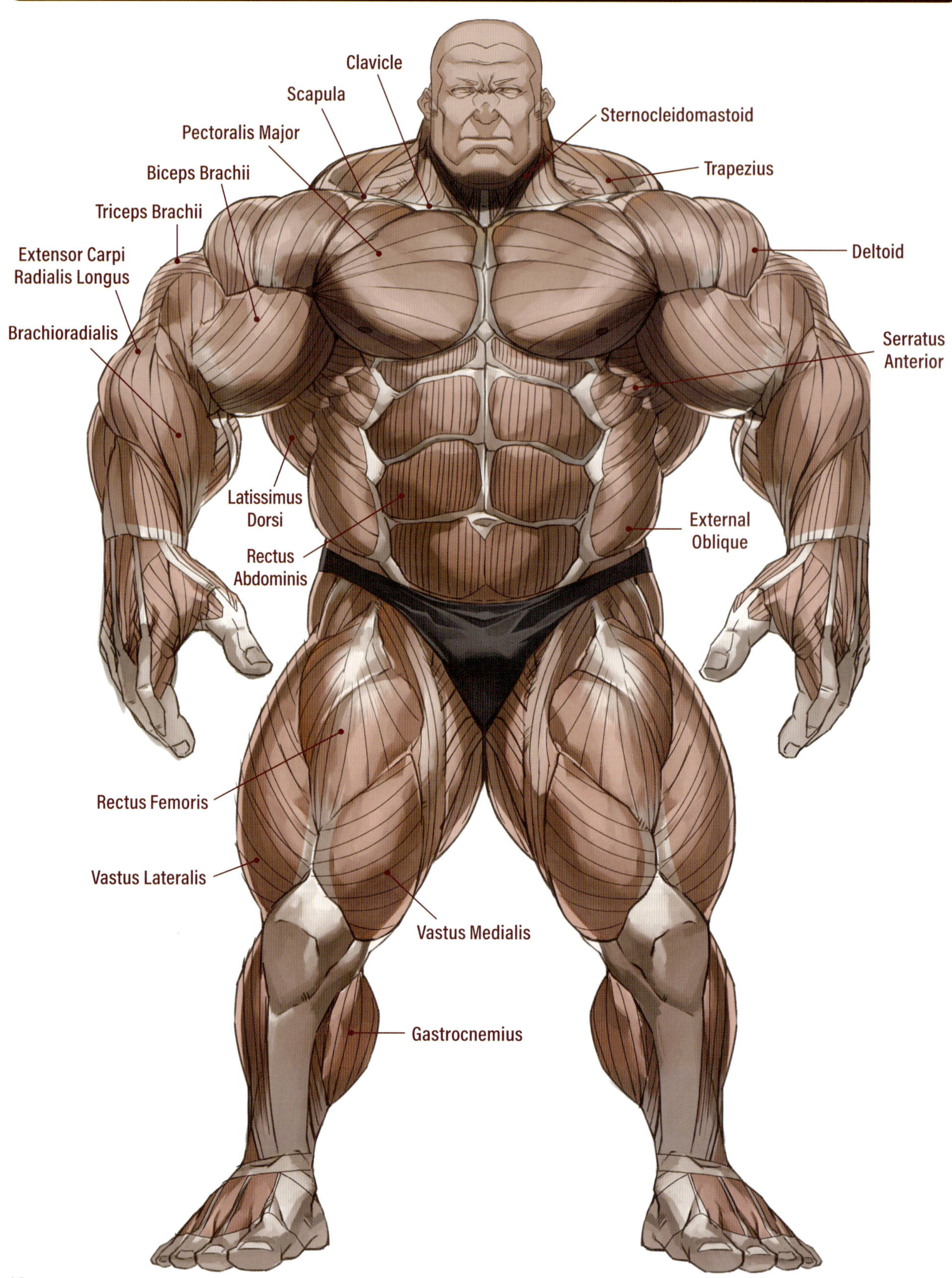

Muscles Viewed from the Front

First, let's look at the entire body's muscles from the front. In the exaggerated muscular body types found in manga, each muscle is clearly depicted in relief. You can create a silhouette that is radically different from the usual body type by explicitly detailing the muscles around the neck, shoulders and legs. The exaggerated body type does not completely adhere to actual human physiology. However, by tracing the positions of real muscles, the body type gains credibility.

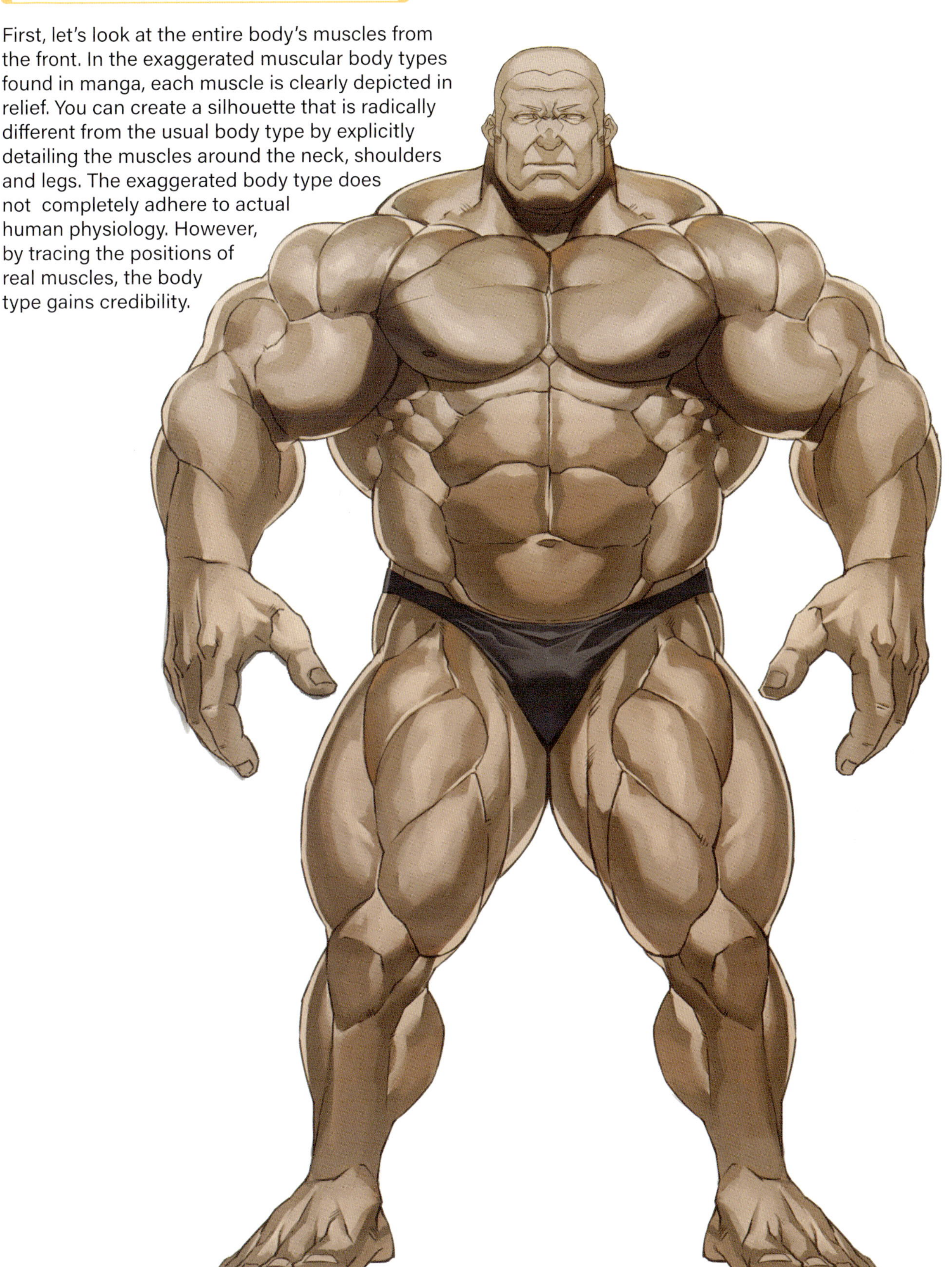

Full-Body Muscle Diagram—Side View

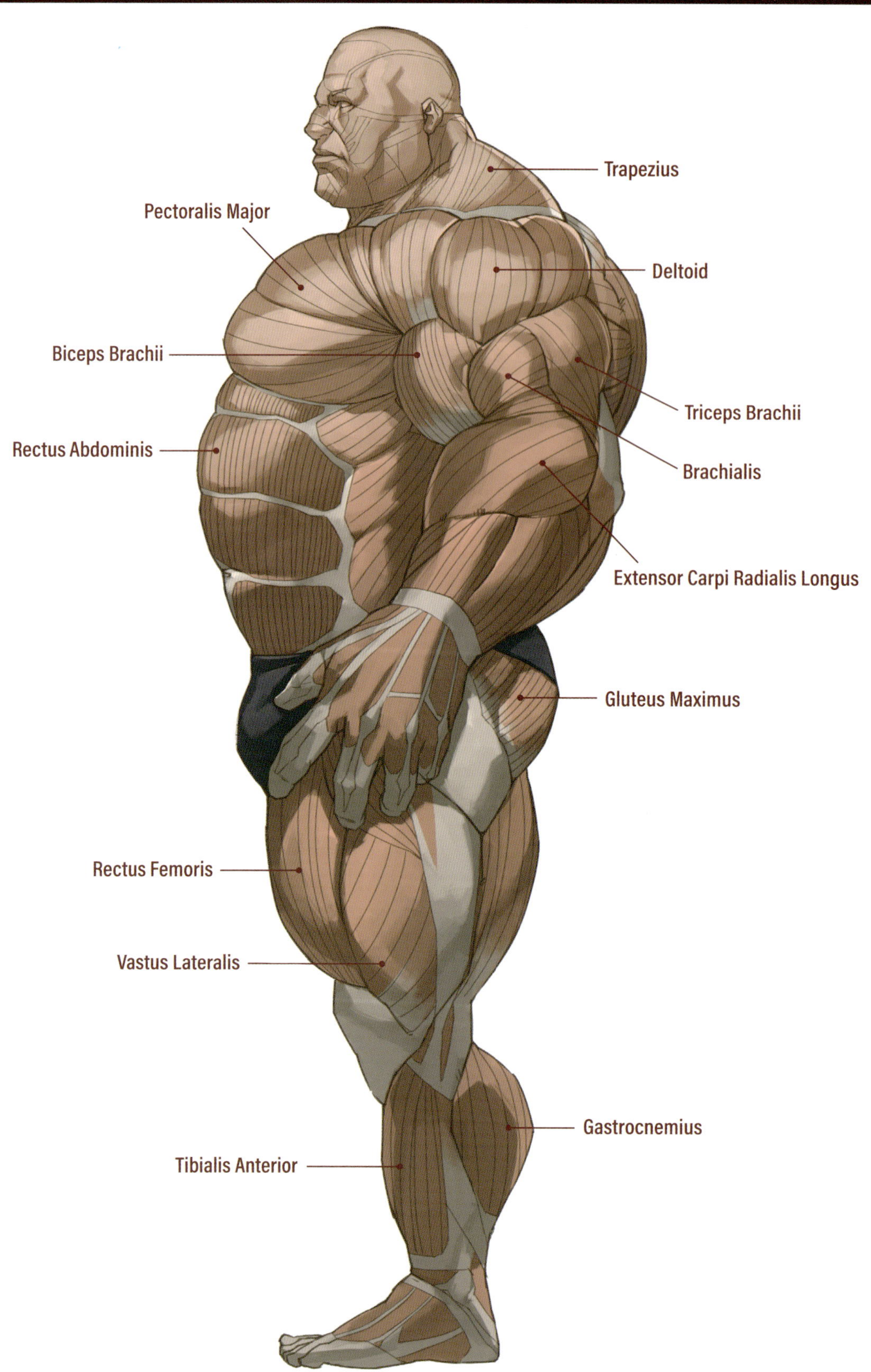

Muscles Viewed from the Side

Let's look at the entire body from the side. The bulges of muscles that were not apparent from the front become prominent. In the upper body, the pectoralis major, deltoid and trapezius muscles bulge significantly, giving the overall silhouette a spindle shape.*

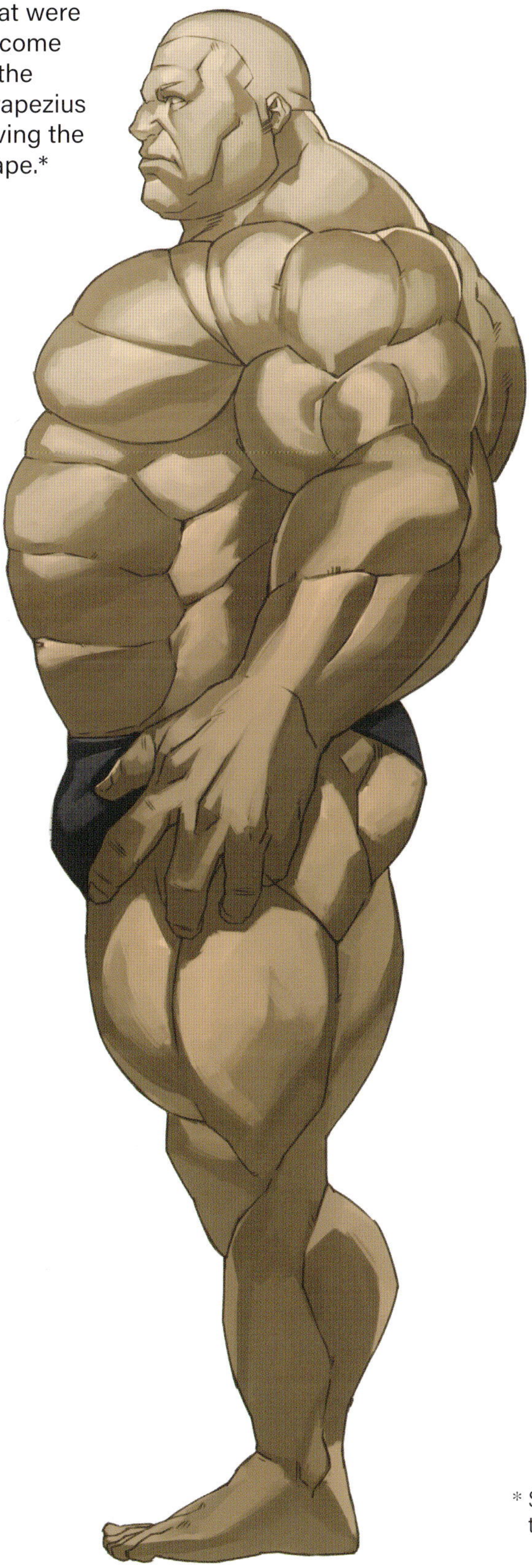

* Spindle-shaped: cylindrical with a thicker central part and thinner ends.

Full-Body Muscle Diagram—Back View

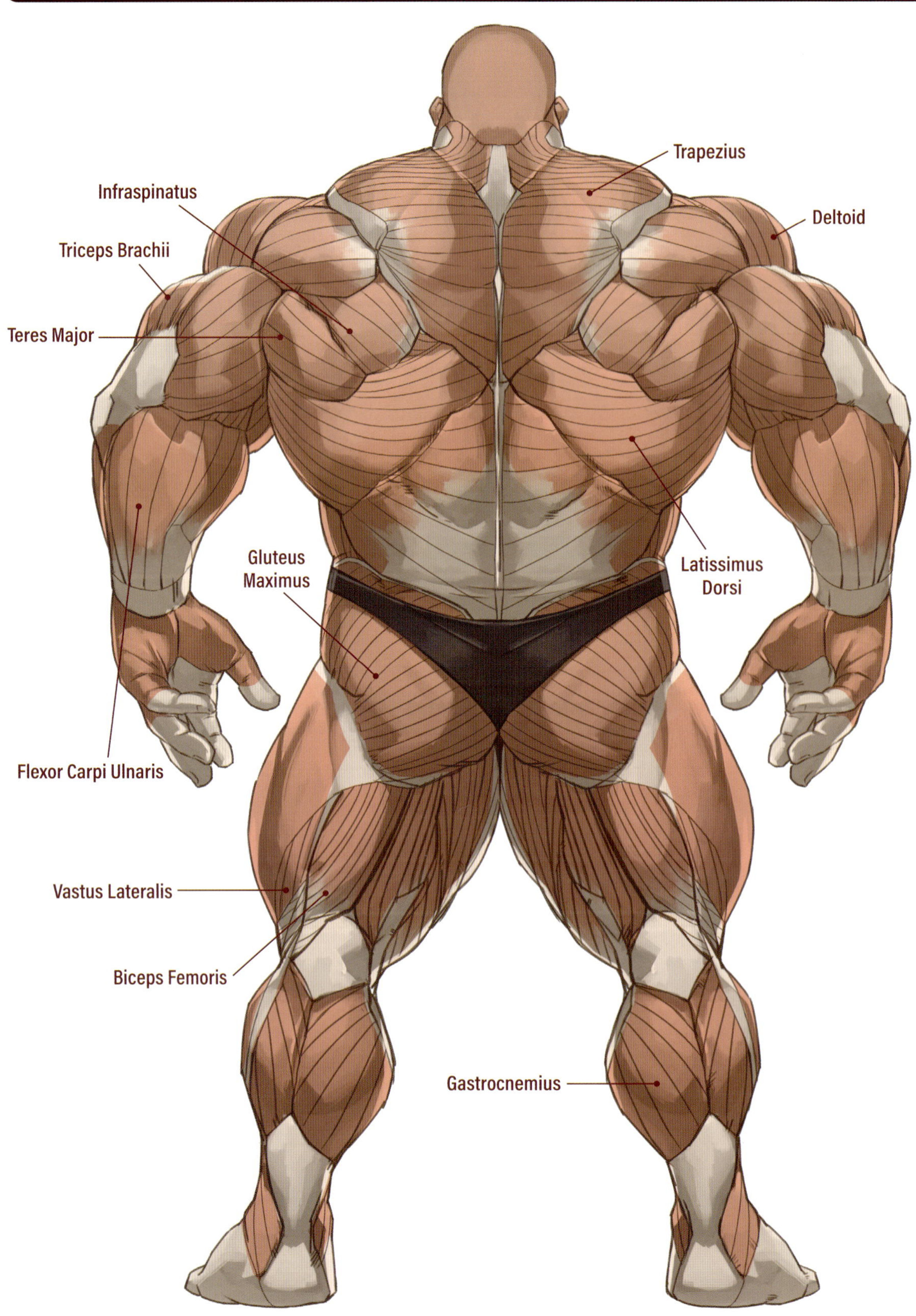

Muscles Viewed from the Back

The back is a region where the prominence of muscles can vary greatly depending on how they are trained. Additionally, the infraspinatus and teres major muscles are typically covered by the latissimus dorsi.

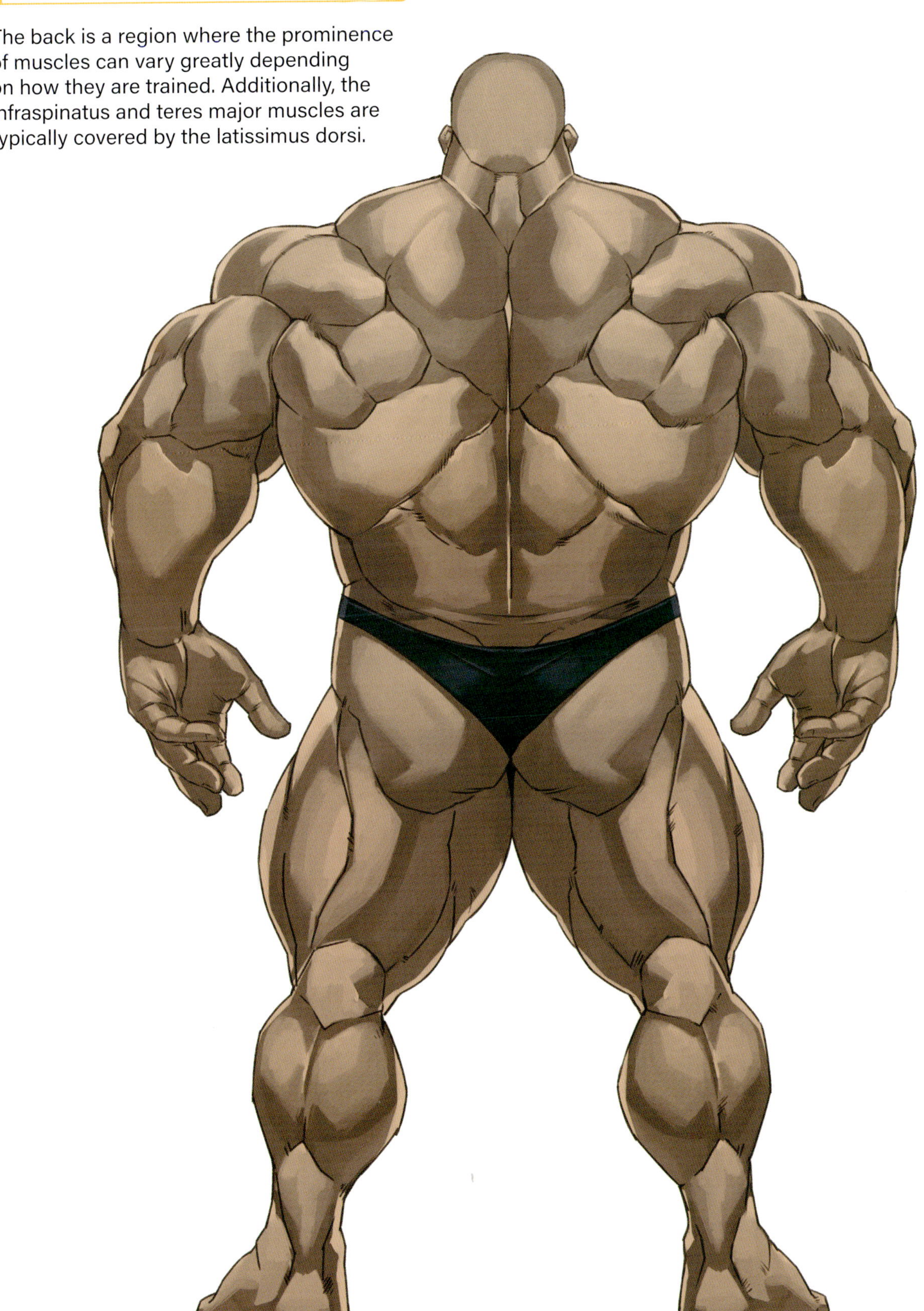

Torso Landmarks

"Landmark" refers to visible markers from an anatomical perspective, such as the layout of bones, muscles, blood vessels and the positions of organs. In the illustration below, the sternum, clavicle, scapula, humerus, iliac crest and femur serve as these markers. Although they are drawn much larger than in an actual skeleton, their proportions and positions remain consistent with basic skeletal anatomy.

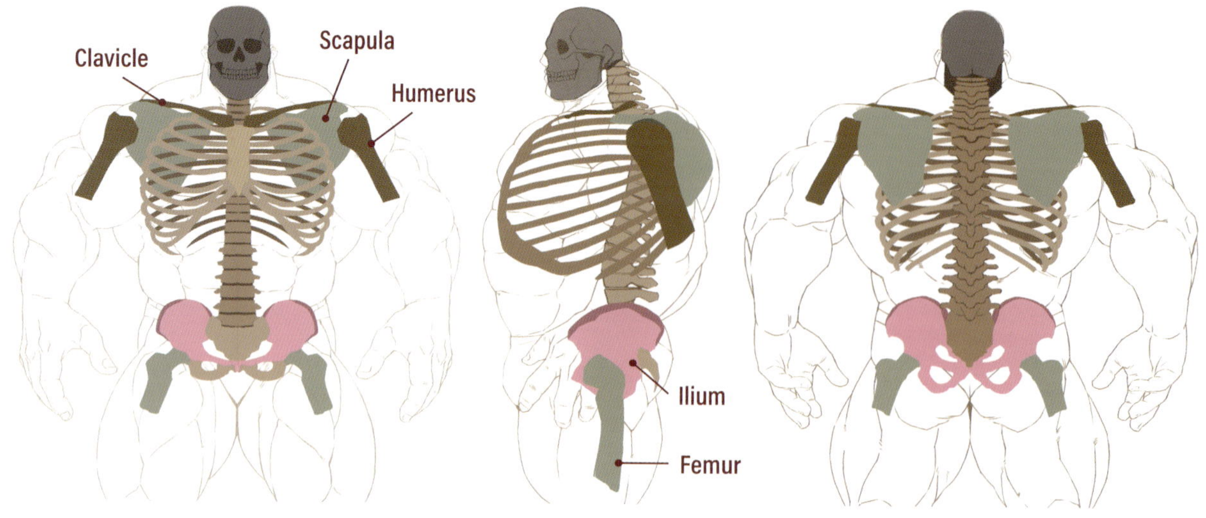

Visible Skeletal Landmarks

The outer edges of the scapula and ilium can be identified even when surrounded by muscle. The edges of bones appear at the boundaries between different muscle groups. In this case, they are visible at the boundaries between the shoulder and back muscles, and between the waist and leg muscles.

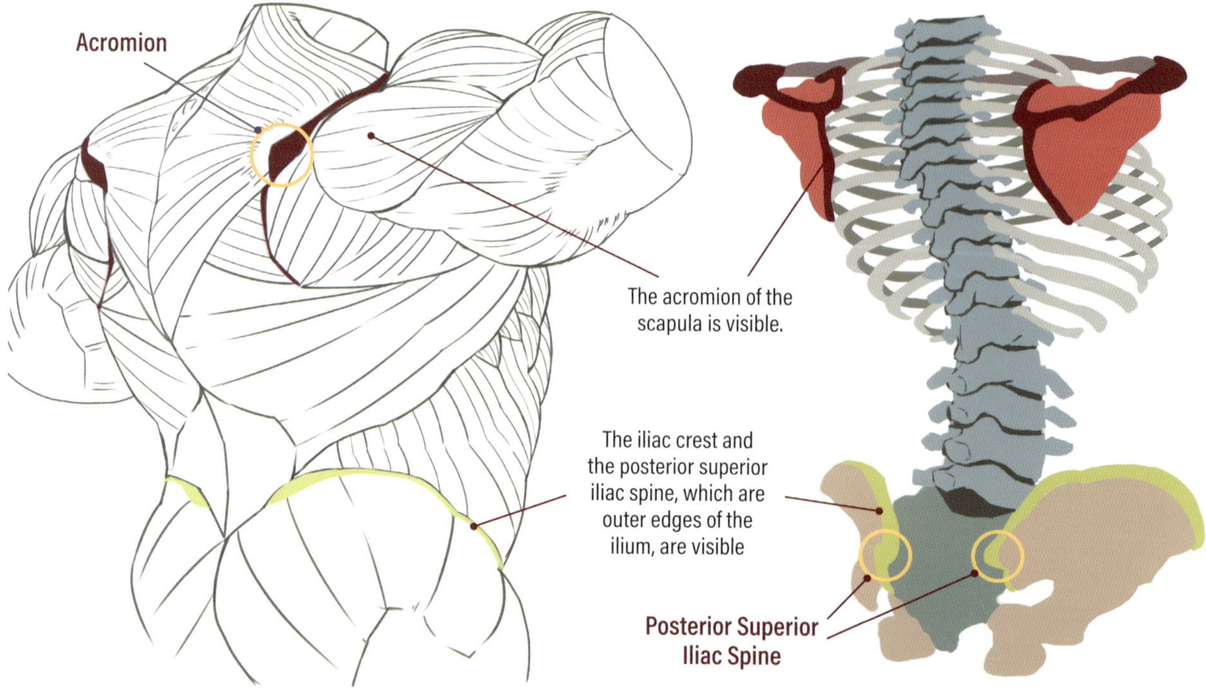

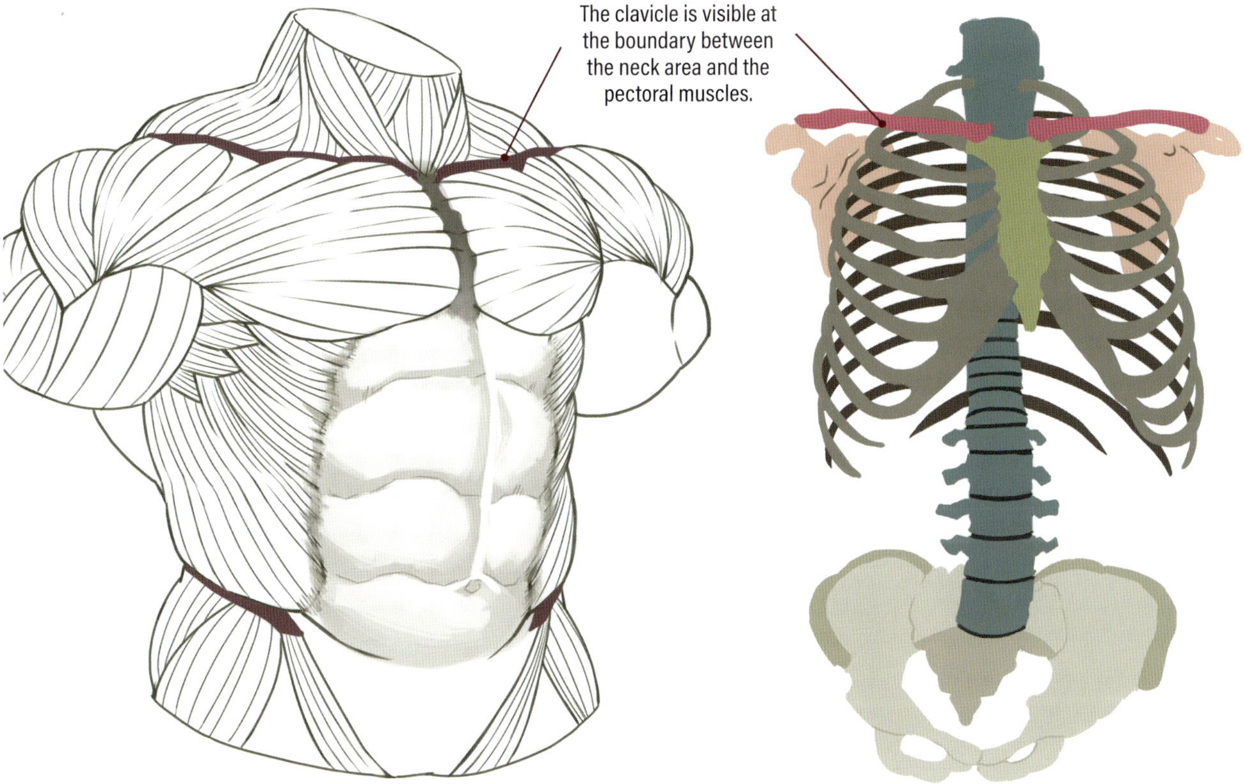

The clavicle is visible at the boundary between the neck area and the pectoral muscles.

Visibility of Landmarks Depending on Muscle Mass

As muscle mass increases, the bones that serve as landmarks become less visible. This is because each muscle thickens, covering the bones.

In the illustrations below, as you move from left to right, muscle mass increases, and the visibility of the clavicle decreases. This happens because the muscles around the clavicle become thicker, causing the prominence of the clavicle to be buried under the muscle.

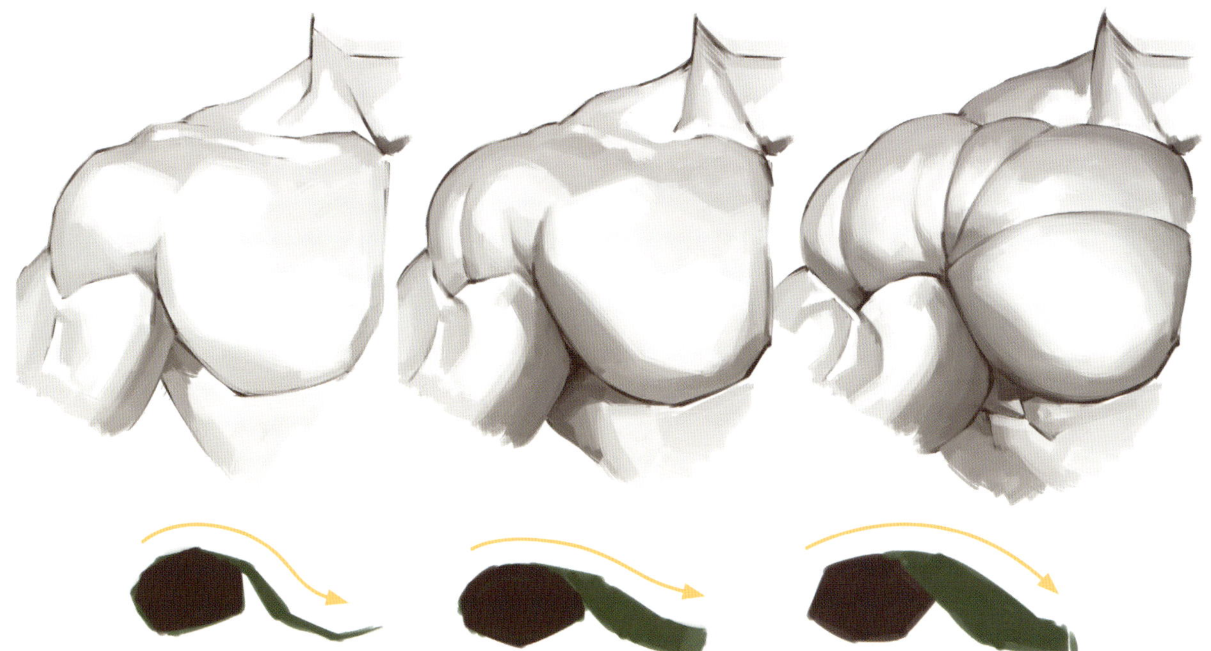

Muscle Attachment of the Torso—Front

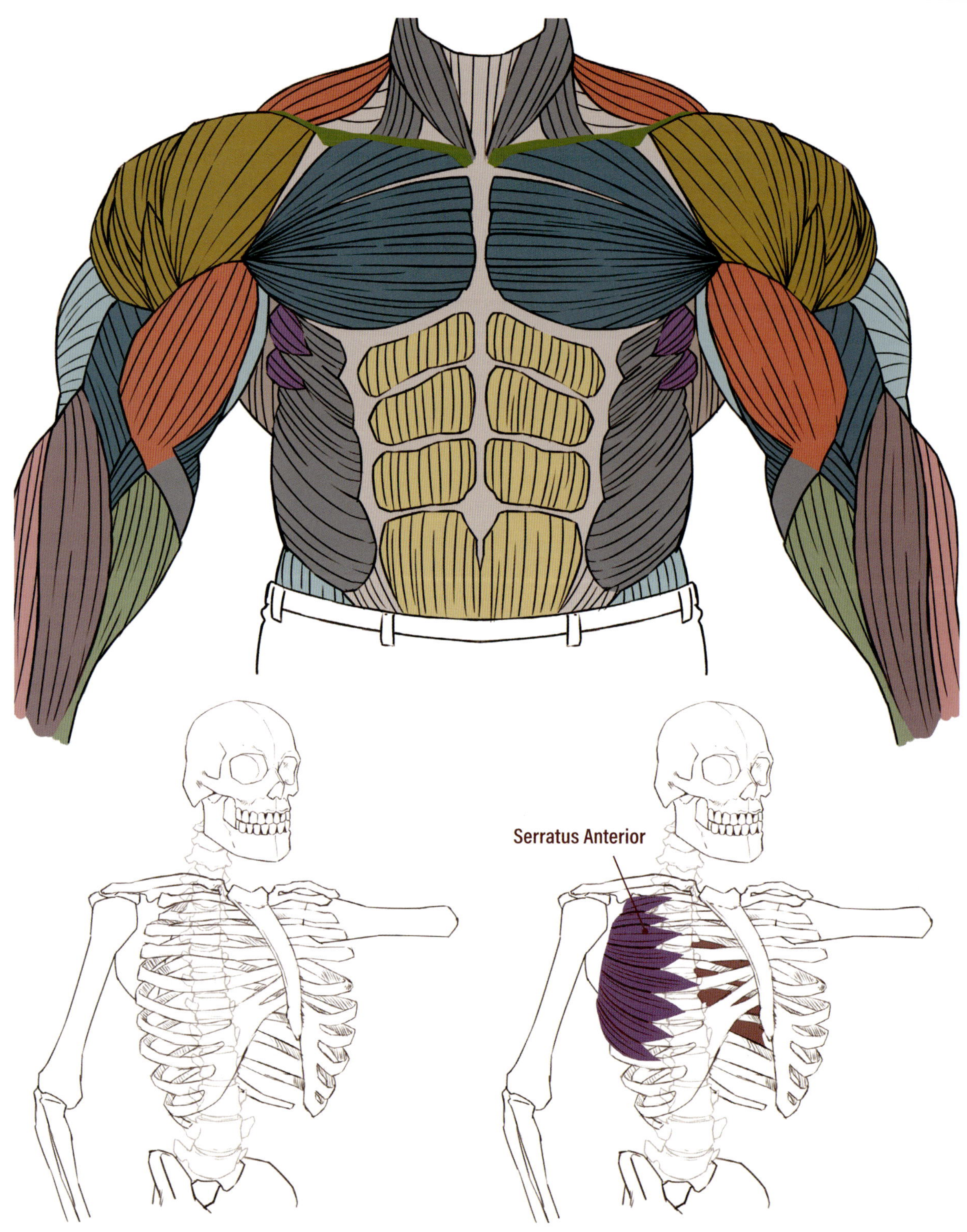

The serratus anterior originates from the first to ninth ribs and spreads across the front of the thorax. It attaches to the inner side of the scapula and plays a role in pulling the scapula forward.

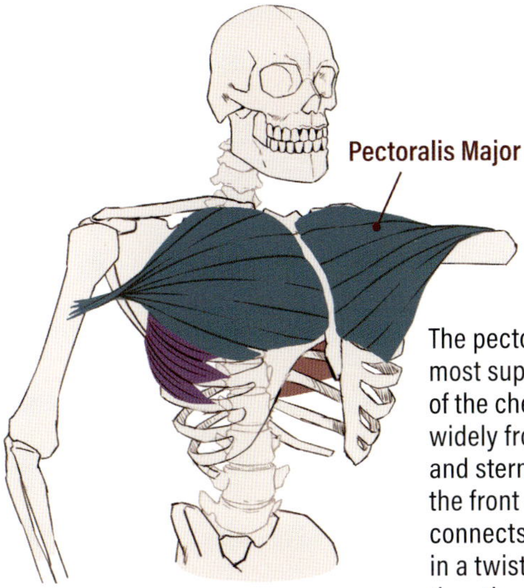

Pectoralis Major

The pectoralis major is the most superficial muscle of the chest, spreading widely from the clavicle and sternum, covering the front of the ribs. It connects to the humerus in a twisted bundle, rather than the shoulder.

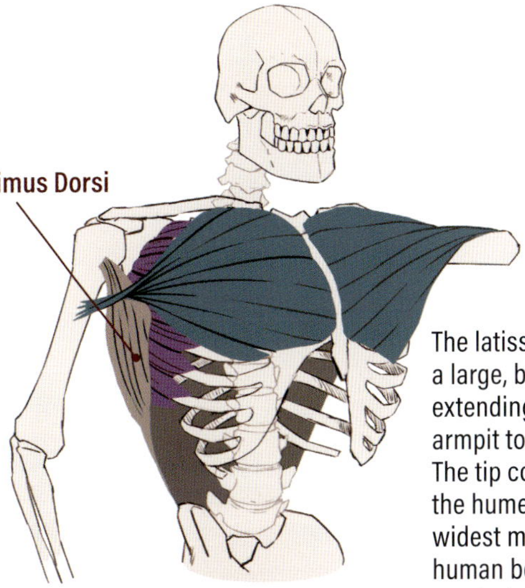

Latissimus Dorsi

The latissimus dorsi is a large, broad muscle extending from the armpit to the pelvis. The tip connects to the humerus. It is the widest muscle in the human body and is used when pulling objects toward you.

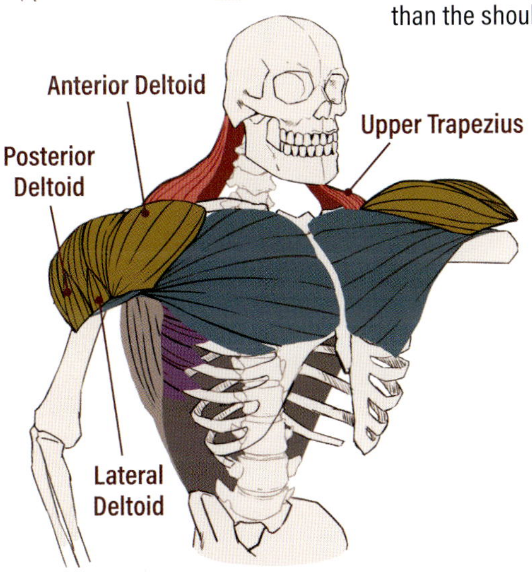

Anterior Deltoid

Posterior Deltoid

Upper Trapezius

Lateral Deltoid

The trapezius muscle connects the back and shoulder joints. Most of it spreads across the back, and from the front of the body, you can see the upper trapezius, which is the closest to the neck. This muscle is located from the upper part of the scapula to the neck and is useful for movements that lift the clavicle and scapula. The deltoid muscle is a group of muscles that cover the shoulder with three parts: anterior, middle and posterior. It is the largest muscle in the arm and helps raise the arm laterally.

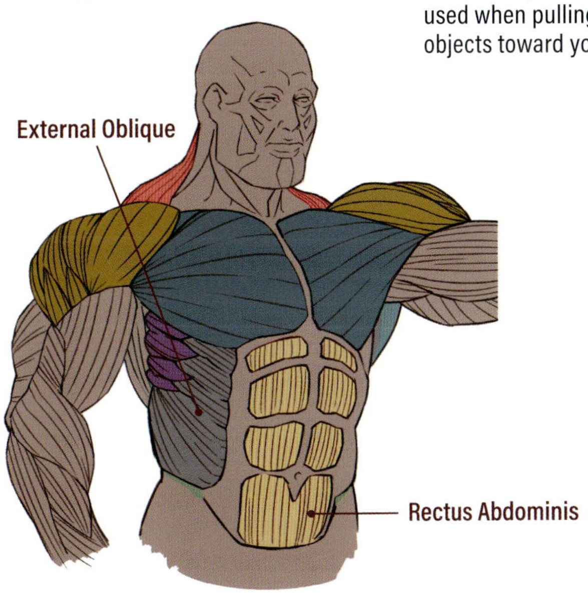

External Oblique

Rectus Abdominis

The external oblique muscle originates from the lower ribs (fifth to twelfth ribs) and extends diagonally downward. This muscle is positioned to overlap with the serratus anterior (purple in the diagram).

The rectus abdominis covers the front of the abdomen. It is surprisingly long, extending from the ribs to the pubic bone. Commonly known as the "six-pack," it is one of the most well-known abdominal muscles.

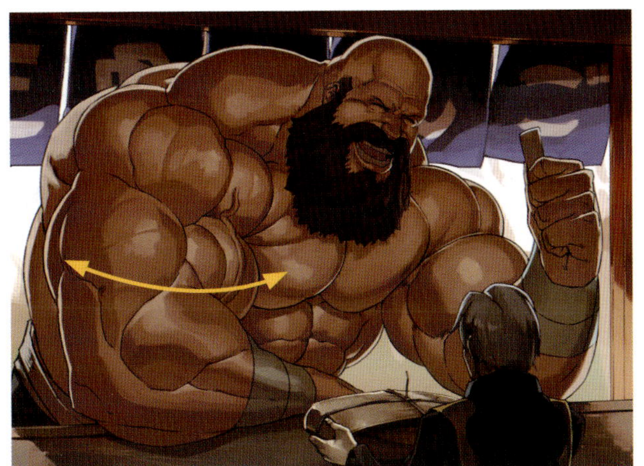

Muscles of the Very Muscular Body Types

While it is important to thicken and enlarge the skeletal landmarks, it is even more crucial to draw the muscles themselves thicker and larger. The skeleton serves as the foundation for depicting the human body. Keep in mind that the muscles are hypertrophied based on this skeleton as you draw.

Muscle Attachment of the Torso—Back

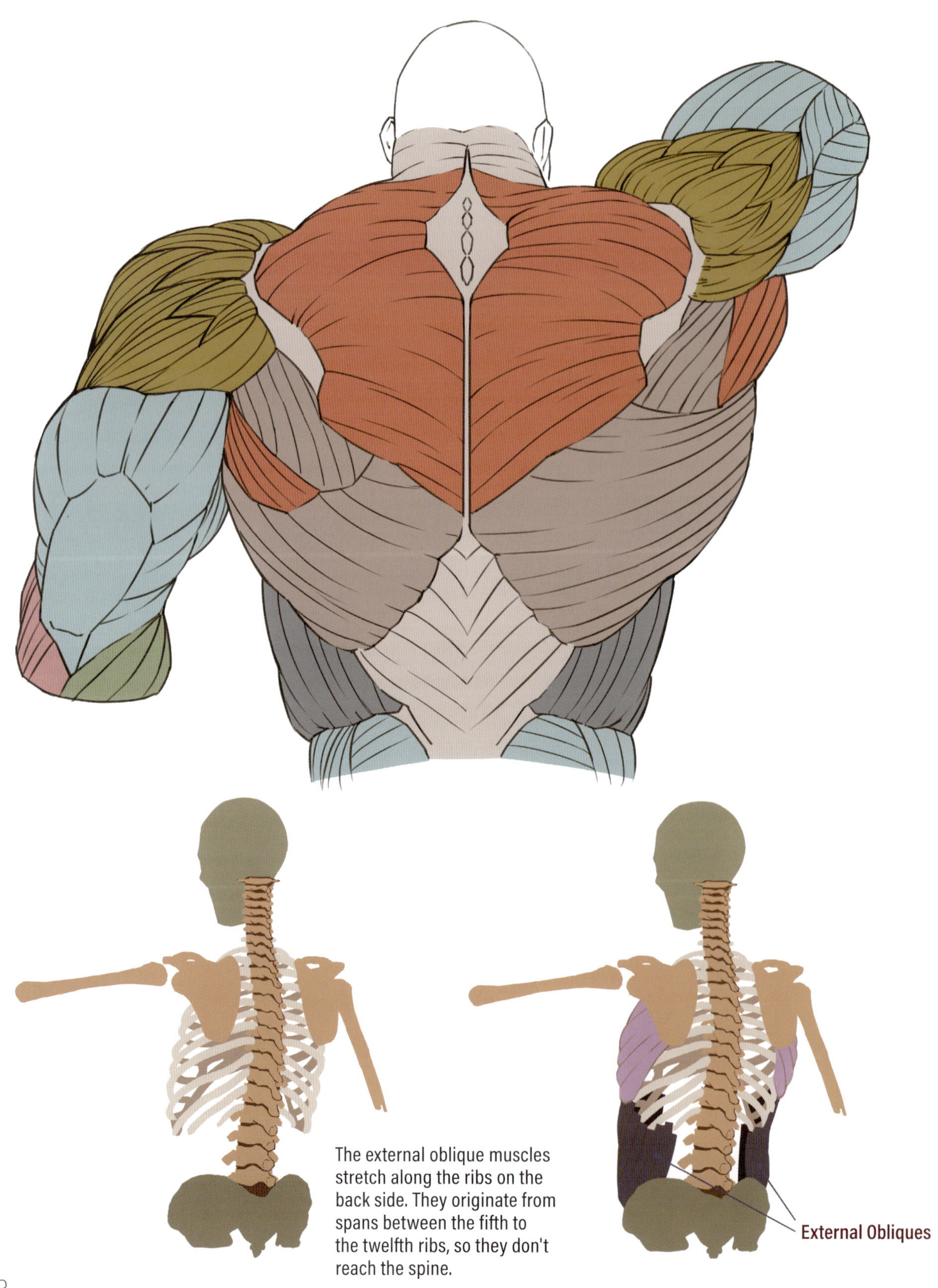

The external oblique muscles stretch along the ribs on the back side. They originate from spans between the fifth to the twelfth ribs, so they don't reach the spine.

The teres minor muscle is below the infraspinatus muscle and above the teres major muscle. Part of it is covered by the infraspinatus muscle and it connects from the outer edge of the shoulder blade to the upper arm bone.

The teres major muscle is under the armpit and connects from the lower part of the shoulder blade to the upper arm bone. It works like the latissimus dorsi muscle and mainly supports it.

The infraspinatus muscle is covered by the deltoid and trapezius muscles. Along with the teres minor and teres major muscles, it helps stabilize the shoulder joint. It is the strongest of these muscles and the only one on the surface. It mainly helps rotate the shoulder joint outward.

The rhomboid minor and rhomboid major muscles are part of the rhomboid muscle group, located between the shoulder blades. The rhomboid minor is at the top and the rhomboid major is at the bottom.

The latissimus dorsi muscle is a large muscle that spreads from the armpit to the pelvis. Its tip connects to the upper arm bone. It is the widest muscle in the body and is used when pulling things toward you.

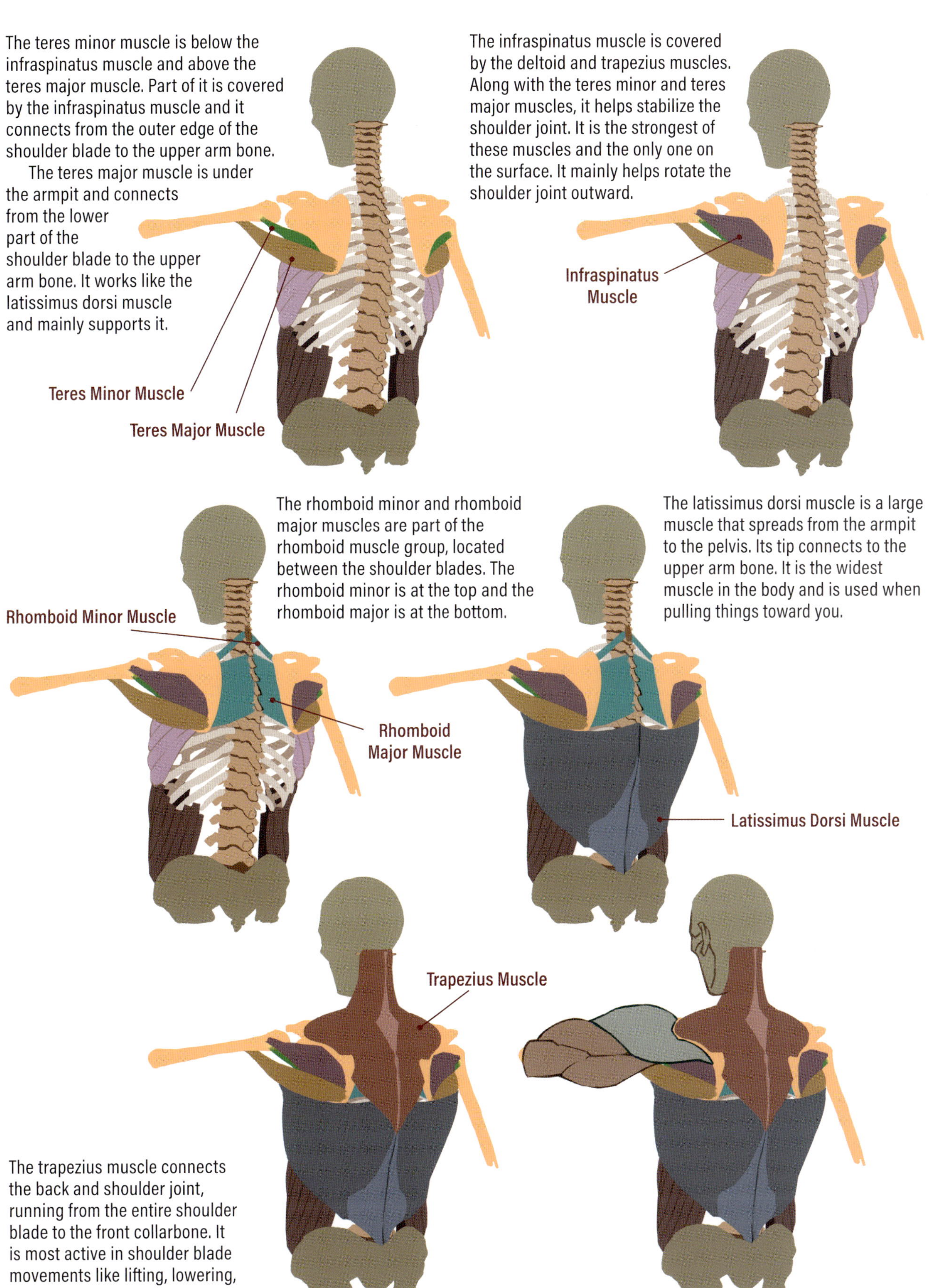

The trapezius muscle connects the back and shoulder joint, running from the entire shoulder blade to the front collarbone. It is most active in shoulder blade movements like lifting, lowering, and pulling back the arms.

Chest Muscles

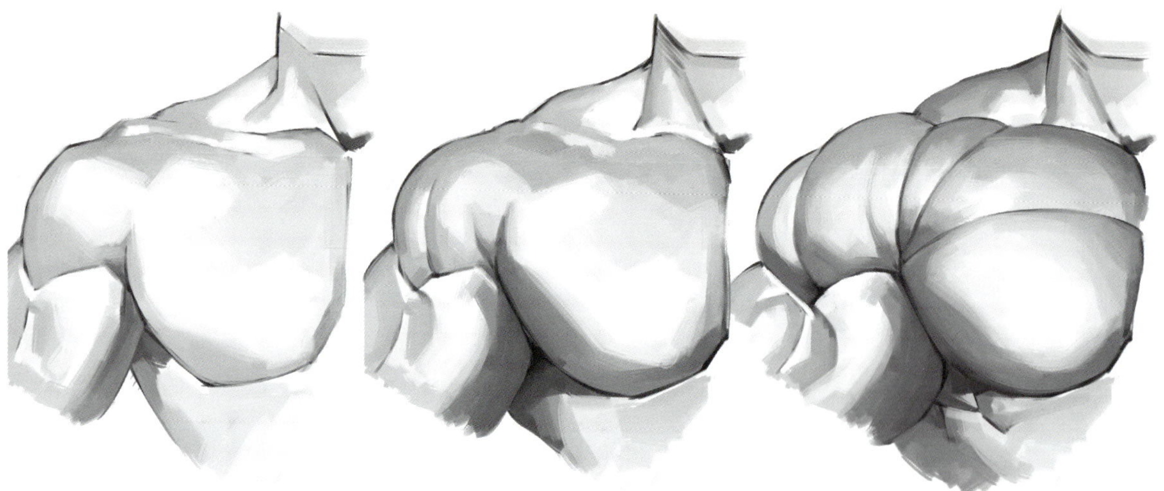

The pectoralis major is the strongest muscle in the upper body and is the most superficial muscle that shapes the chest. It greatly influences the appearance of the chest and bust. When the pectoralis major develops, it covers the collarbone, making it less visible (as seen on the right, above).

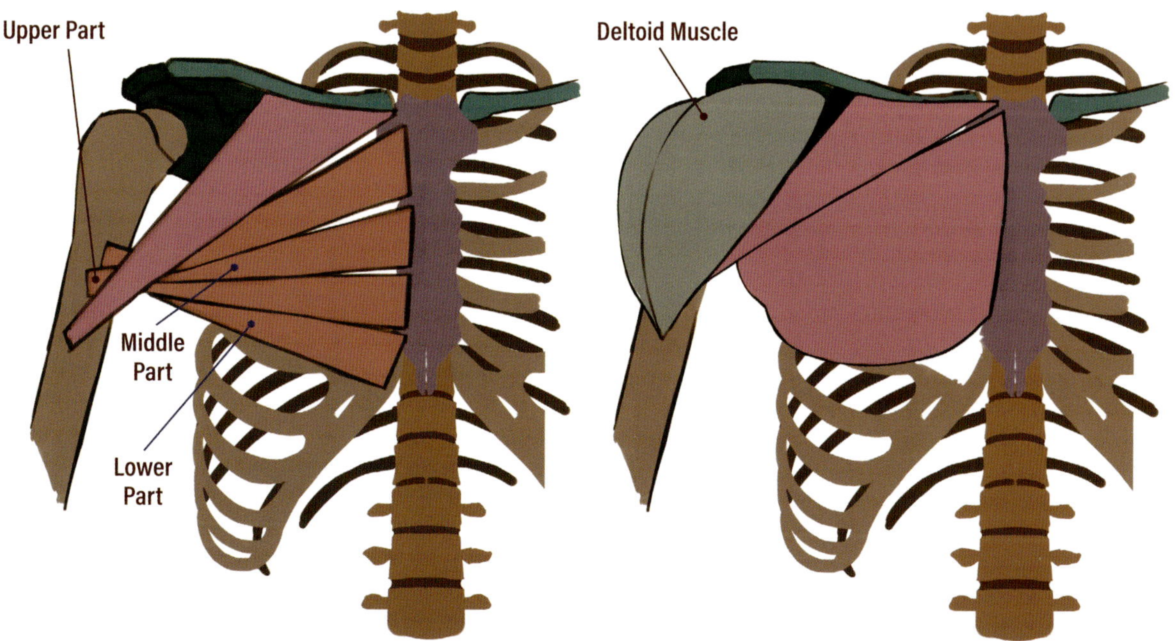

The pectoralis major is divided into the upper, middle and lower parts. The direction of the muscle fibers is different in each part. The upper-part fibers run diagonally downward from the shoulder blade to the upper arm bone. The middle-part fibers run horizontally from the sternum to the upper arm bone. The lower-part fibers run diagonally upward from the ribs and abdominal muscle sheath to the upper arm bone.

The starting points of the muscles are different, but they all attach to the same spot on the upper arm bone. The order in which they attach to the arm is reversed from the order in which they start from the chest, creating a twisted configuration. When the arm is raised straight up, the three muscle bundles line up in order. It is thought to be this way because humans transitioned from walking on all fours to standing upright, with arms hanging down. The parts of the pectoralis major near their attachment points are covered by the deltoid muscle.

Appearance from Different Angles

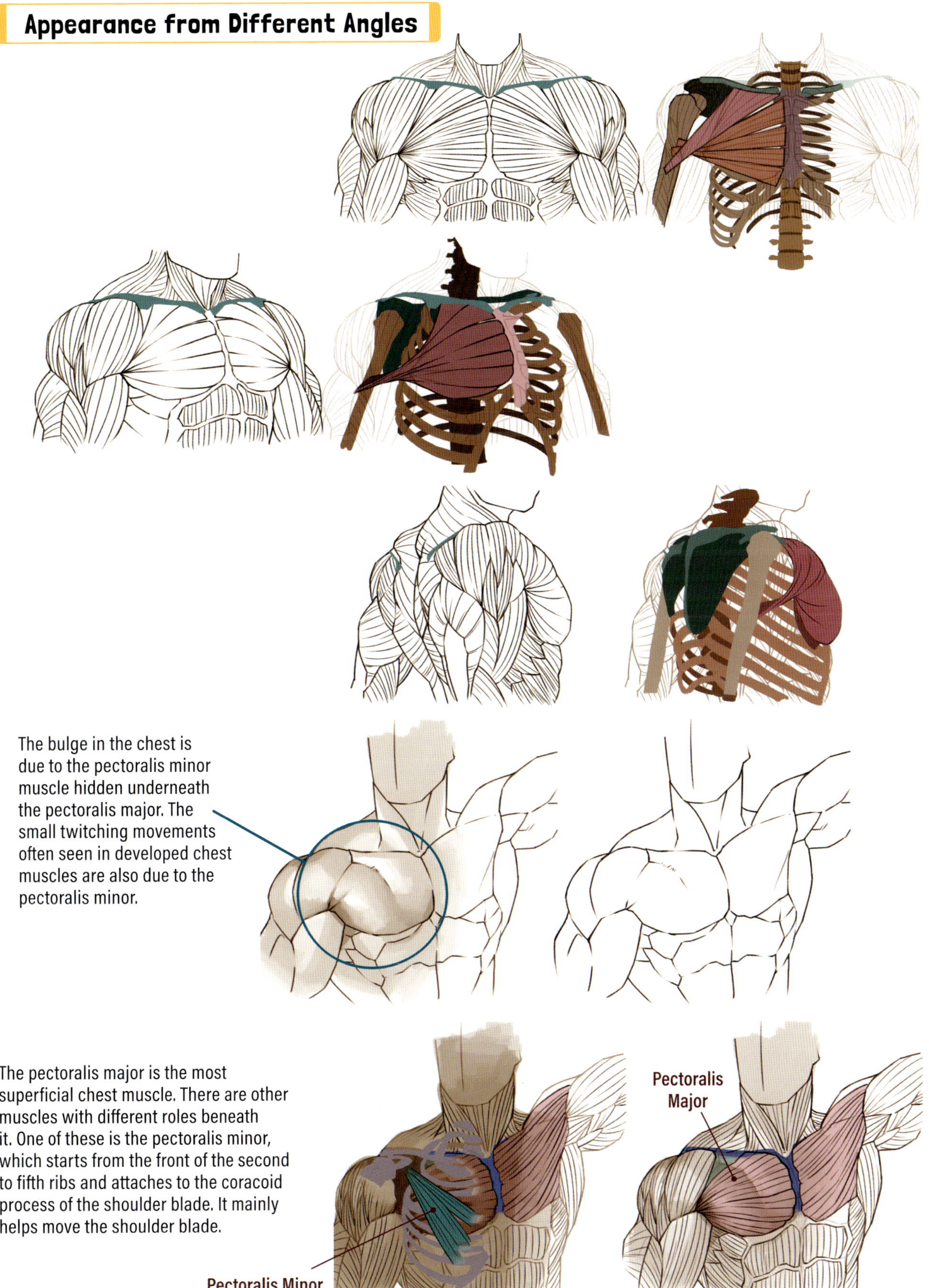

The bulge in the chest is due to the pectoralis minor muscle hidden underneath the pectoralis major. The small twitching movements often seen in developed chest muscles are also due to the pectoralis minor.

The pectoralis major is the most superficial chest muscle. There are other muscles with different roles beneath it. One of these is the pectoralis minor, which starts from the front of the second to fifth ribs and attaches to the coracoid process of the shoulder blade. It mainly helps move the shoulder blade.

Shoulder Muscles

Deltoid

The deltoid is the largest muscle in the upper limb by volume, and is positioned to roundly cover the shoulder from the front and back of the body. The deltoid is composed of three parts: anterior, middle and posterior. Each part originates from the outer clavicle (anterior), acromion (middle) and scapular spine (posterior). The muscle bundles extend over the shoulder joint toward the arm and insert at the deltoid tuberosity of the humerus. The deltoid muscle plays a role in moving the arm forward, backward, up and down.

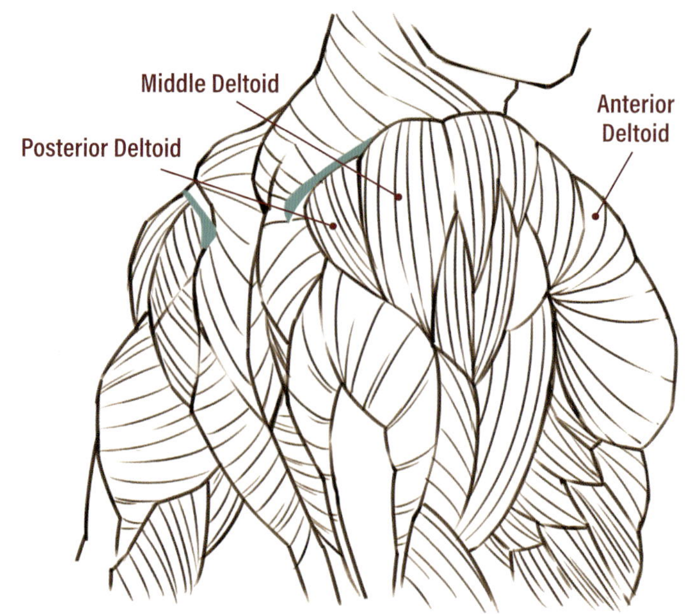

Shape of the Deltoid

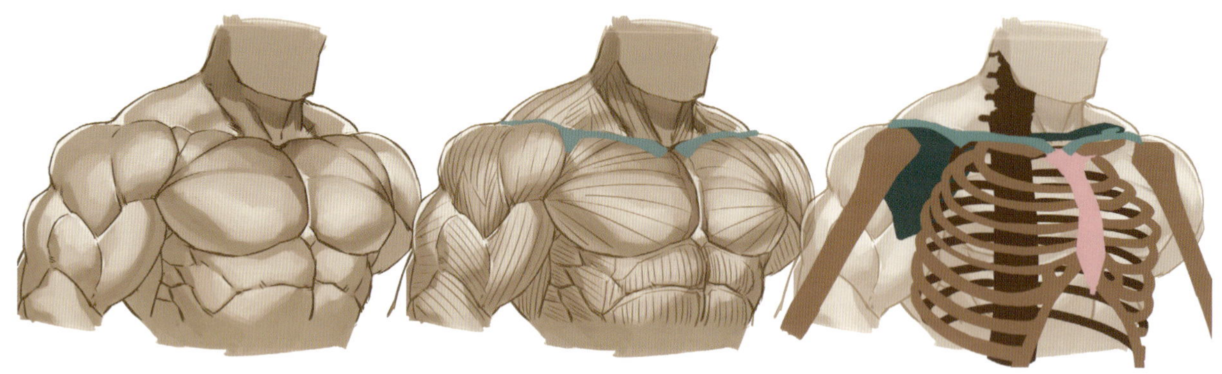

Silhouette of a Developed Deltoid

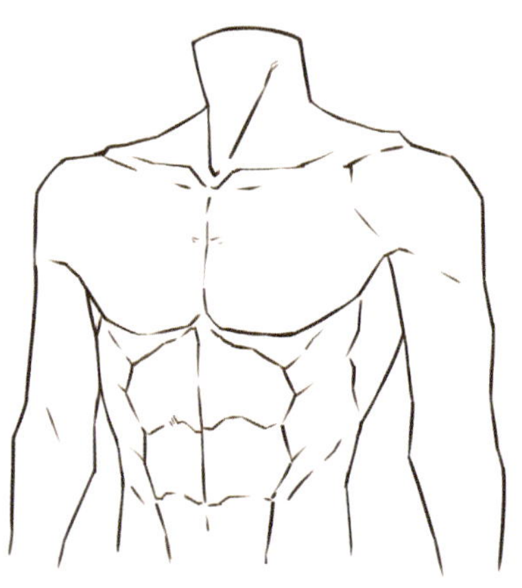

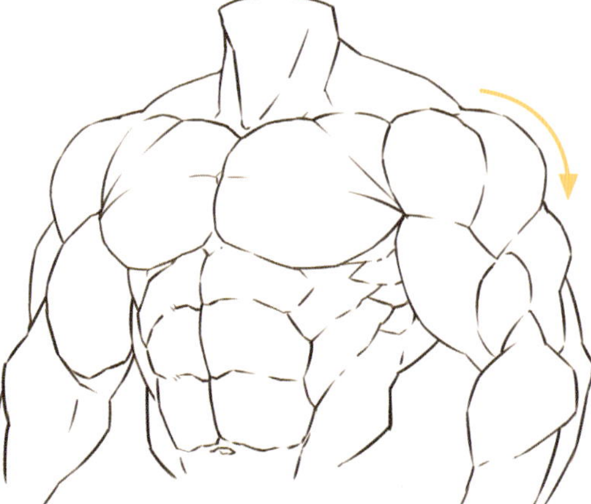

The deltoid wraps around the shoulder in a rounded shape from the front and back of the body. Therefore, when developed, it significantly bulges not only from the front and back but also from the sides.

Details of the Deltoid

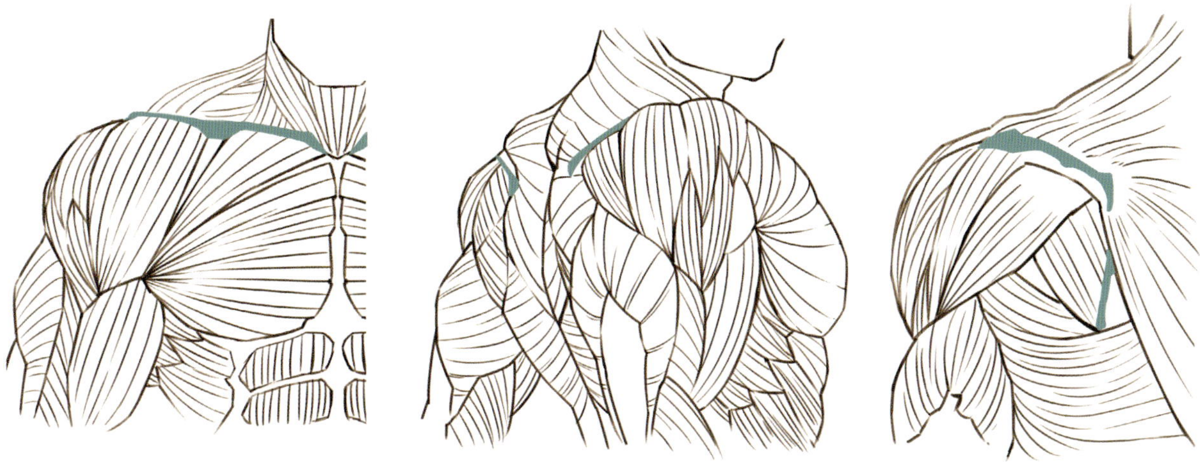

Expanding in a Manga Style

When expressing muscles in a manga style that are hypertrophied to an unrealistic degree, simply drawing the arms thicker and rounder, with exaggerated muscles, can look odd. As mentioned on page 26, the deltoid is divided into anterior, middle and posterior parts.

Therefore, each part should be hypertrophied as individual muscles and then fitted around the shoulder. This way, even though the muscles themselves are abnormally bulging, you can still depict a well-proportioned human figure.

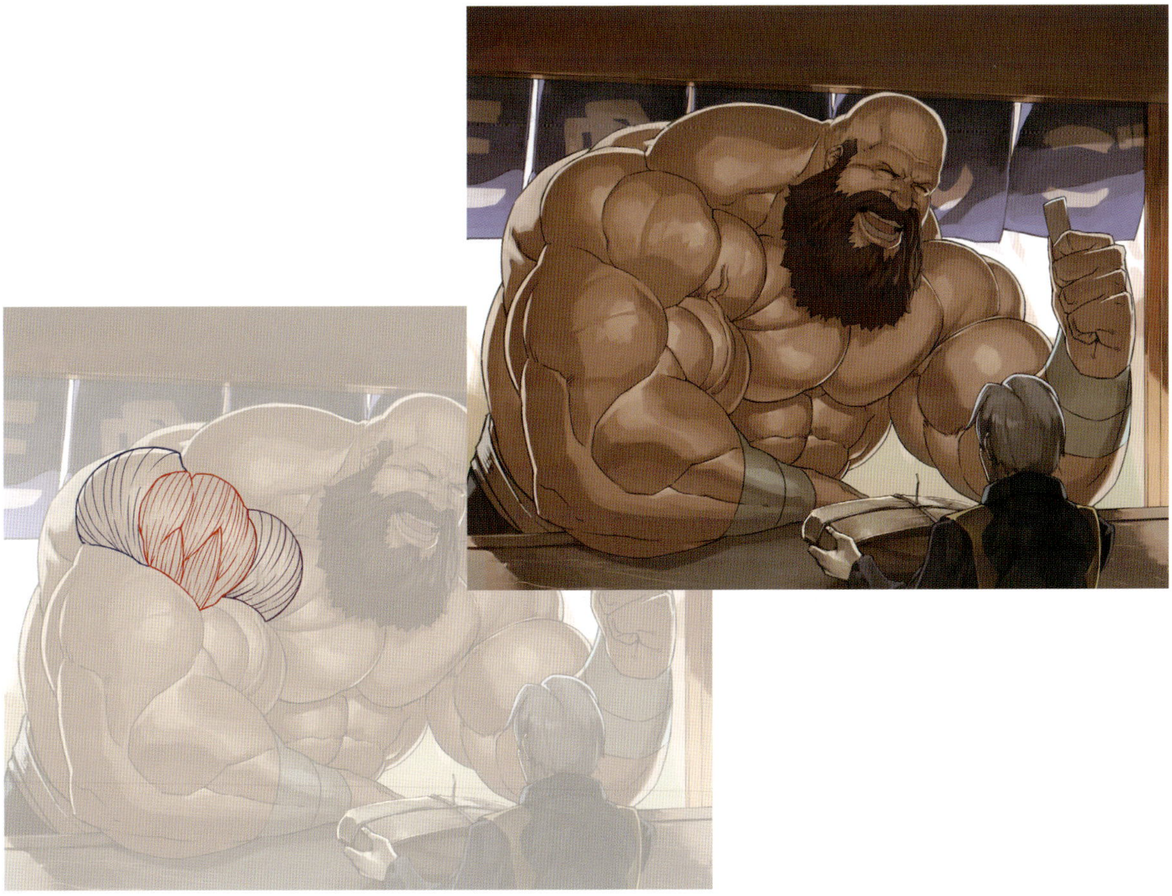

Shoulder Muscles

Trapezius

The trapezius muscle is known as the primary muscle responsible for shoulder stability. It also plays a significant role in arm movements. This muscle is located at the most superficial layer of the back and is divided into the upper trapezius, middle trapezius and lower trapezius. Due to its extensive reach, the trapezius has various functions.

The upper trapezius is relatively weak and does not significantly contribute to neck movements. It mainly helps in lifting the clavicle and scapula. The middle trapezius is thick and strong, and it functions to pull the scapula backward. Weakness in this area can cause the scapula to open outward, leading to a hunched back. The lower trapezius works to pull the scapula downward. The most important function of the trapezius is to assist the deltoid muscles and stabilize the scapula. Each part of the muscle originates and inserts at specific points: the upper trapezius originates from the occipital bone and inserts at the lateral clavicle, the middle trapezius originates around the seventh cervical vertebra and inserts at the acromion and spine of the scapula, and the lower trapezius originates from the spinous processes of the fourth to twelfth thoracic vertebrae and inserts at the triangular area of the scapular spine.

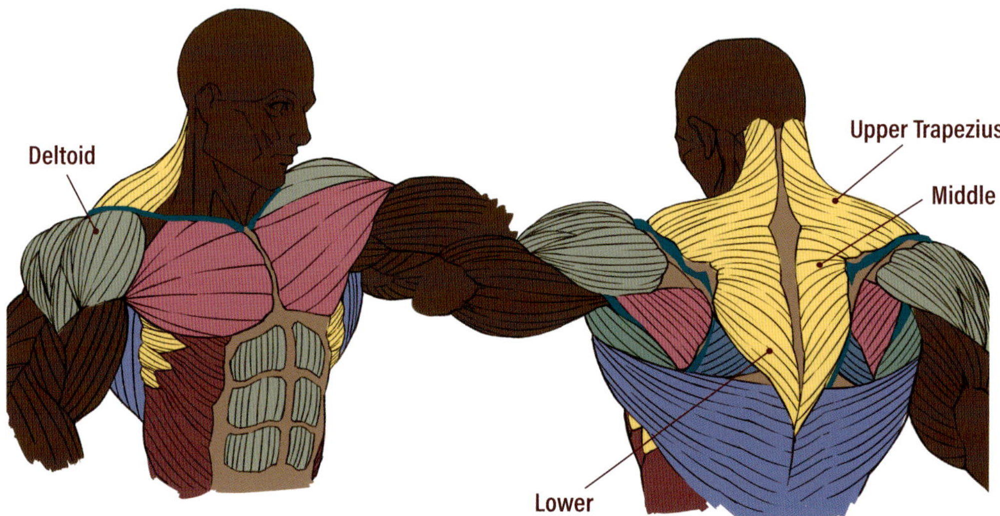

Trapezius and Body Thickness

The upper trapezius, part of the trapezius muscle, connects from the occipital bone to the lateral clavicle. This portion is visible from the front and is part of the back muscle known as the trapezius. Strengthening this area can enlarge the muscles from the neck to the clavicle, making it appear as if there is an additional shoulder on top of the original shoulder!

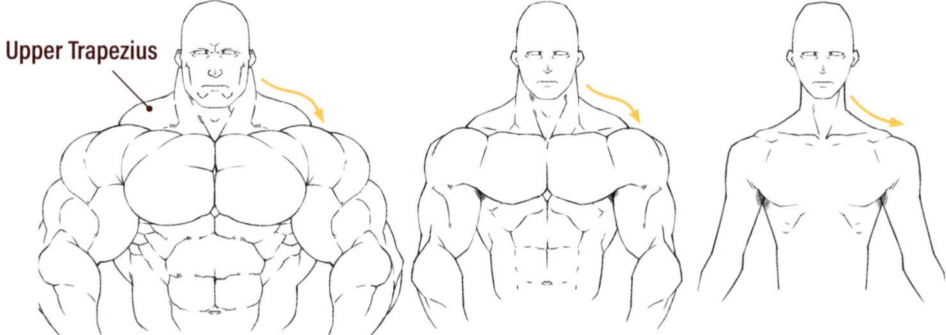

Shoulder Muscles Viewed from Various Angles

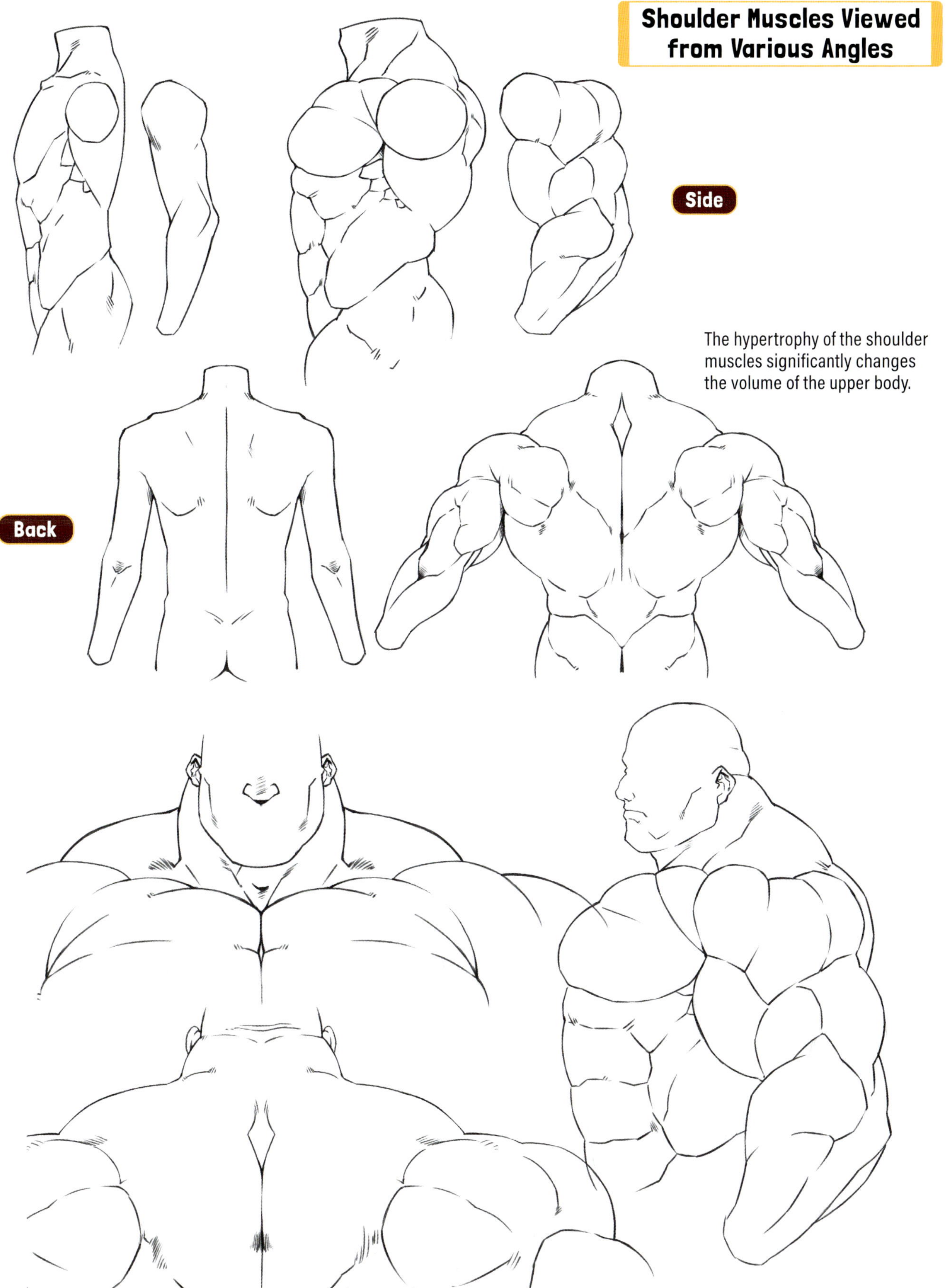

The hypertrophy of the shoulder muscles significantly changes the volume of the upper body.

Shoulder and Back Muscles

Muscles That Make up the Back

The erector spinae is a group of muscles consisting of the iliocostalis, longissimus and spinalis muscles. It includes the thoracic longissimus, thoracic spinalis, thoracic iliocostalis and lumbar iliocostalis. The erector spinae is the longest and largest muscle group in the back, stretching vertically on both sides of the spine from the neck to the lower back.

This muscle group helps lift and support the body in its upright position. Humans can maintain an upright posture because the erector spinae supports the spine. Even when in a hunched position, the erector spinae keeps the back from bending farther by stabilizing the body. It starts from the back of the sacrum and the iliac crest, and attaches to the temporal bone's mastoid process along the vertebrae and ribs.

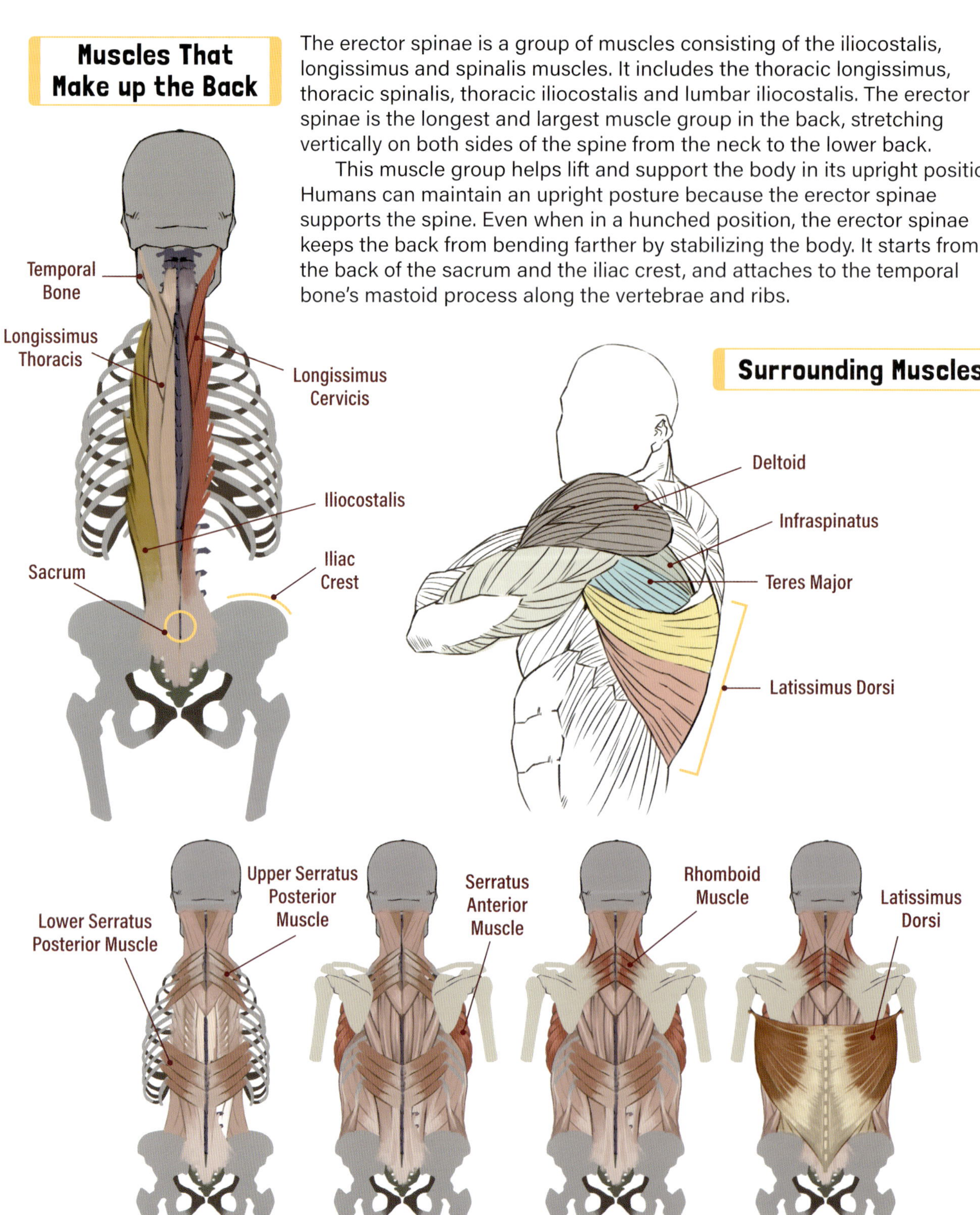

How Muscles Look Depending on Training

The appearance of muscles can vary depending on how they are trained and their natural structure. By building muscle mass and creating a well-defined body, shadows and chiseled definition between muscle boundaries become visible.

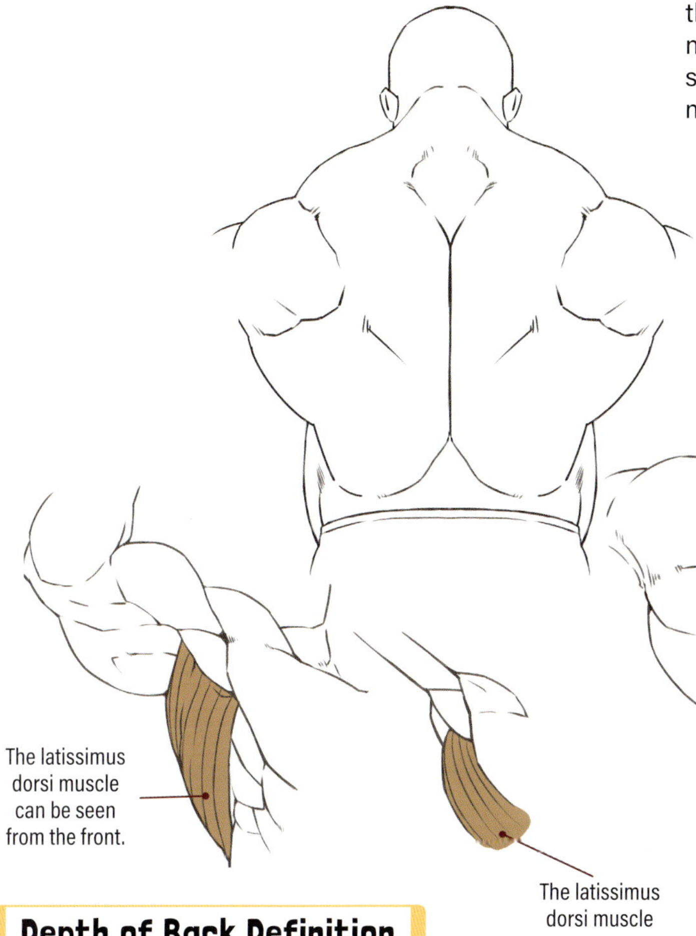

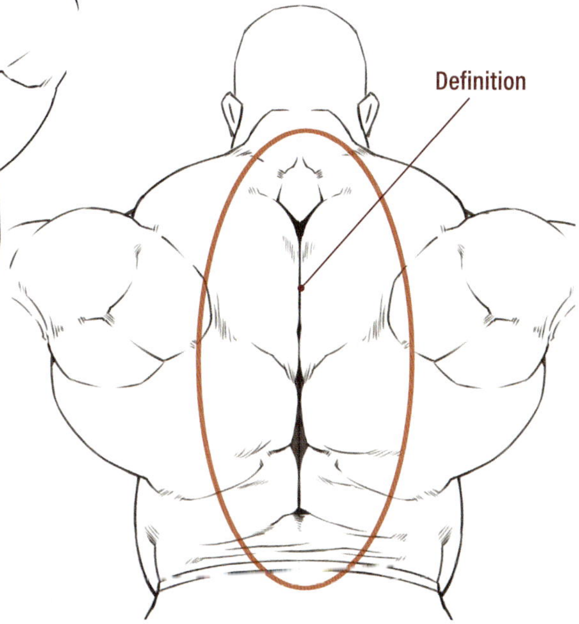

Definition

The latissimus dorsi muscle can be seen from the front.

The latissimus dorsi muscle

Depth of Back Definition

"Definition" refers to the boundaries between muscles. Highlighting the muscle lines and creating shadows makes the definition deeper. Training the trapezius and latissimus dorsi muscles can create deep "cuts" along the spine when the arms are spread out. This happens because raising the trapezius and latissimus dorsi muscles makes the boundaries between the muscles more distinct.

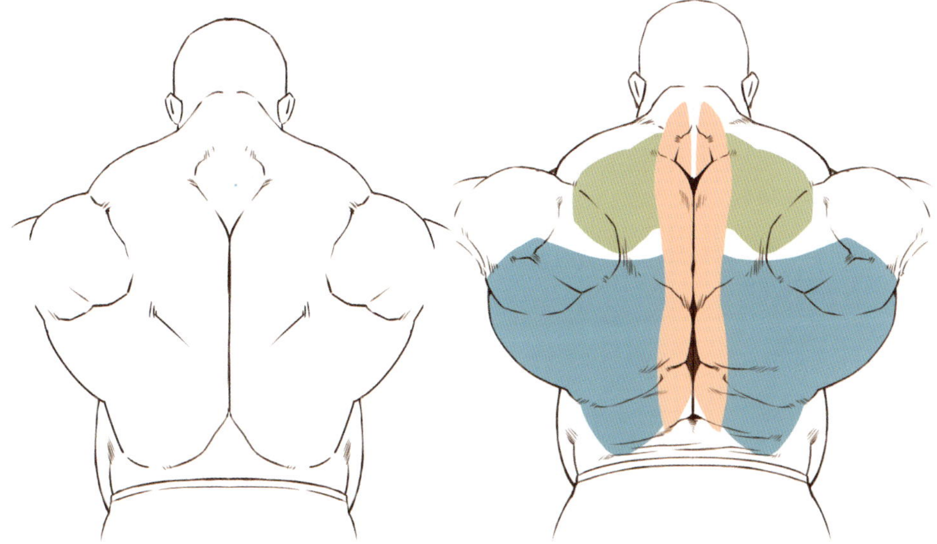

Shoulder and Back Muscles

Infraspinatus, Teres Minor, Teres Major

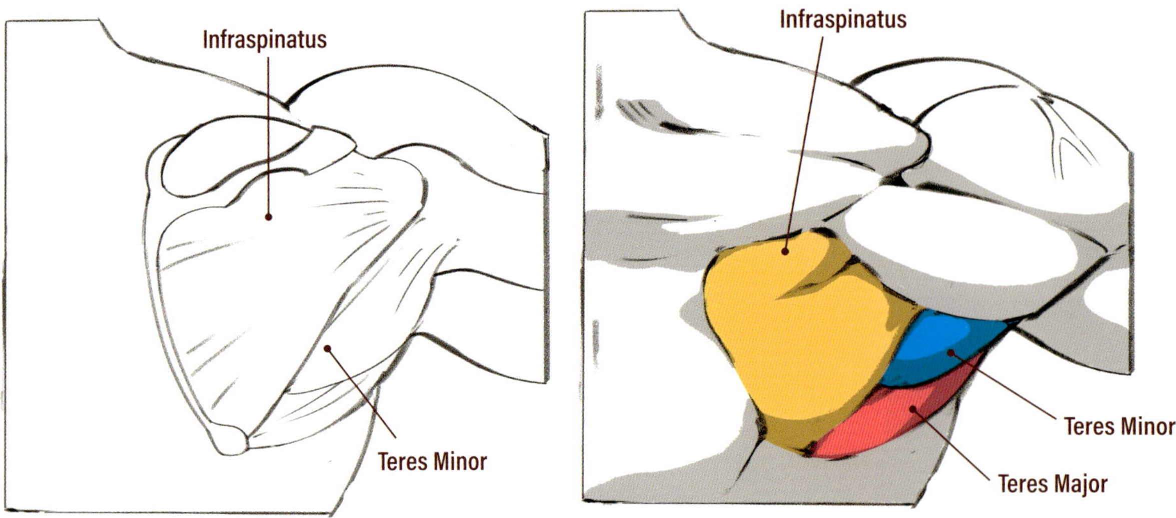

The infraspinatus and teres minor belong to the group of muscles that stabilize the shoulder joint. Both start from the shoulder blade. Specifically, the infraspinatus originates in the lower inside posterior part of the shoulder blade, and the teres minor originates the outer edge of the shoulder blade, both attaching to the upper humerus. These muscles help to rotate the shoulder outward. The teres major starts from the outer lower corner of the shoulder blade and attaches to the lesser tubercle of the humerus. It works similarly to the latissimus dorsi, helping to lower and pull back the arm.

Serratus Anterior

The serratus anterior is the only muscle involved in moving the shoulder blade outward. It originates from the first to the ninth ribs and extends toward the inner side of the shoulder blade. Because it attaches along the ribs, it is often mistaken for the ribs themselves.

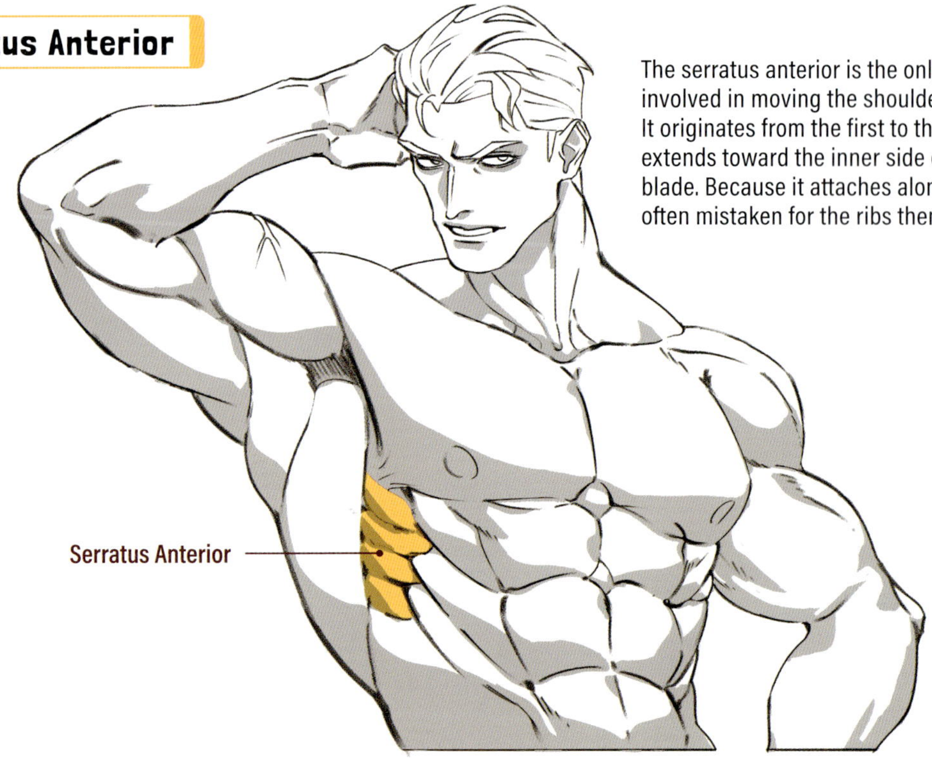

Serratus Anterior

Serratus Anterior and Other Muscles

The serratus anterior is close to the external oblique, and their starting points overlap. Both muscles attach along the ribs, creating finger-like shapes. This makes them look like interlaced fingers.

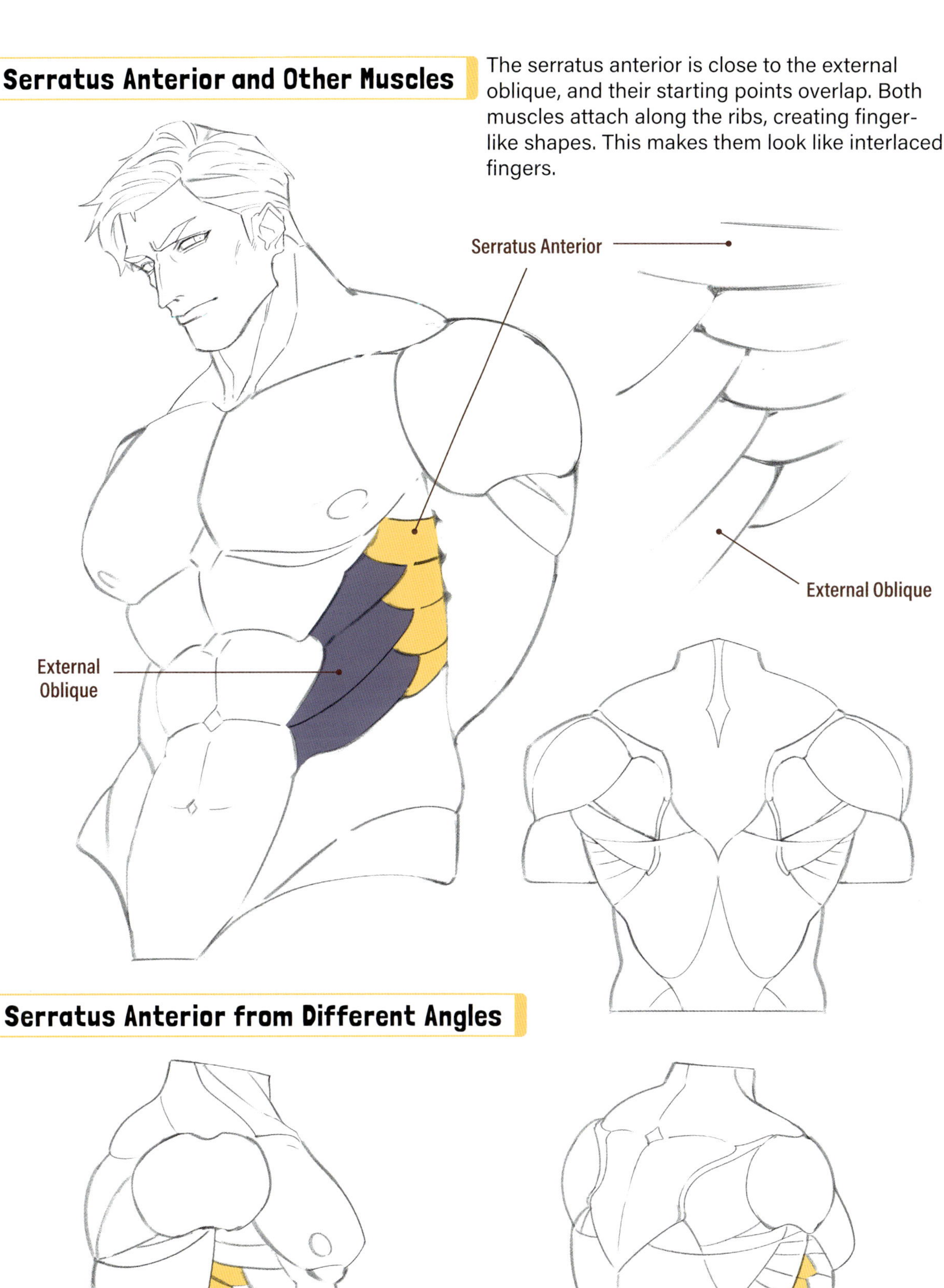

Serratus Anterior from Different Angles

Torso and Waist Muscles

External Oblique

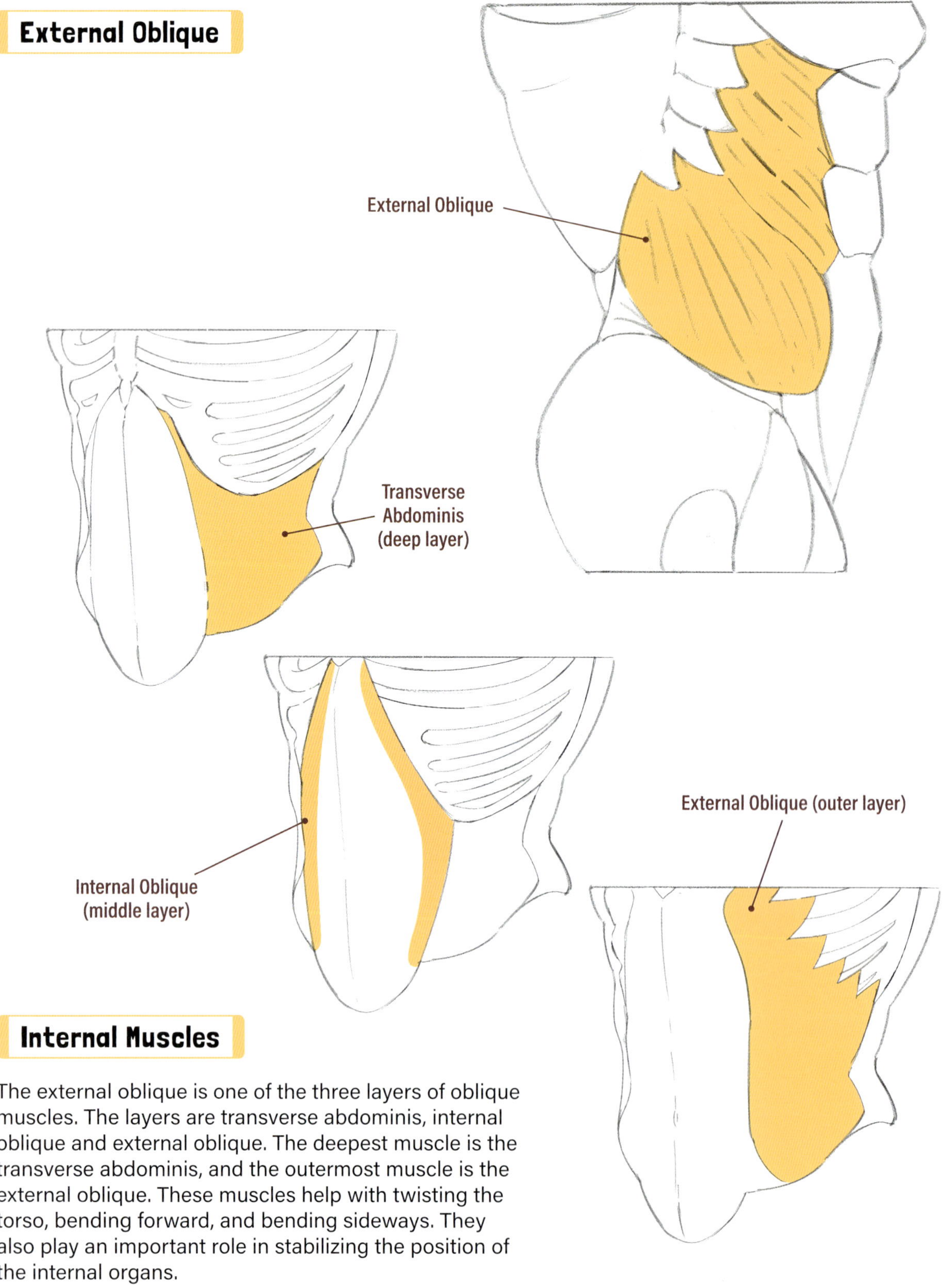

Internal Muscles

The external oblique is one of the three layers of oblique muscles. The layers are transverse abdominis, internal oblique and external oblique. The deepest muscle is the transverse abdominis, and the outermost muscle is the external oblique. These muscles help with twisting the torso, bending forward, and bending sideways. They also play an important role in stabilizing the position of the internal organs.

Changes in External Oblique with Different Body Types

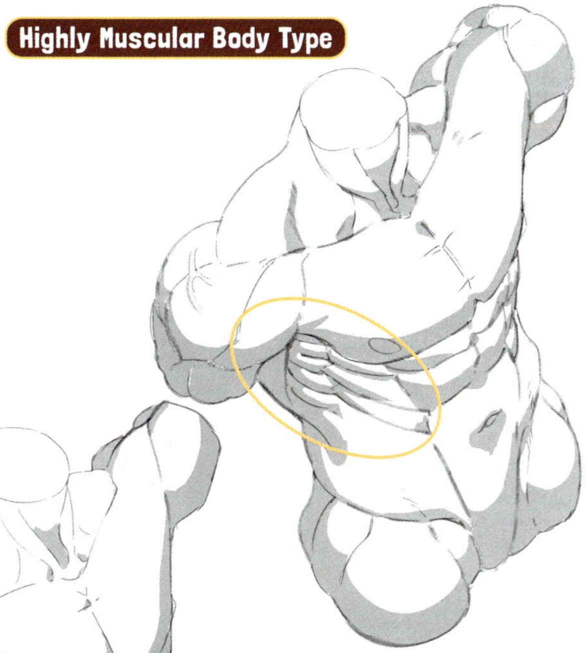

Highly Muscular Body Type

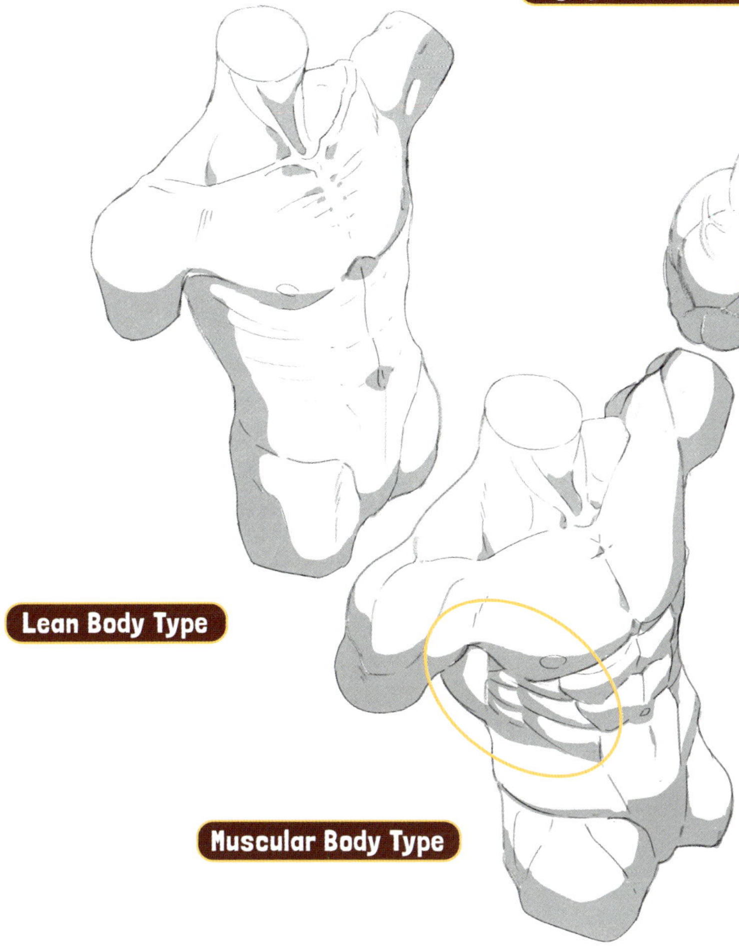

Lean Body Type

Muscular Body Type

The external oblique is the muscle on the side of the abdomen and is the outermost muscle. Therefore, changes in this muscle are immediately visible on the surface. Shadows form between the external oblique muscles, making each muscle bundle appear thicker. Because the muscle follows the ribs, it can make the bones appear more prominent. When the muscle grows, it creates noticeable bulges from under the armpits down to the waist.

Direction of Internal Muscle Fibers

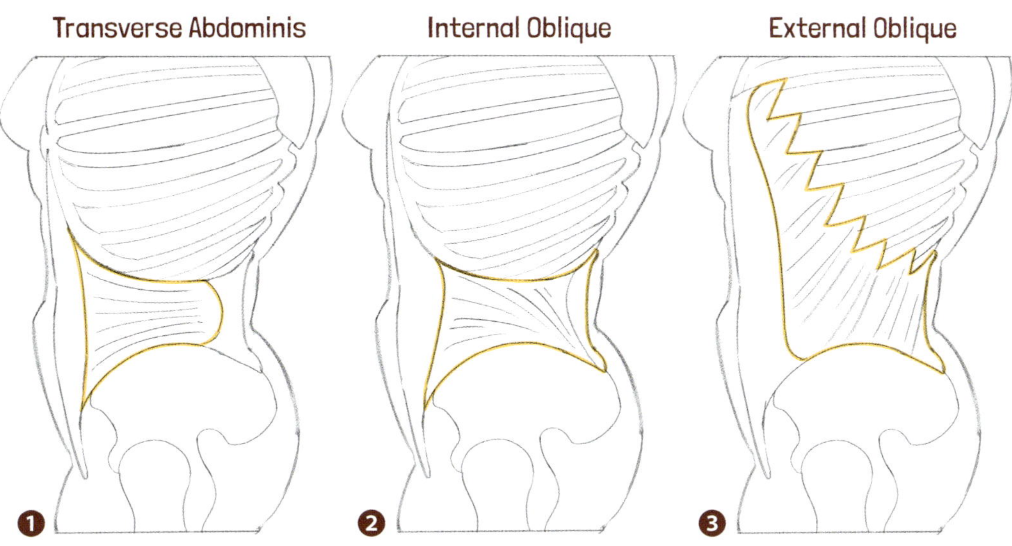

Neck Muscles

Structures of the Neck

1. Mylohyoid
2. Stylohyoid
3. Omohyoid
4. Digastric
5. Sternohyoid
6. Laryngeal prominence
7. Sternocleidomastoid
8. Sternohyoid
9. Trapezius
10. Hyoglossus

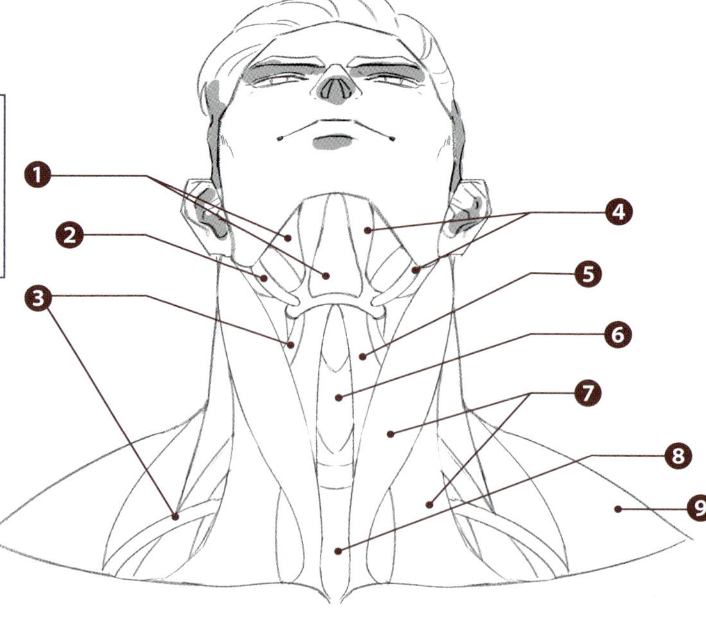

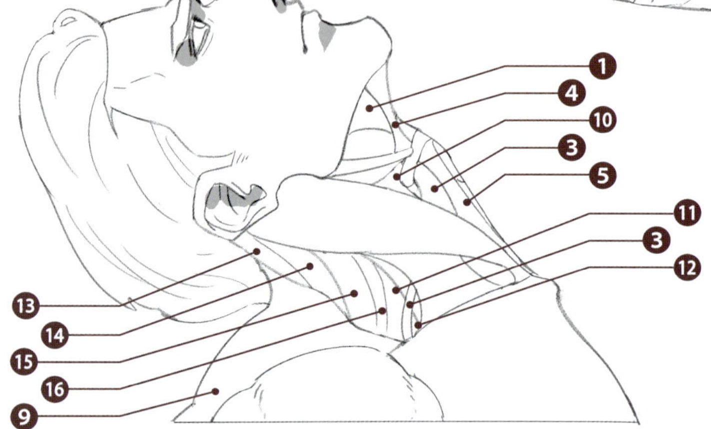

11. Middle Scalene
12. Anterior Scalene
13. Semispinalis Capitis
14. Splenius Capitis
15. Levator Scapulae
16. Posterior Scalene

The Sternocleidomastoid looks like this from the back.

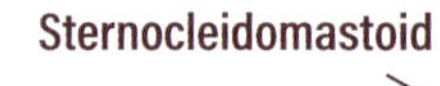

Neck Movement and the Sternocleidomastoid

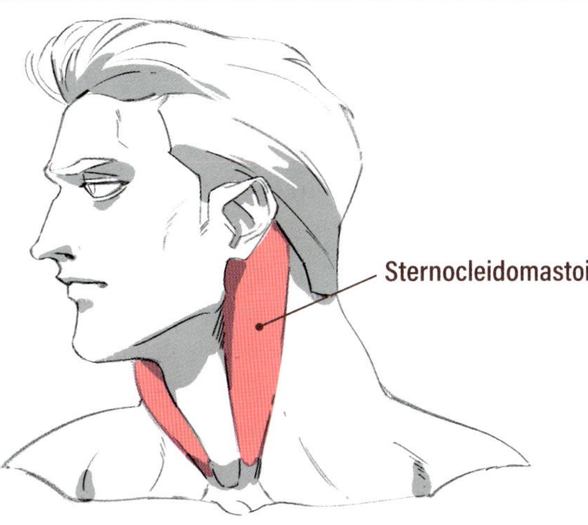

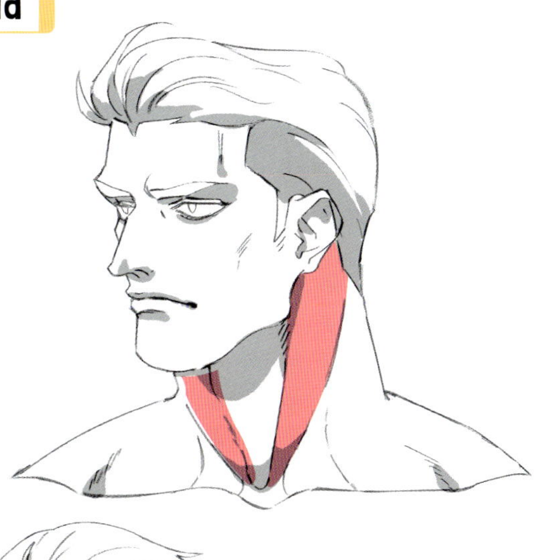

The sternocleidomastoid is a key muscle for "agonist" and "antagonist" movements. The agonist muscle is the primarily mover for a given action, while the antagonist muscle moves in the opposite direction. When you twist or tilt your neck, the muscle on the side of the movement is the agonist muscle, and the opposite muscle is the antagonist muscle. Therefore, both sternocleidomastoid muscles move simultaneously but with different roles when the neck moves to one side or the other.

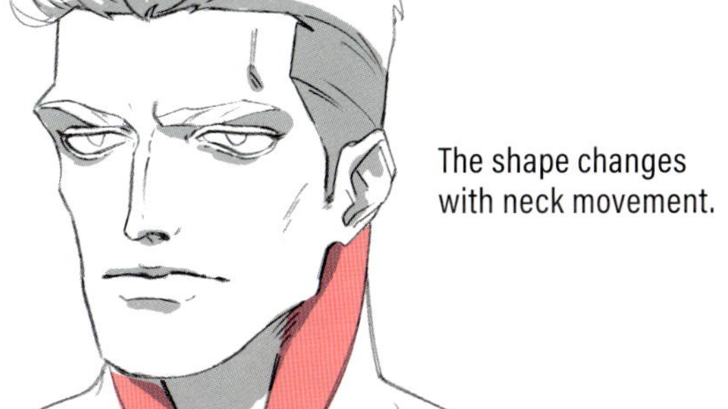

The shape changes with neck movement.

Sternocleidomastoid Size and Body Shape Changes

The sternocleidomastoid is an essential muscle for drawing the neck. Even in a lean body type, illustrating the sternocleidomastoid greatly enhances the appearance. In a muscular body type, the neck is thicker. Additionally, making the sternocleidomastoid itself thicker ensures that the neck's appearance is in proportion with the rest of the body.

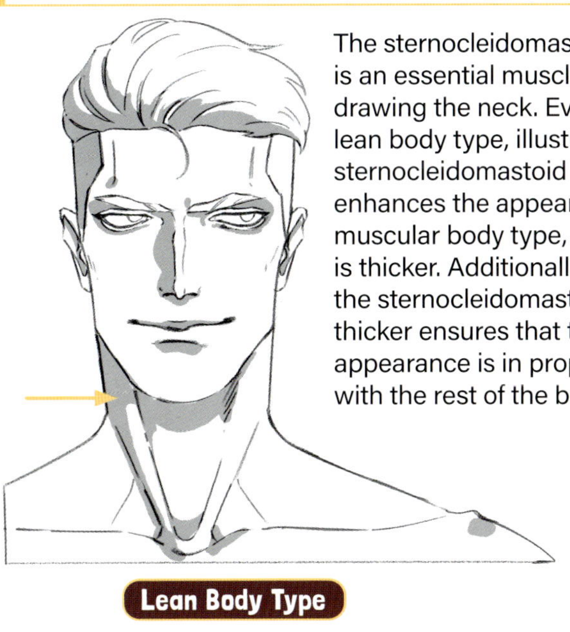

Lean Body Type

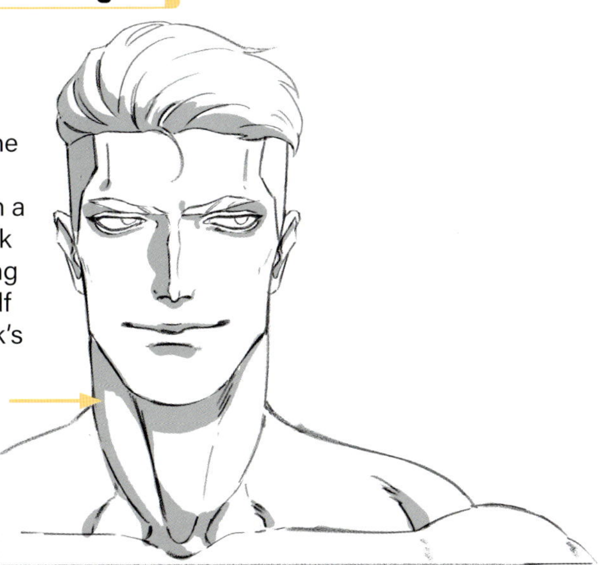

Muscular Body Type

Arm Muscles

Structure of the Arm Muscles

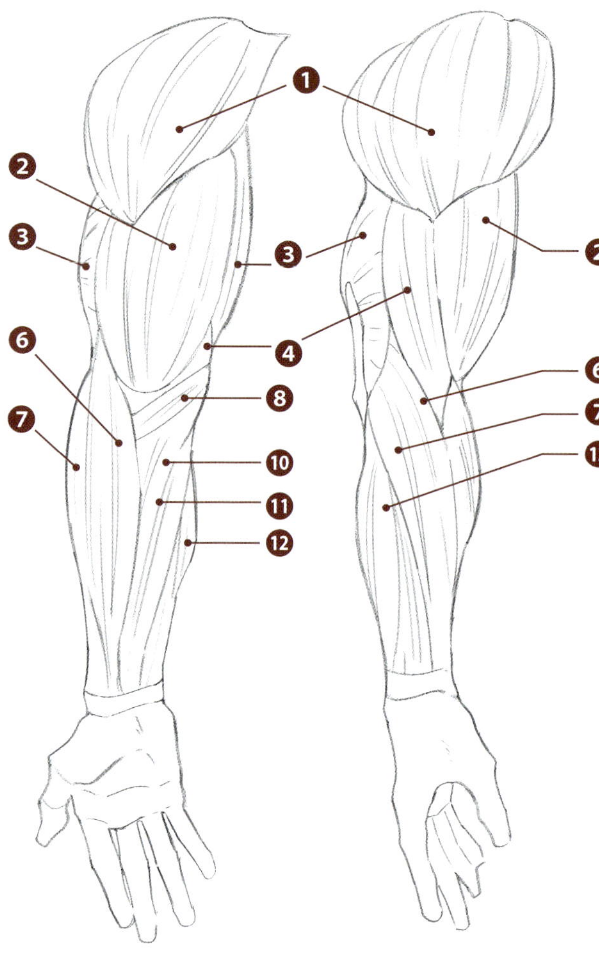

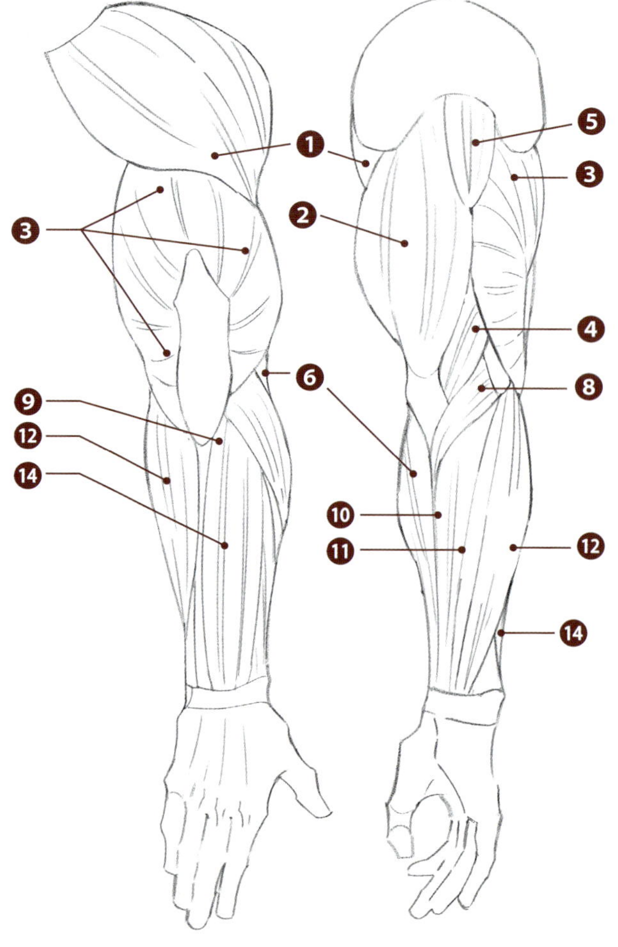

1. Deltoid
2. Biceps
3. Triceps
4. Brachialis
5. Coracobrachialis
6. Brachioradialis
7. Extensor Carpi Radialis Longus
8. Pronator Teres
9. Anconeus
10. Flexor Carpi Radialis
11. Palmaris Longus
12. Flexor Carpi Ulnaris
13. Extensor Digitorum
14. Extensor Carpi Ulnaris

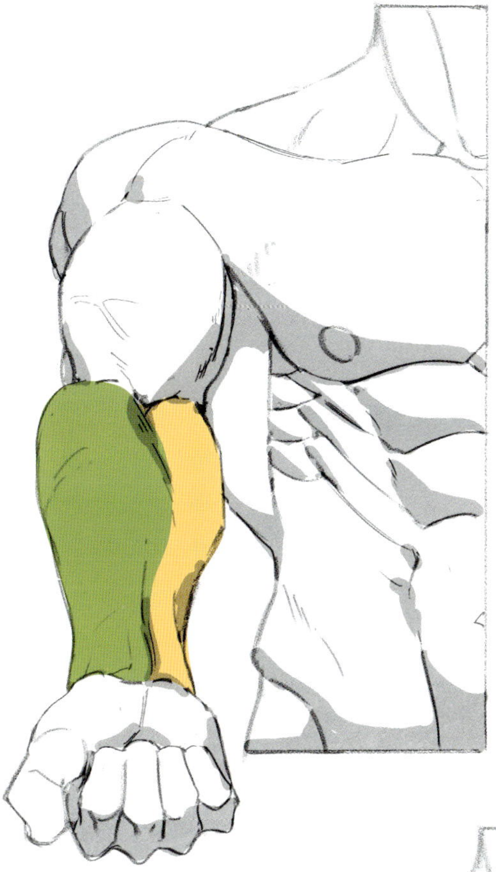

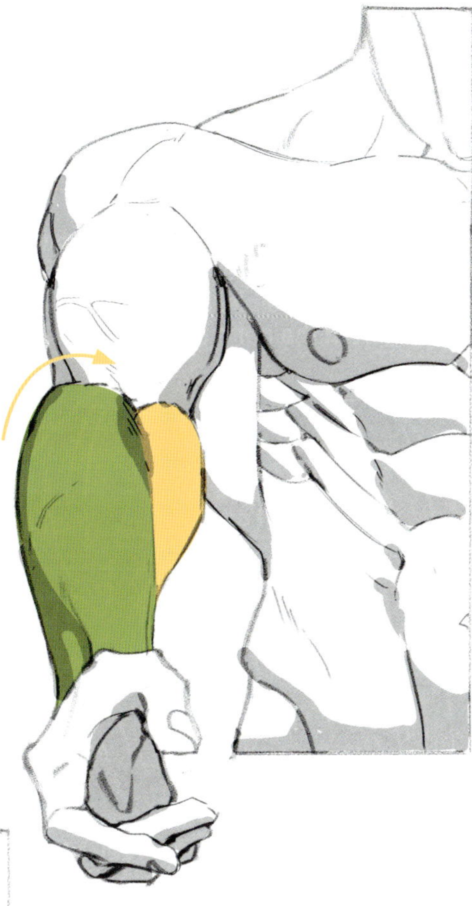

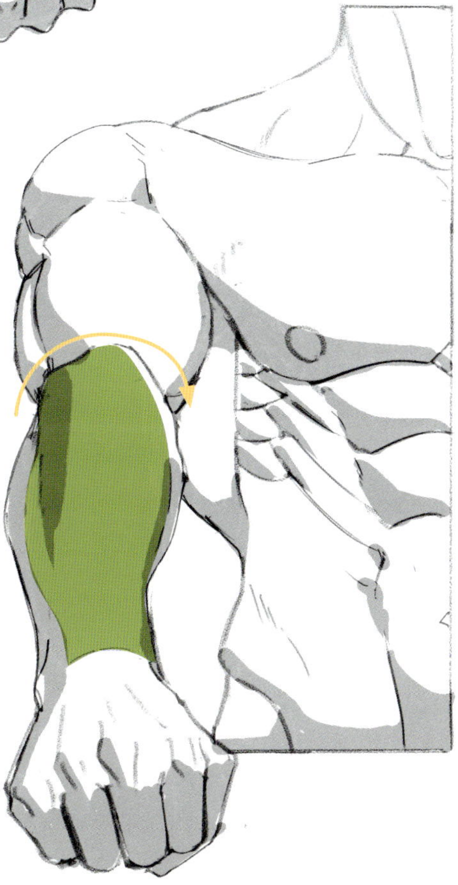

Arm Rotation and Muscle Twisting

The illustration shows muscle positions when the arm is rotated. This rotation changes how the arm muscles appear, even in the same pose and angle.

Arm Muscles

Arm Direction

The arm is a collection of many muscles. The visible muscles change depending on the view. From the front, the brachioradialis and extensor muscles are prominent. From the back, the flexor muscles, like the flexor carpi ulnaris, are visible. From the back of the hand, the extensor group can be seen, while the flexor group is seen from the palm side.

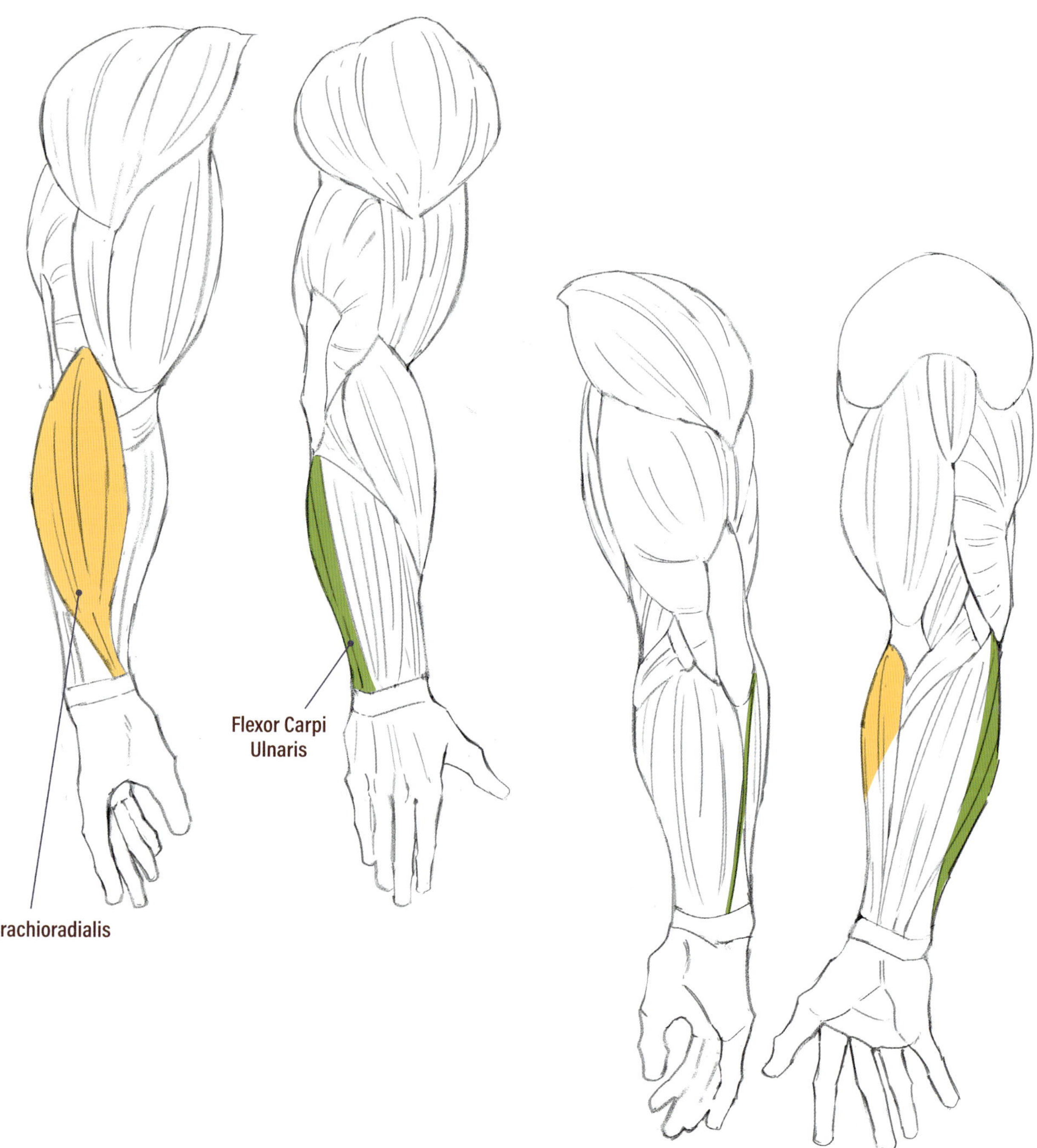

Forearm Turned Backward

Muscle distribution with the palm turned backward 90 degrees. The shapes of the muscles change slightly, and some muscles become invisible.

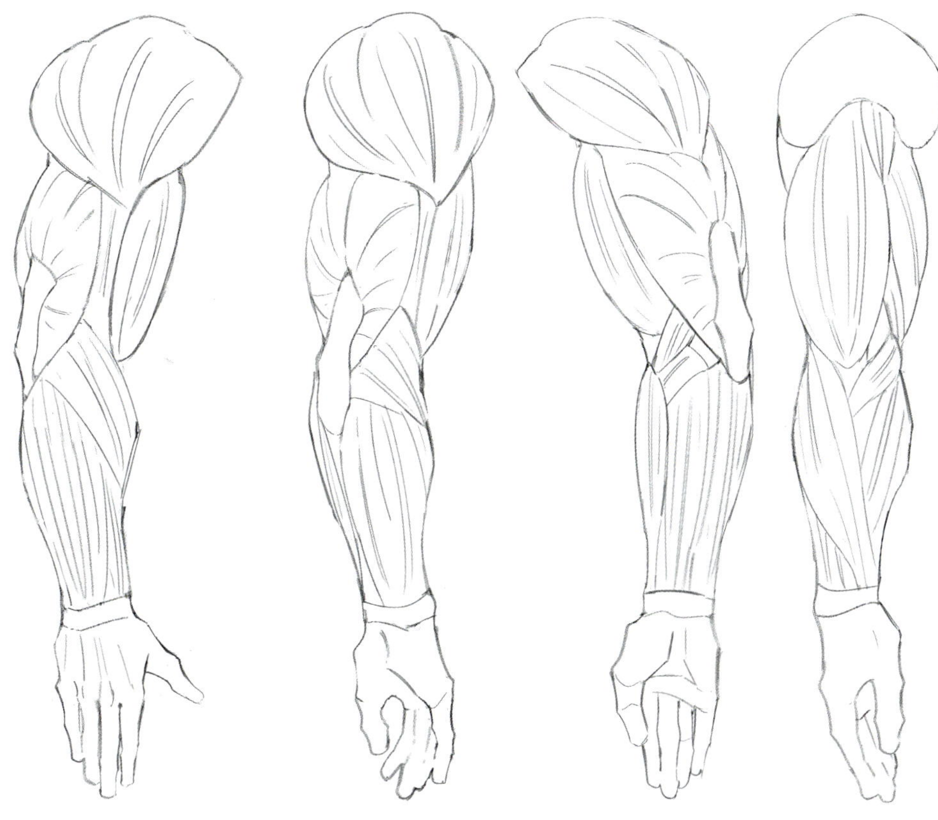

Forearm Turned Outward

Muscle distribution with the palm forced to face away from the body.

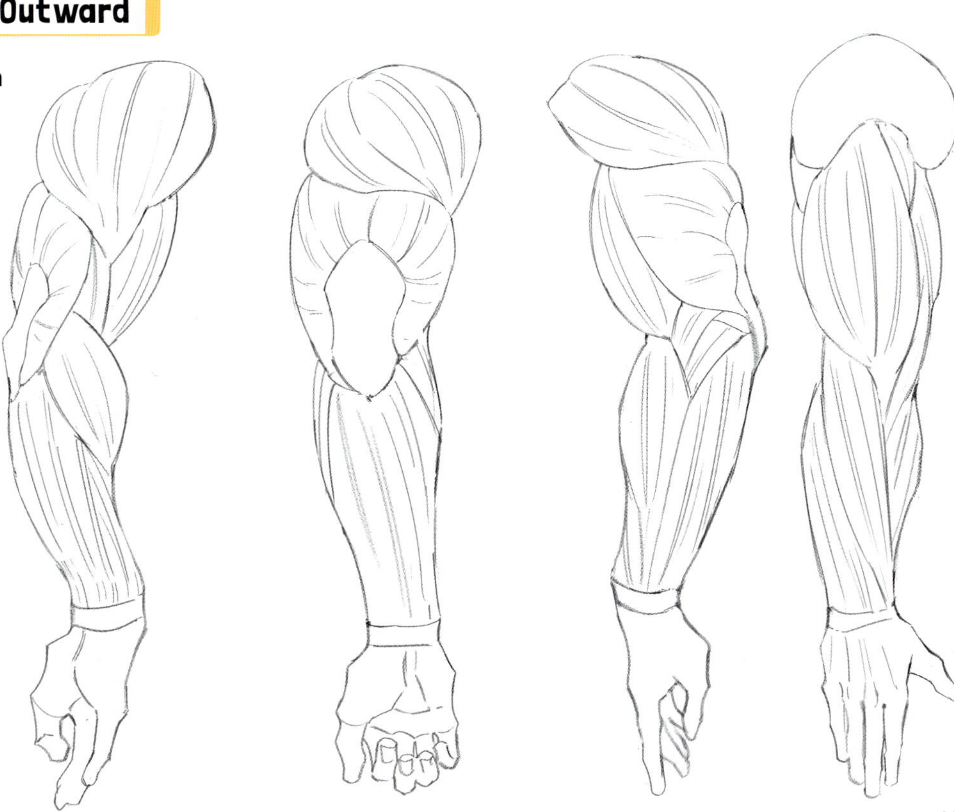

Arm Muscles

Biceps

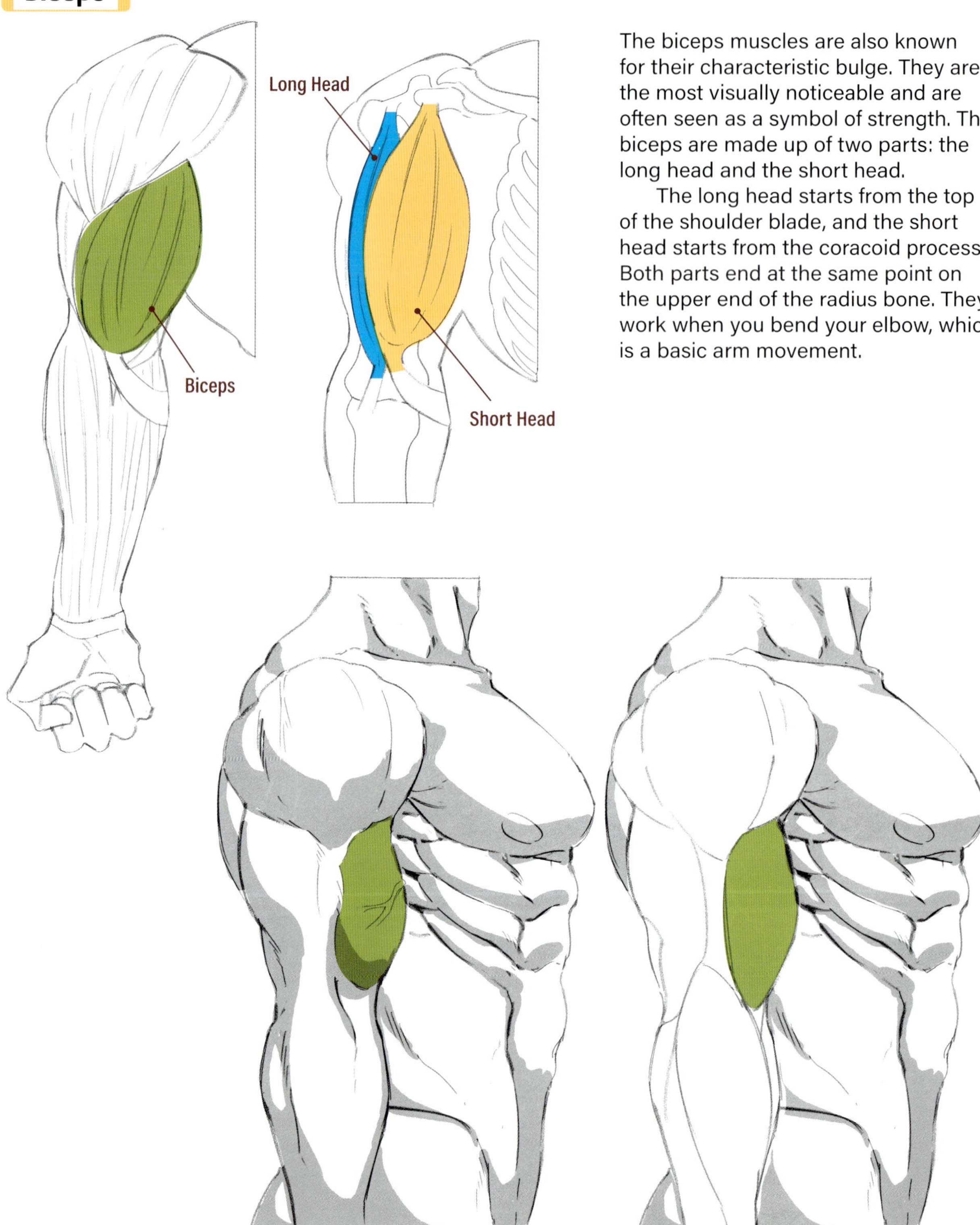

The biceps muscles are also known for their characteristic bulge. They are the most visually noticeable and are often seen as a symbol of strength. The biceps are made up of two parts: the long head and the short head.

The long head starts from the top of the shoulder blade, and the short head starts from the coracoid process. Both parts end at the same point on the upper end of the radius bone. They work when you bend your elbow, which is a basic arm movement.

Movement of Biceps and Triceps

Pronation and Direction of Biceps

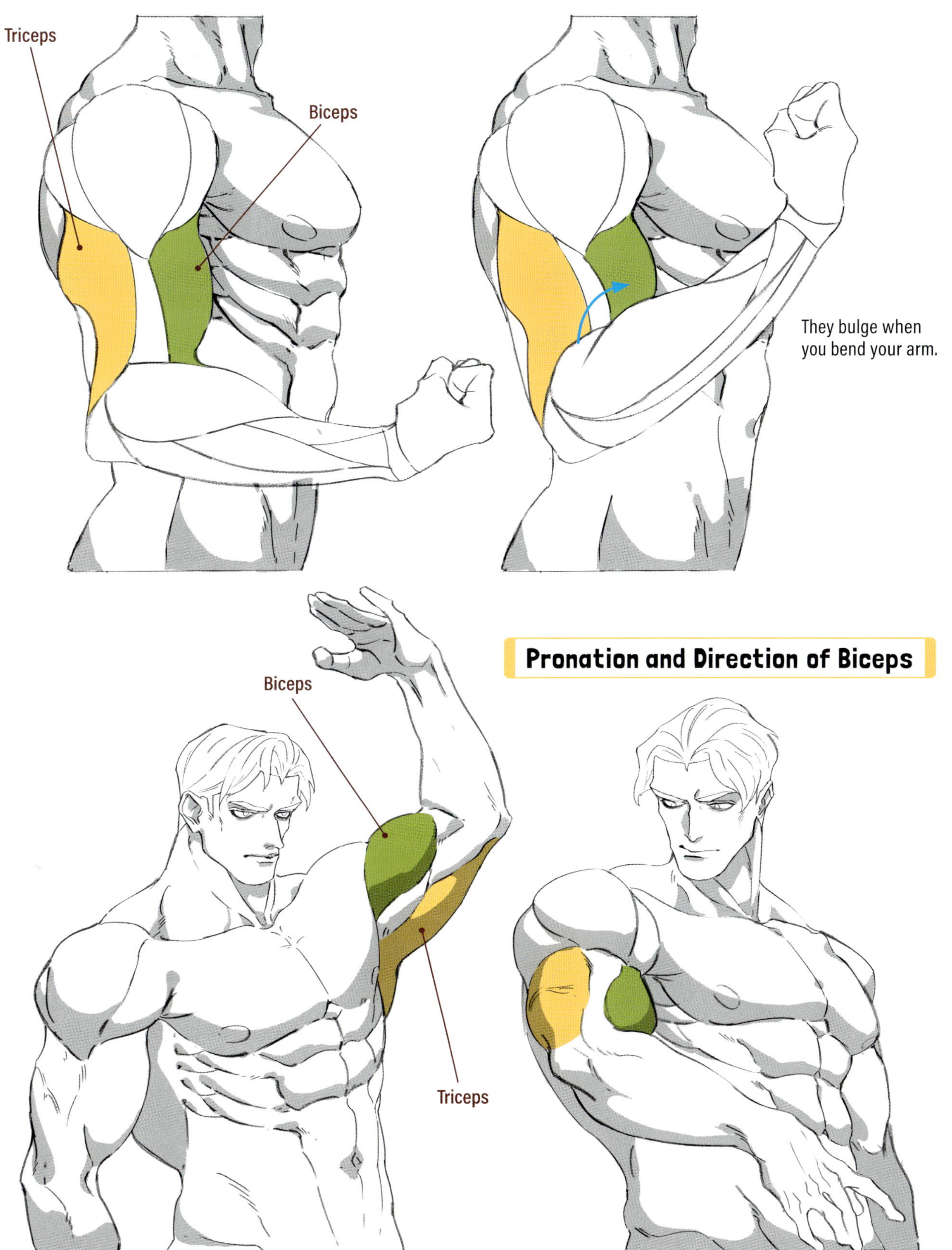

Arm Muscles

Triceps

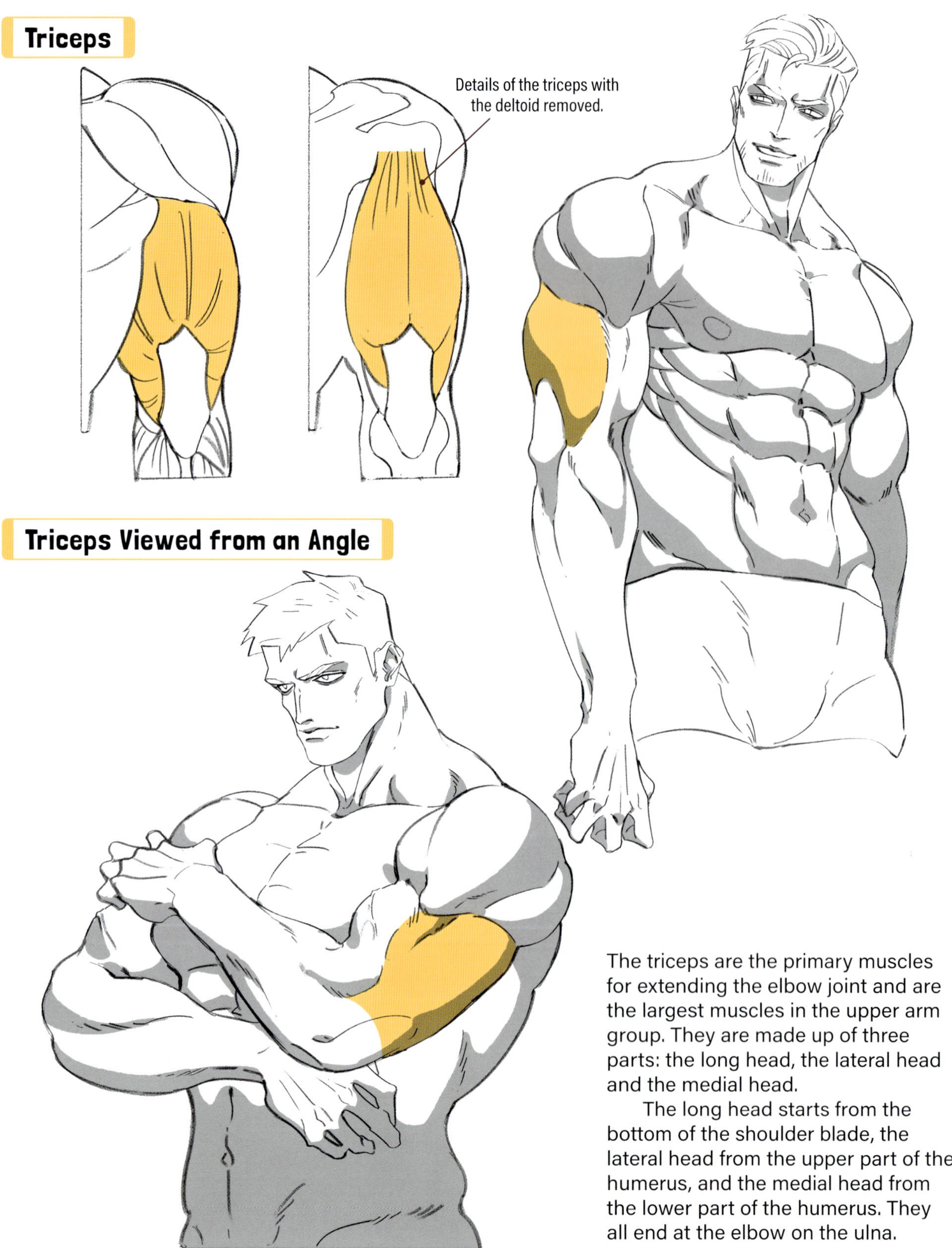

Triceps Viewed from an Angle

The triceps are the primary muscles for extending the elbow joint and are the largest muscles in the upper arm group. They are made up of three parts: the long head, the lateral head and the medial head.

The long head starts from the bottom of the shoulder blade, the lateral head from the upper part of the humerus, and the medial head from the lower part of the humerus. They all end at the elbow on the ulna.

Tension and Relaxation of Biceps and Triceps

The triceps muscles extend the elbow joint, opposite to the biceps. When you pull your arm down strongly, the triceps contracts while the biceps relaxes.

When you bend your elbow, the biceps contracts and the triceps relaxes.

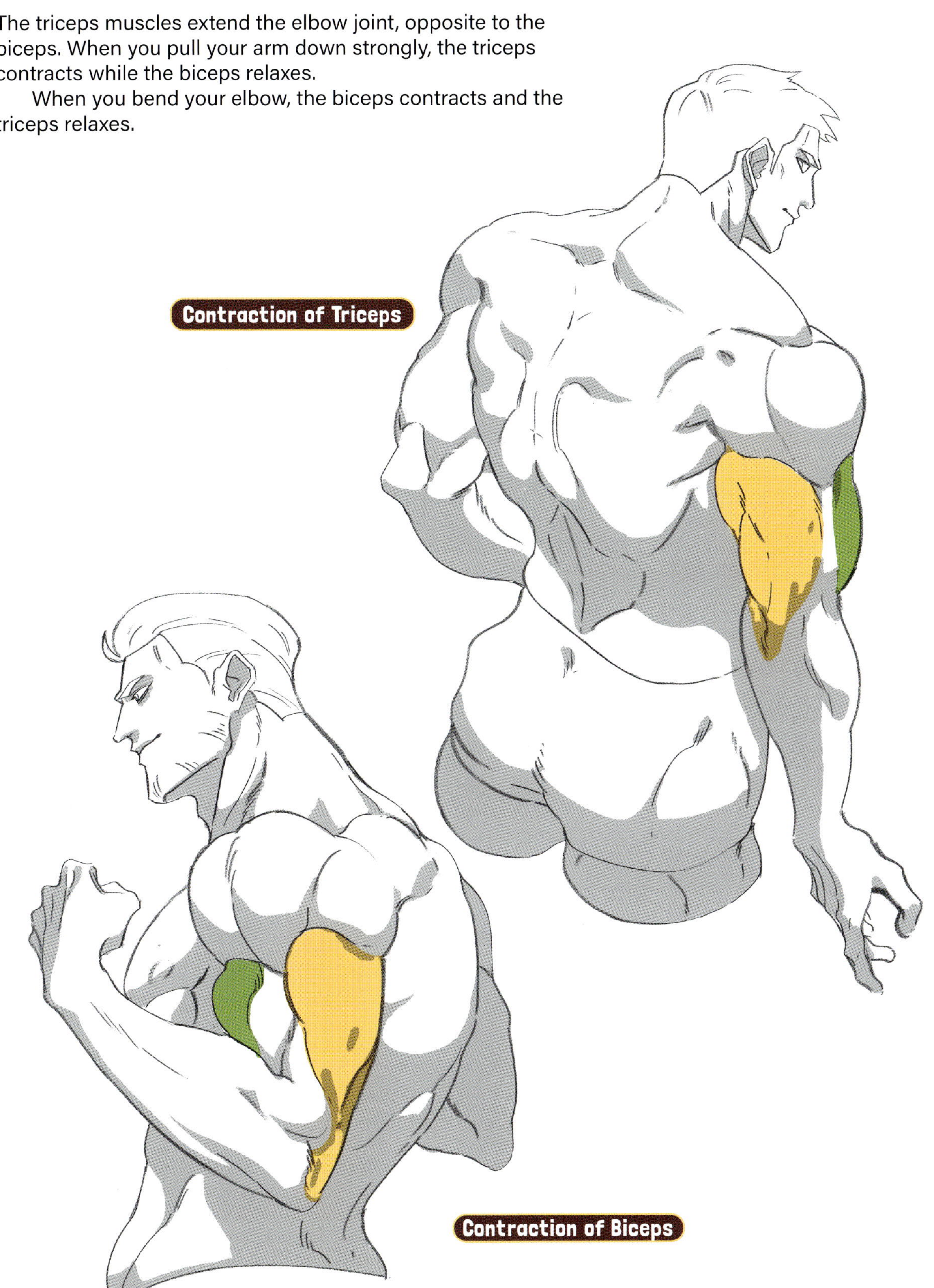

Upper Arm Muscles

Brachialis and Coracobrachialis

The coracobrachialis starts from the coracoid process on the inside of the shoulder blade and ends on the inside of the humerus. It helps the brachialis and biceps when bending the shoulder or pulling down.

It is important when lifting the arm inward.

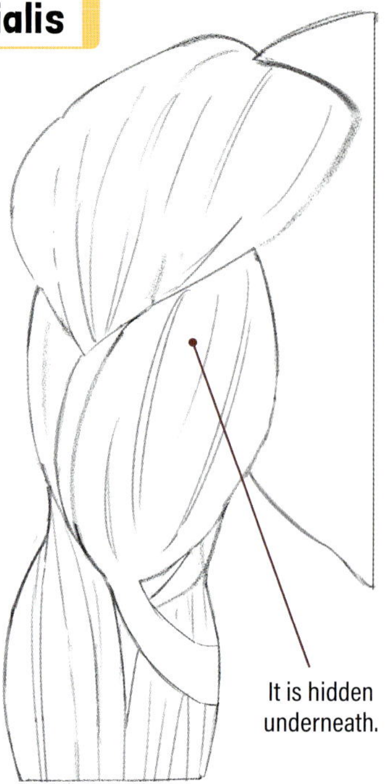

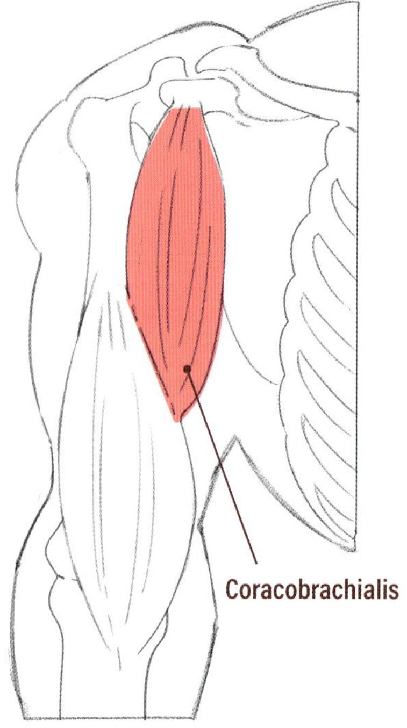

Appearance of Brachialis

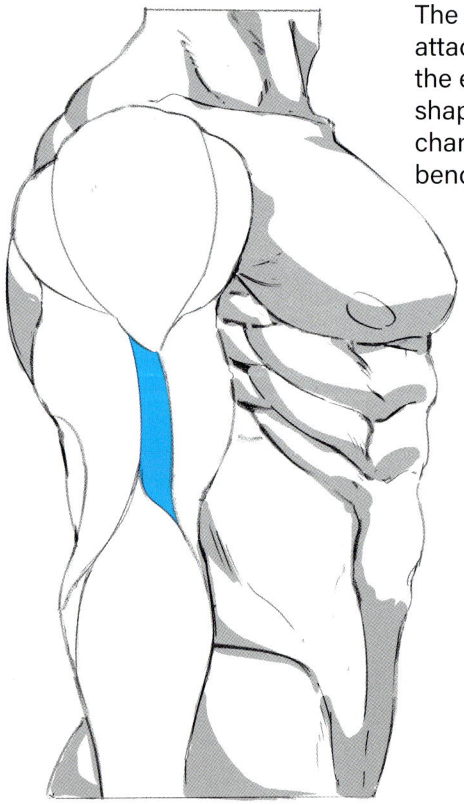

The brachialis is attached across the elbow joint. The shape of the muscle changes when you bend your arm.

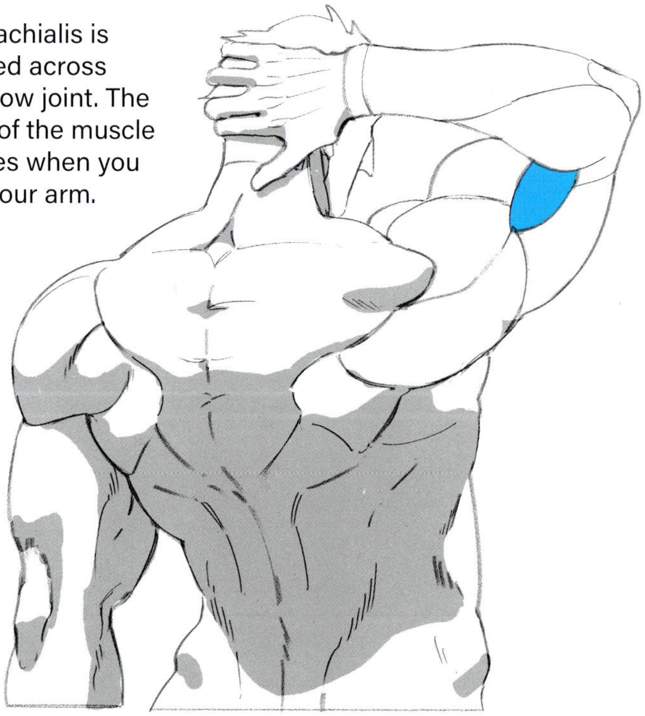

Appearance of Coracobrachialis

The coracobrachialis is inside and under the biceps and triceps. It is usually hidden but can be seen under the deltoid when the arm is raised.

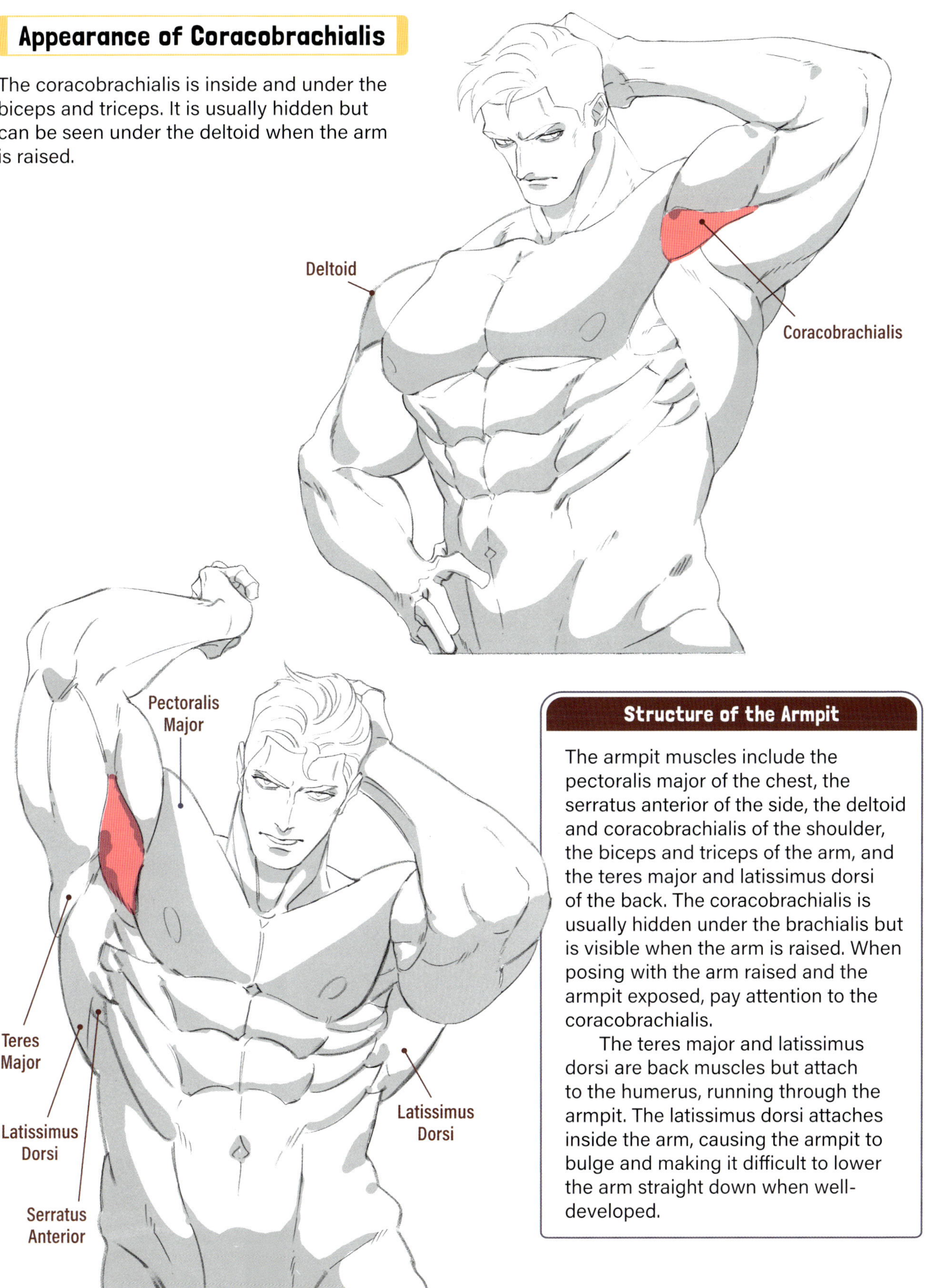

Structure of the Armpit

The armpit muscles include the pectoralis major of the chest, the serratus anterior of the side, the deltoid and coracobrachialis of the shoulder, the biceps and triceps of the arm, and the teres major and latissimus dorsi of the back. The coracobrachialis is usually hidden under the brachialis but is visible when the arm is raised. When posing with the arm raised and the armpit exposed, pay attention to the coracobrachialis.

The teres major and latissimus dorsi are back muscles but attach to the humerus, running through the armpit. The latissimus dorsi attaches inside the arm, causing the armpit to bulge and making it difficult to lower the arm straight down when well-developed.

Forearm Muscles

Brachioradialis and Extensor Carpi Radialis Longus

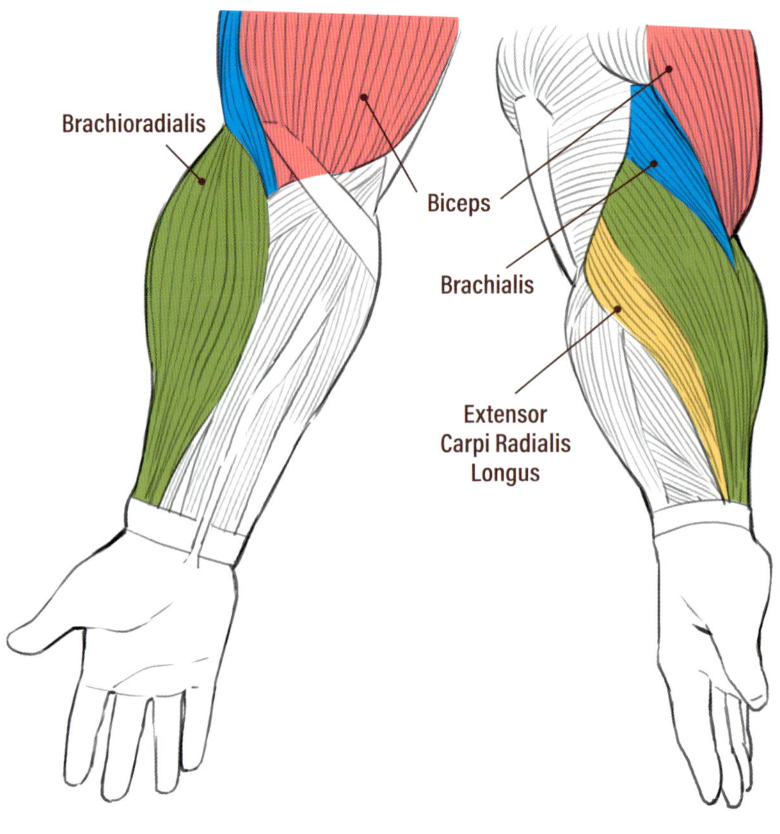

Brachioradialis is a muscle located on the front side of the forearm, on the thumb side. It starts from the outer ridge of the upper arm bone and ends at the styloid process of the radius bone. Unlike other forearm muscles, it doesn't help with wrist movement. Instead, it works with the brachialis and biceps to bend the elbow from below.

Extensor Carpi Radialis Longus is a muscle that helps to extend the wrist. It starts near the outer side of the upper arm bone and ends at the base of the second metacarpal bone. This muscle is on the back of the forearm and is the outermost muscle, playing a key role in extending the wrist.

Look at the three images below, keeping in mind the muscles discussed above. You can make various observations.

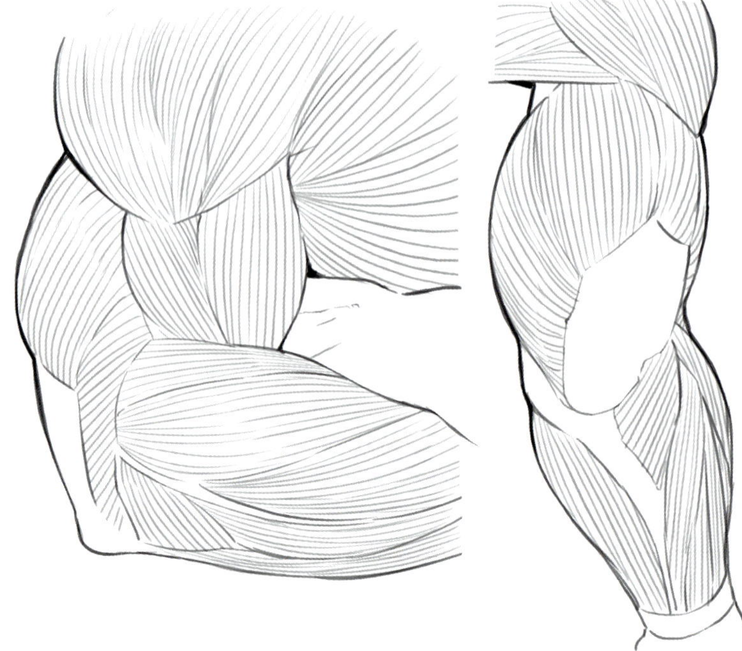

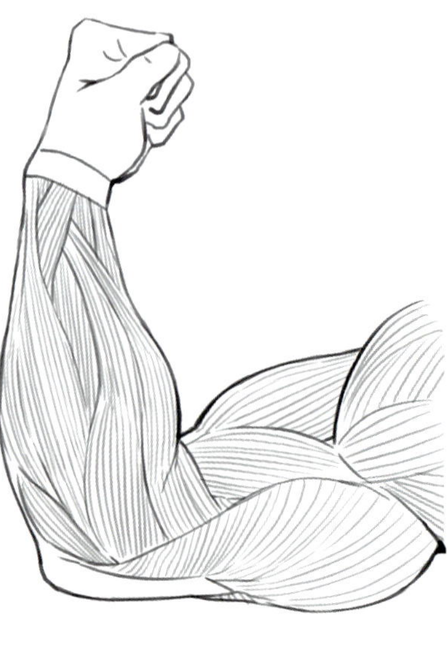

Anconeus and Forearm Extensors

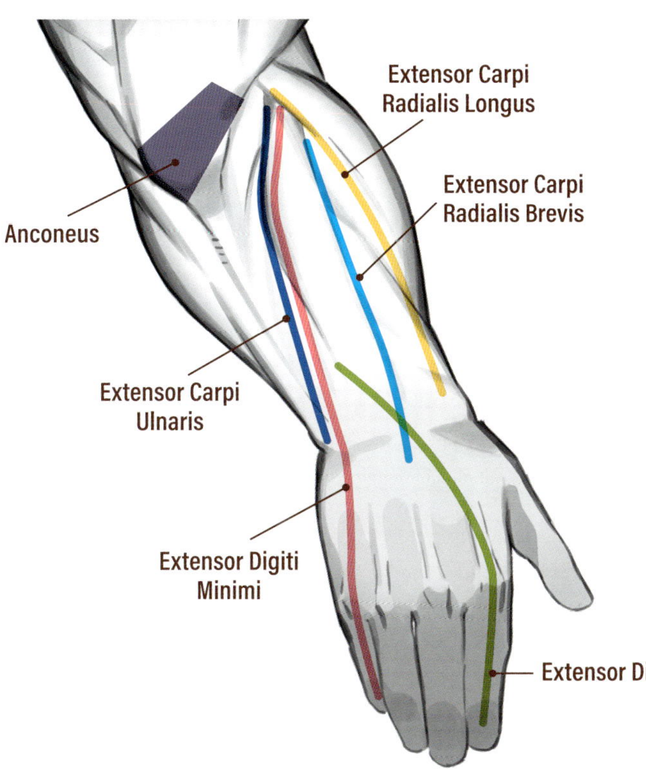

The anconeus is a small muscle located under the elbow joint. It mainly assists the triceps in extending the elbow. The forearm extensor group consists of muscles on the back-of-the-hand side of the forearm, including the extensor carpi radialis longus, extensor carpi radialis brevis, extensor carpi ulnaris, extensor digitorum and extensor digiti minimi.

The extensor carpi radialis longus, extensor carpi radialis brevis and extensor carpi ulnaris help to extend the wrist. The extensor digitorum helps extend the fingers at the wrist joint, and the extensor digiti minimi specifically helps to extend the little finger.

These muscles all originate on the outer side of the humerus, but terminate in different locations.

Emphasize These Forearm Muscles When Drawing

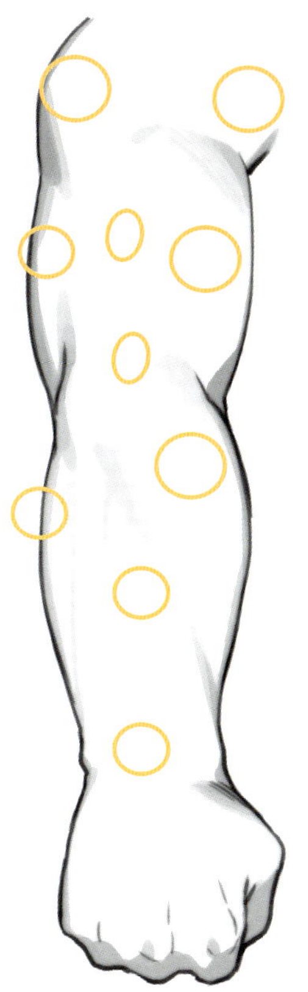

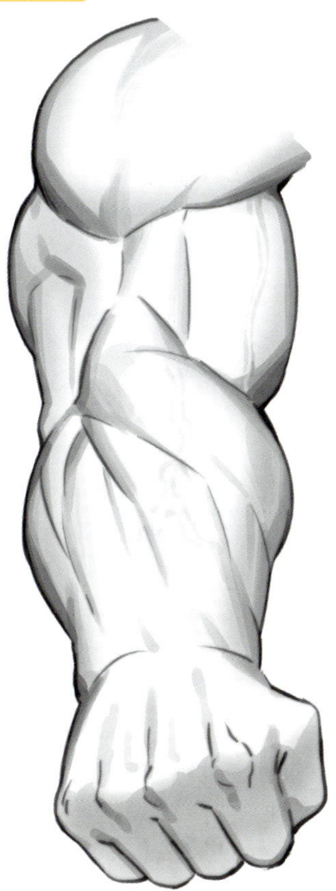

Forearm Muscles

Flexor Group (viewed from the inside)

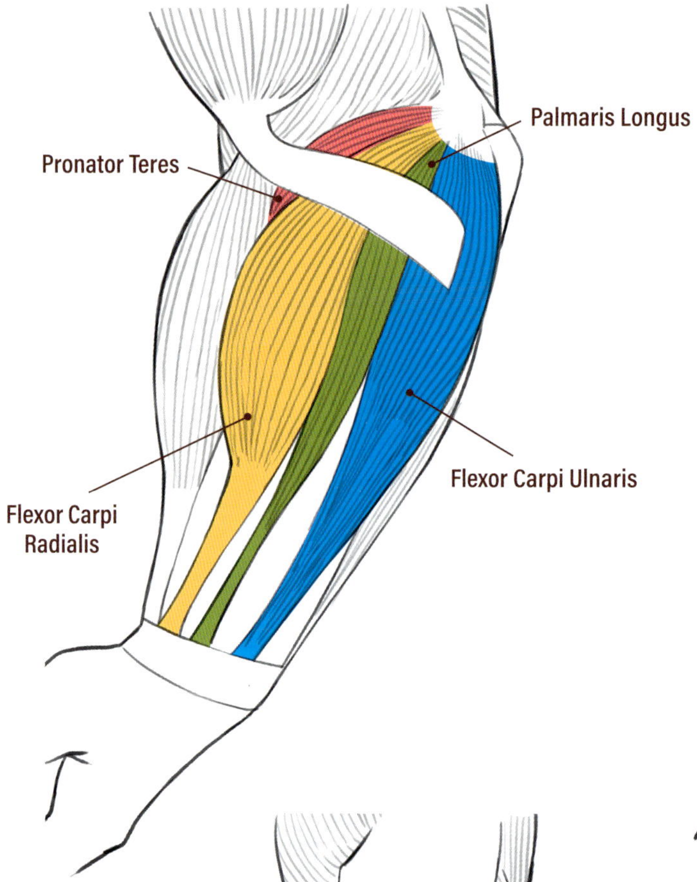

Palmaris Longus

Pronator Teres

Flexor Carpi Ulnaris

Flexor Carpi Radialis

Flexor Group (viewed from the front)

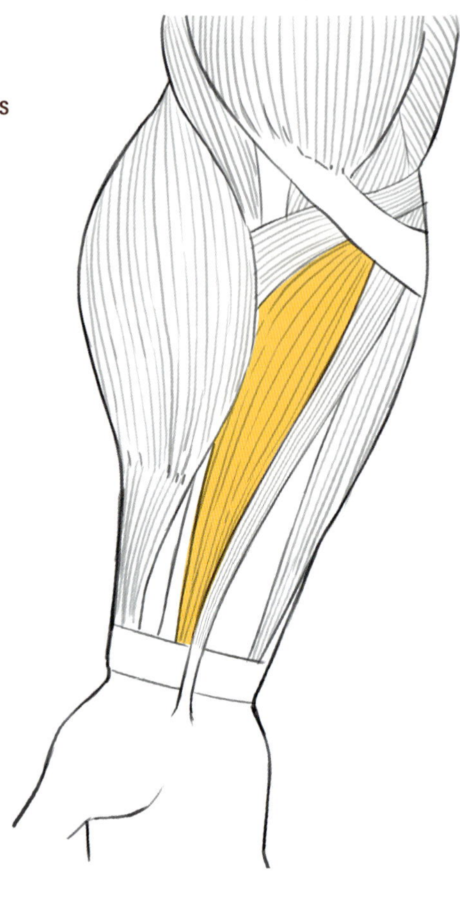

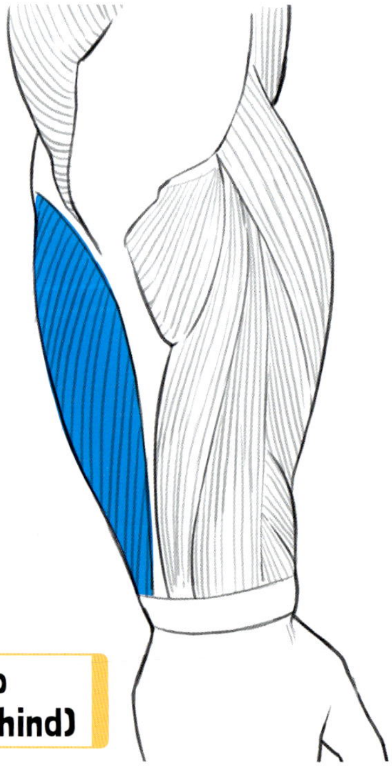

Flexor Group (viewed from behind)

Flexor muscles work opposite to extensor muscles, helping to bend joints. The flexor group in the forearm includes four muscles: pronator teres, palmaris longus, flexor carpi radialis and flexor carpi ulnaris. These muscles are located in the superficial layer of the forearm and connect the wrist and elbow joints.

The main function of the pronator teres is to bend the elbow and twist the wrist inward. The flexor carpi radialis, palmaris longus, and flexor carpi ulnaris mainly work to bend the wrist. These muscles have different ending points, but they all start from the inner side of the humerus.

Twisting of Forearm Muscles

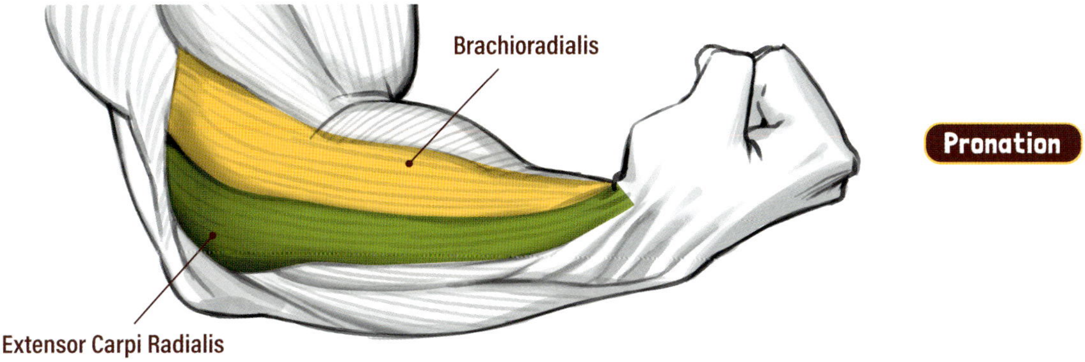

Brachioradialis

Pronation

Extensor Carpi Radialis

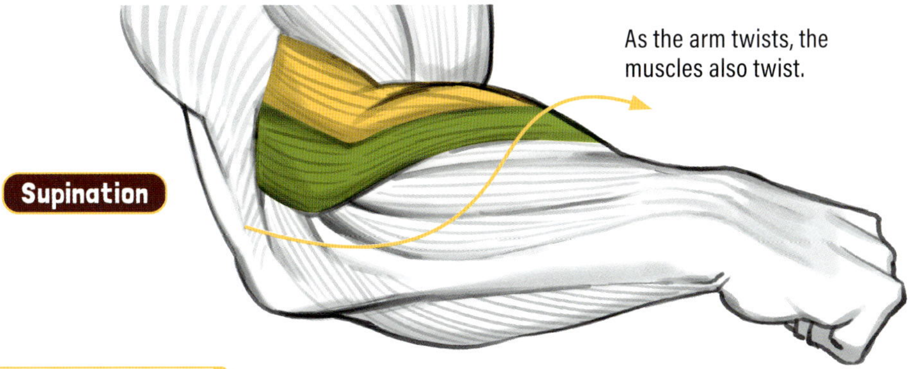

As the arm twists, the muscles also twist.

Supination

Emphasizing Forearm Muscles

The forearm muscles, including the extensors and flexors, run along the front and back of the arm. Emphasizing these muscles when drawing can make the arm appear much thicker due to the combined effect of the muscles.

When doing this, it's important to also enlarge the upper arm, shoulder and neck muscles in proportion with the thickened forearm.

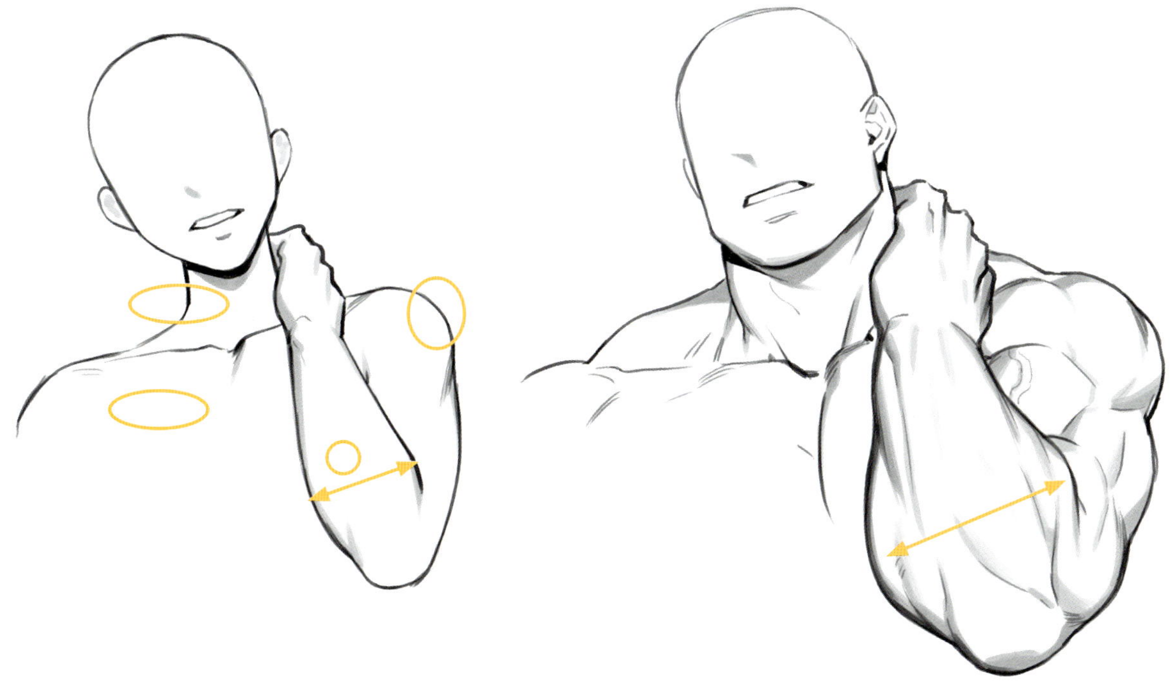

Forearm Muscles

Abductor Pollicis Longus, Extensor Pollicis Brevis

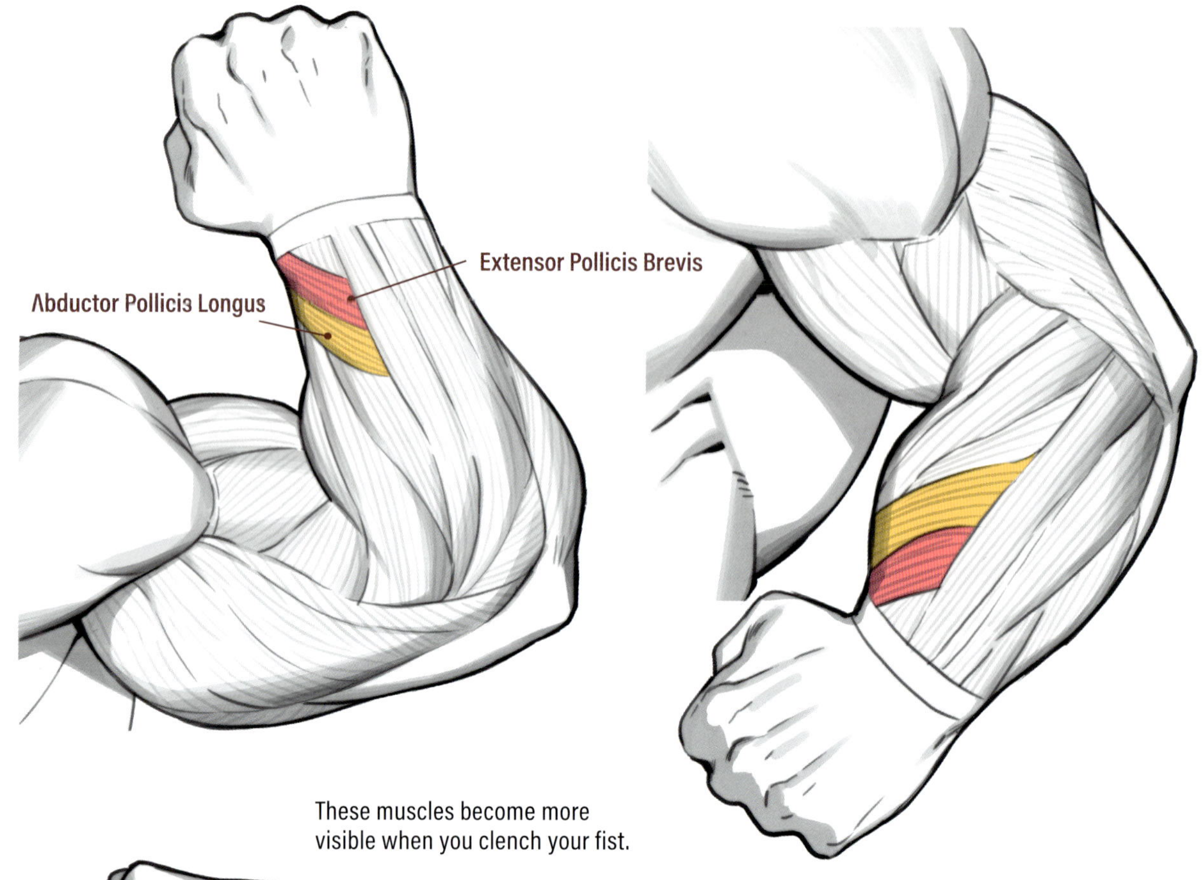

These muscles become more visible when you clench your fist.

Both the abductor pollicis longus and extensor pollicis brevis are part of the forearm extensor group that runs underneath the extensor digitorum. Their main function is to move the thumb outward. The abductor pollicis longus starts from the middle back of the radius and ulna bones and ends on the outer side of the base of the first metacarpal bone. The extensor pollicis brevis starts from the middle back of the radius and ends at the base of the thumb's proximal phalanx on the back side.

Ulna and Silhouette

The ulna is the bone that forms the axis for basic arm movements like bending and extending the forearm. It is located on the pinky side of the two forearm bones and connects to the humerus. The upper part is thick, while the lower part is thin. The top end sticks out and is called the olecranon. Because the ulna is the bone that forms the axis of the forearm, its position doesn't change during pronation and supination. During pronation, the head of the ulna becomes visible at the base of the wrist on the pinky side, making it easy to spot.

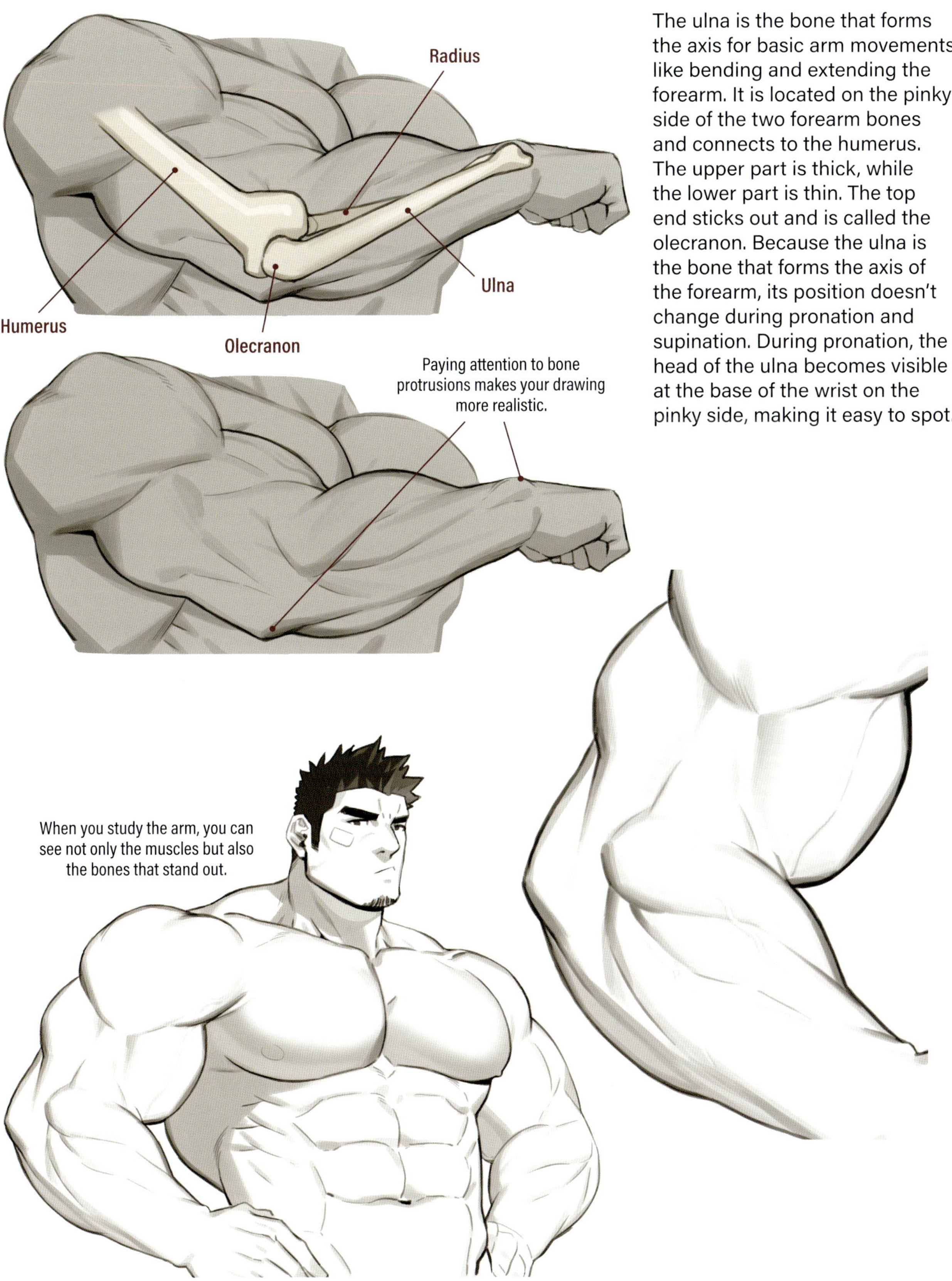

Leg Muscles

Structure of the Leg Muscles

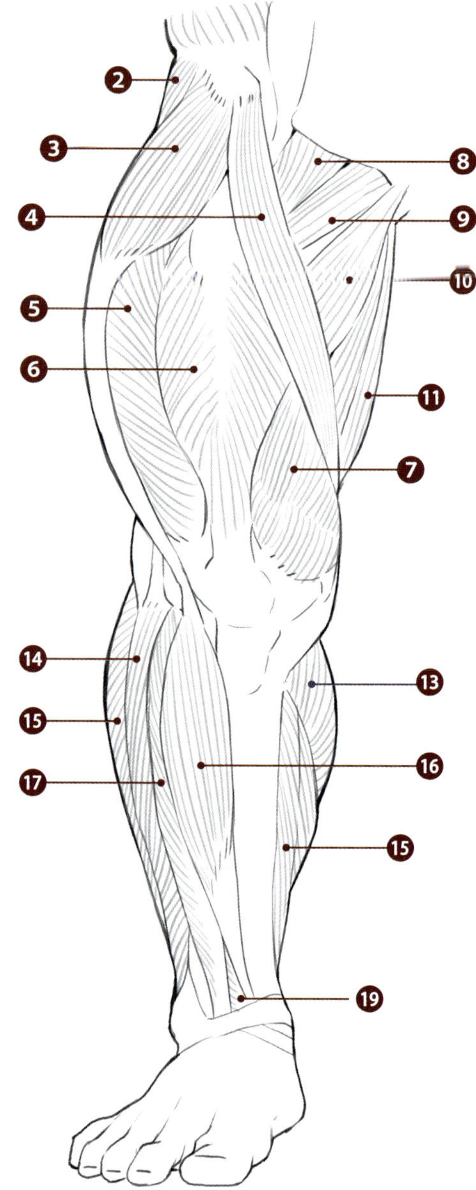

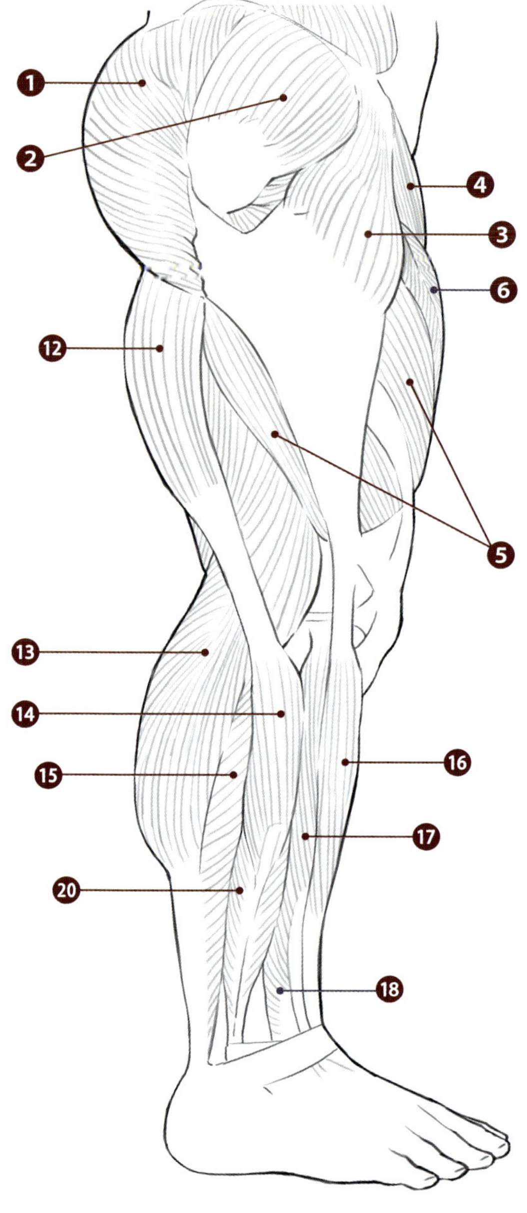

❶ Gluteus Maximus
❷ Gluteus Medius
❸ Tensor Fasciae Latae
❹ Sartorius
❺ Vastus Lateralis
❻ Rectus Femoris
❼ Vastus Medialis
❽ Iliopsoas
❾ Pectineus
❿ Adductor Longus
⓫ Gracilis
⓬ Biceps Femoris
⓭ Gastrocnemius
⓮ Peroneus Longus
⓯ Soleus
⓰ Tibialis Anterior
⓱ Extensor Digitorum Longus
⓲ Peroneus Tertius
⓳ Extensor Hallucis Longus
⓴ Peroneus Brevis
㉑ Adductor Magnus
㉒ Semitendinosus
㉓ Semimembranosus

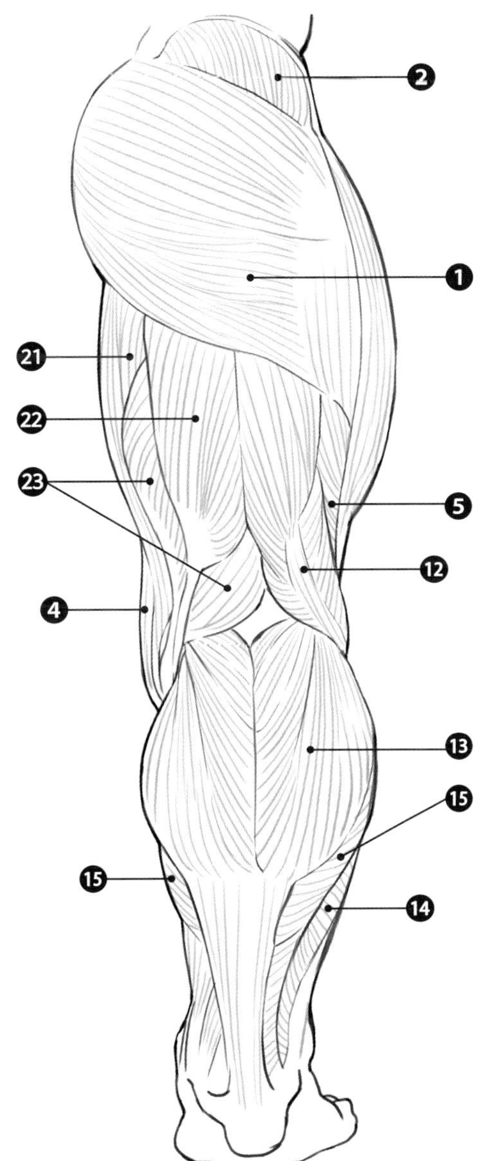
2
1
21
22
23
5
12
4
13
15
15
14

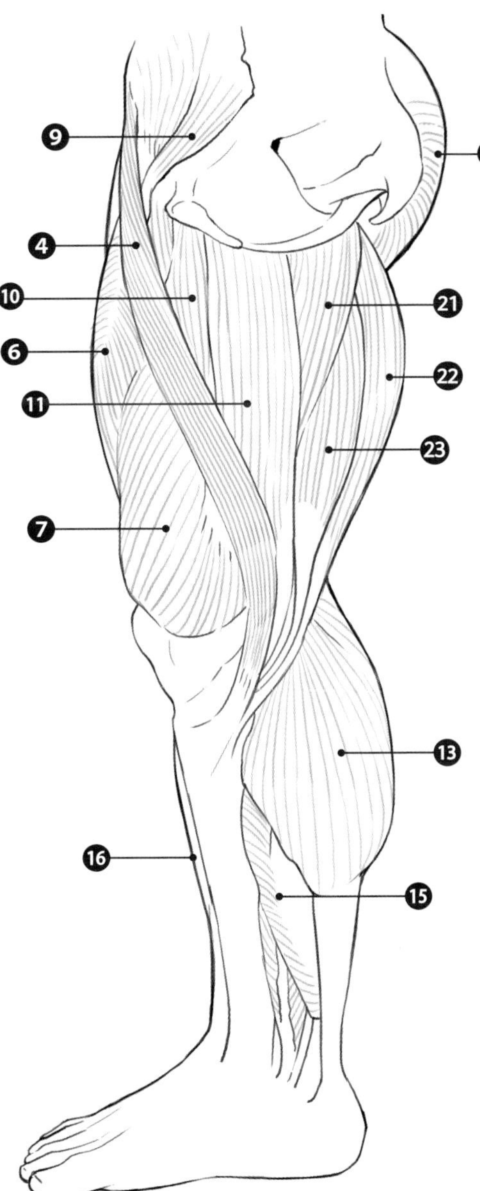
9
1
4
10
21
6
22
11
23
7
13
16
15

Leg Muscles (Buttocks and Thighs)

Gluteus Maximus

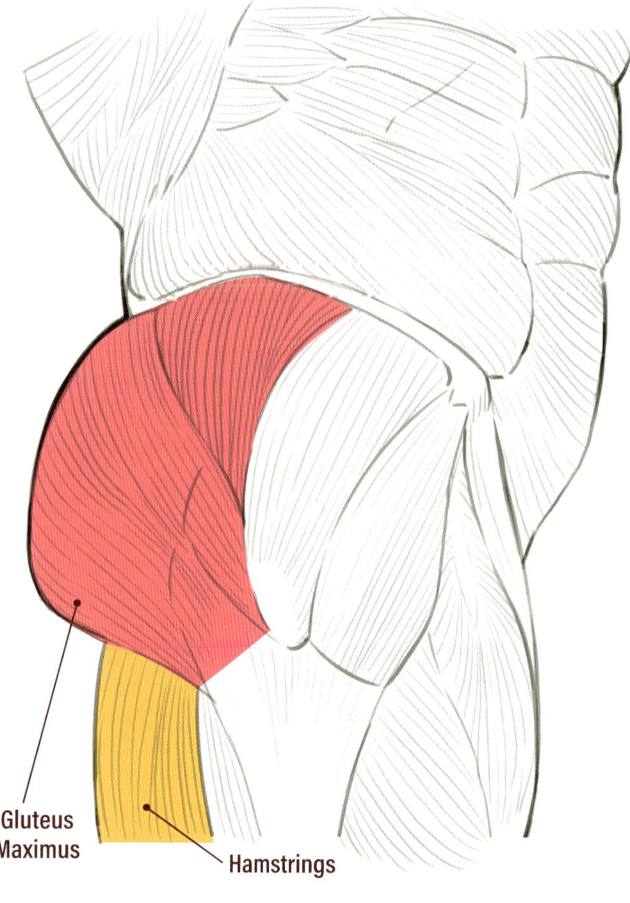

The gluteus maximus is a large muscle that forms the buttocks and is the largest muscle in the human body. It plays an important role in maintaining an upright posture and walking.

Its main function is to work with the hamstrings (page 60) to extend the hip joint. The gluteus maximus starts from the back of the sacrum and ilium, with the upper part attaching to the iliotibial band and the lower part to the gluteal tuberosity of the femur.

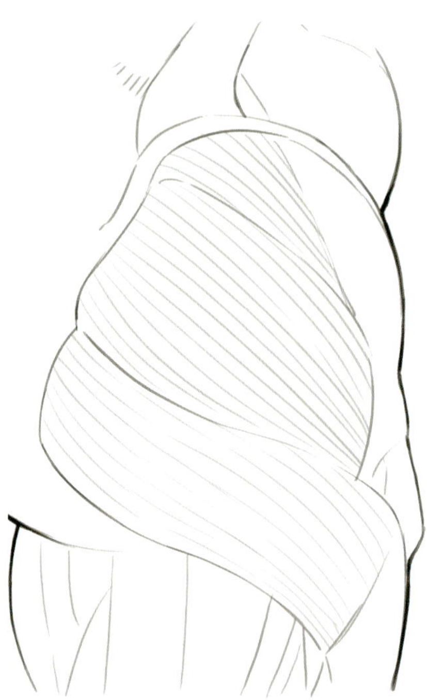

Waist Fat

Subcutaneous fat refers to fat stored just under the skin in the subcutaneous tissue. It acts as a cushion against external impacts and helps retain heat to protect against the cold, making it essential for maintaining the body. Near the waist, it includes areas like the pubic fat pad, side fat on the waist ("love handles"), and fat around the buttocks (see the yellow areas illustrated at left).

Quadriceps

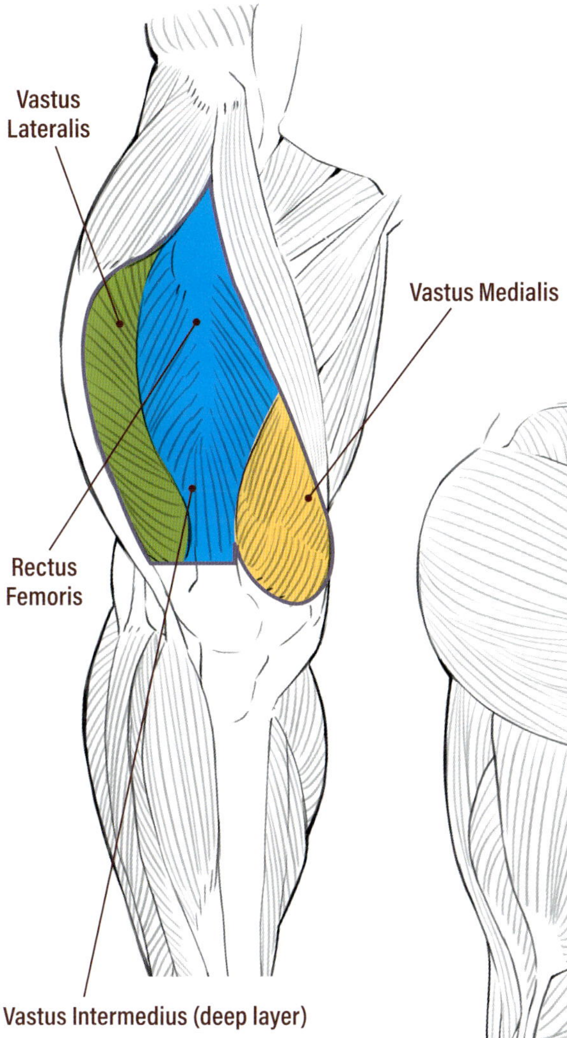

Vastus Lateralis

Vastus Medialis

Rectus Femoris

Vastus Intermedius (deep layer)

The quadriceps consist of the vastus medialis, vastus lateralis and the vastus intermedius in the deep layer. The starting points are different for each muscle: the rectus femoris starts from the anterior inferior iliac spine, the vastus lateralis from the outer side of the femur below the greater trochanter, the vastus medialis from the linea aspera of the femur, and the vastus intermedius from the front of the femur.

However, they all attach to the upper edge of the kneecap, join together through the patellar ligament, and connect to the tibial tuberosity at the upper part of the tibia. Their main function is to extend the knee joint.

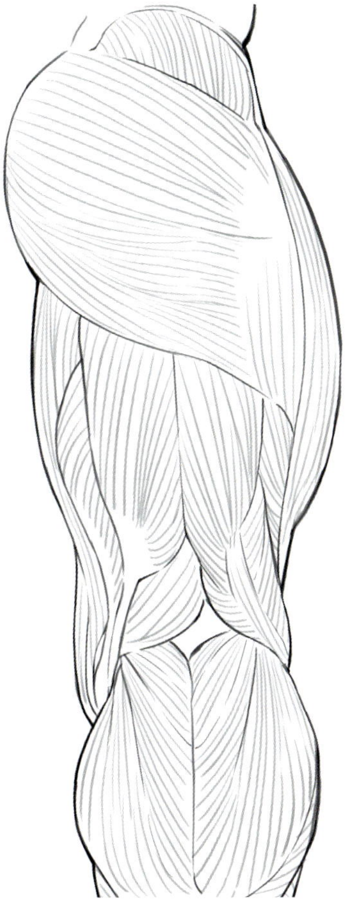

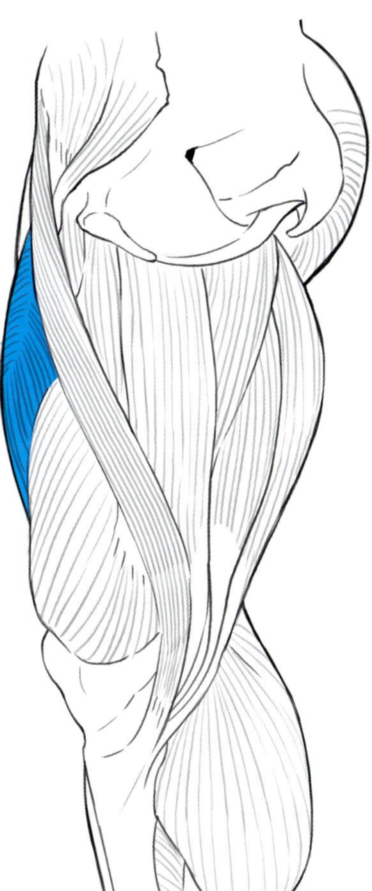

Leg Muscles (Buttocks and Thighs)

Sartorius

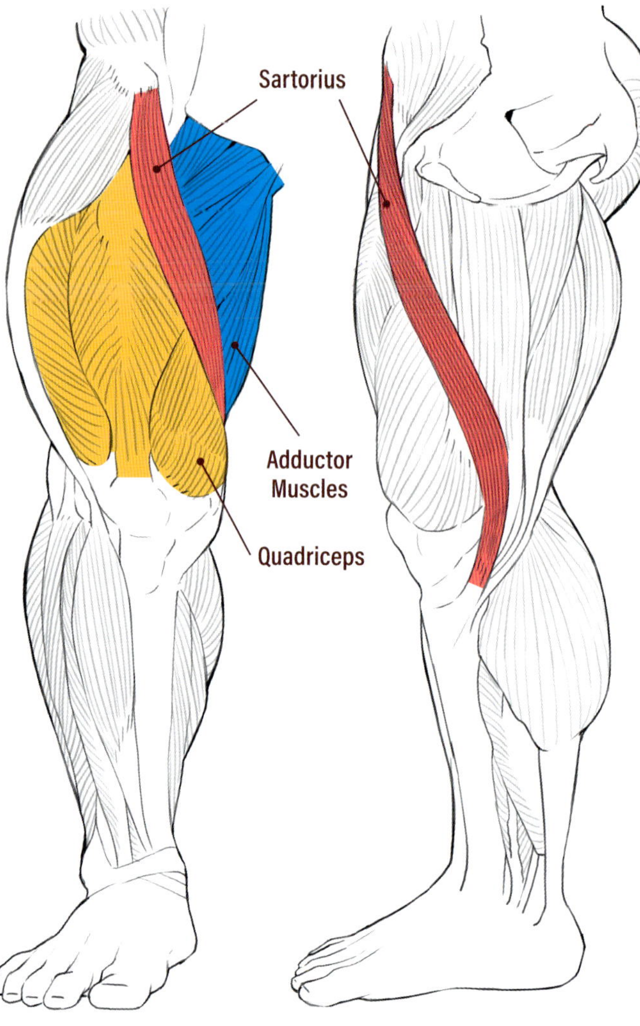

The sartorius is located on the surface of the thigh and is the longest muscle in the human body. It crosses over the quadriceps and is positioned between the adductor muscles and the quadriceps. It mainly helps with bending movements of the hip and knee joints. It starts from the anterior superior iliac spine of the pelvis and ends on the inner side of the tibial tuberosity.

Once you understand the function of the sartorius muscle, you can feature it in your illustrations, like the one shown to the right.

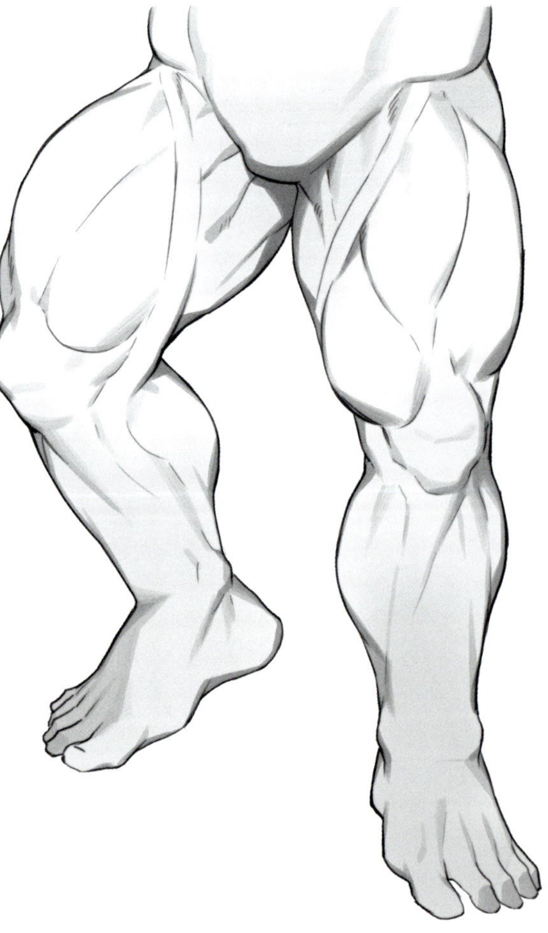

Hip Adductor Muscles

The adductor muscle group includes the adductor magnus, adductor brevis, adductor longus, pectineus and gracilis. These muscles are mainly involved in the adduction movement, which pulls the leg inward.

The adductor magnus starts from the ischial tuberosity, the gracilis from the outer edge of the pubic symphysis, the adductor brevis from the ischiopubic ramus, the adductor longus from the superior pubic ramus, and the pectineus from the pubic crest and surrounding area. All of these muscles connect to the inner side of the femur.

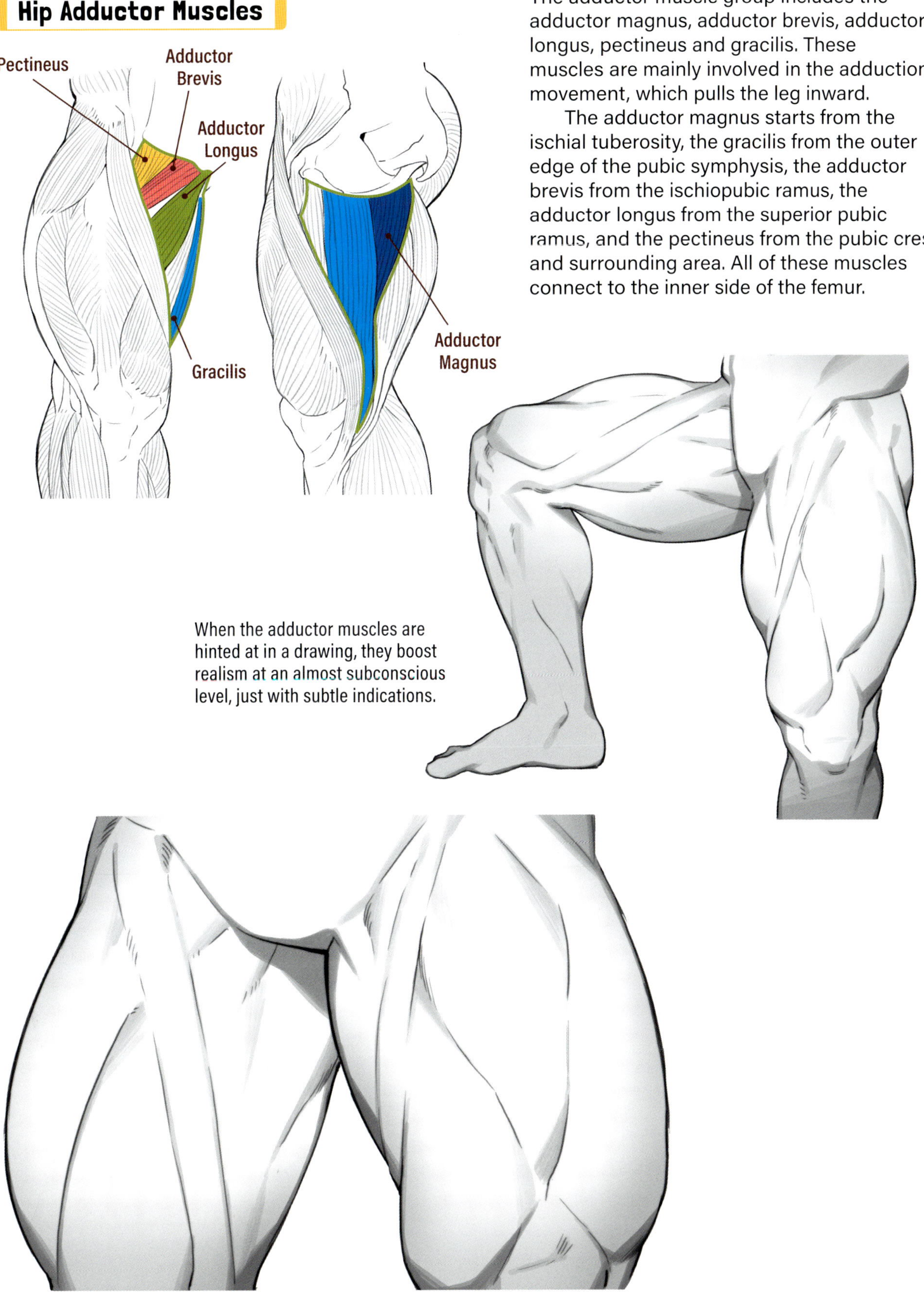

When the adductor muscles are hinted at in a drawing, they boost realism at an almost subconscious level, just with subtle indications.

Leg Muscles (Buttocks and Thighs)

Hamstrings, Semimembranosus, Semitendinosus, Biceps Femoris

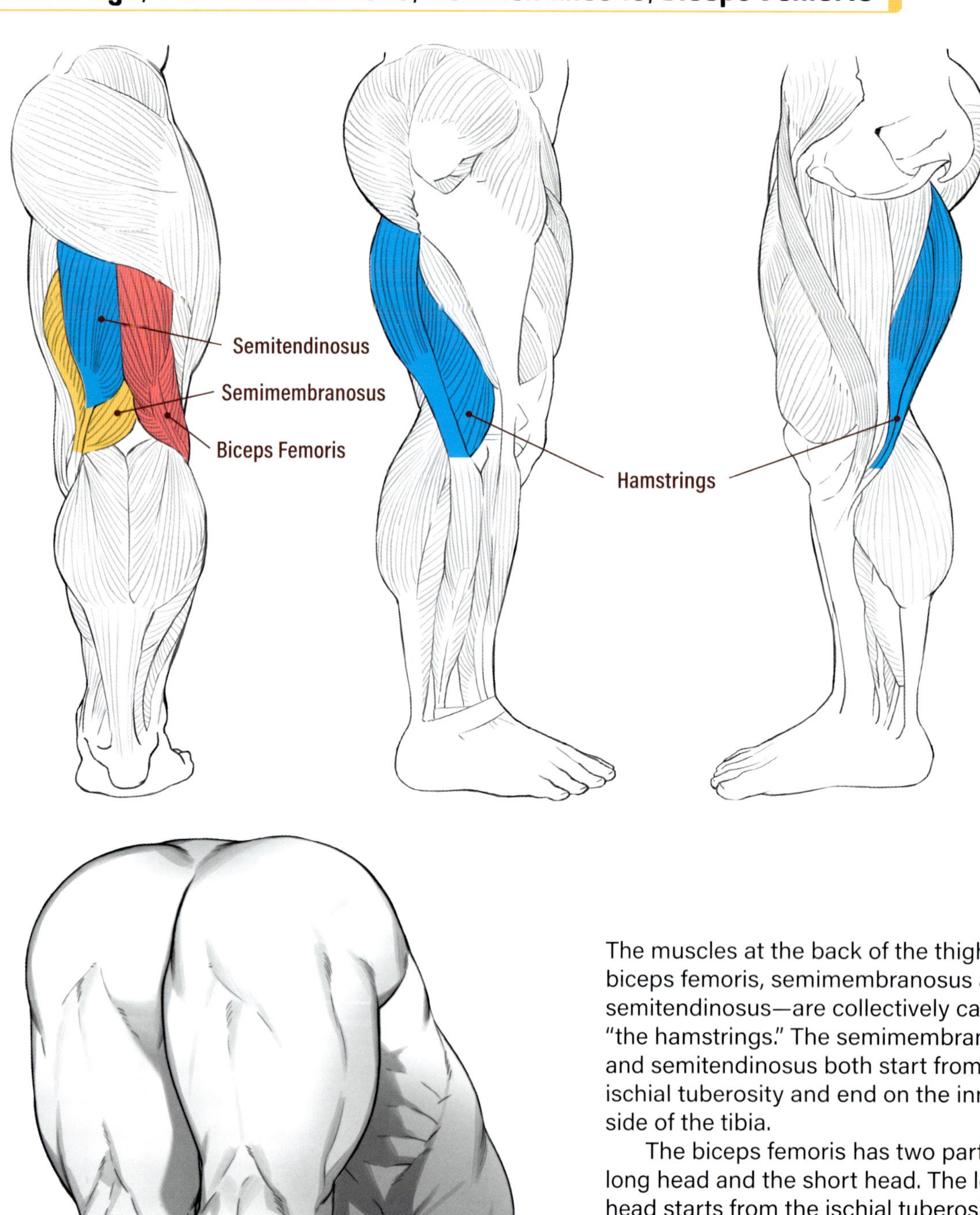

The muscles at the back of the thigh—the biceps femoris, semimembranosus and semitendinosus—are collectively called "the hamstrings." The semimembranosus and semitendinosus both start from the ischial tuberosity and end on the inner side of the tibia.

The biceps femoris has two parts: the long head and the short head. The long head starts from the ischial tuberosity, and the short head starts from the outer side of the linea aspera of the femur. Both end at the head of the fibula. These muscles mainly help to bend the knee and extend the hip joint.

Leg Muscles (Calves)

Gastrocnemius, Soleus

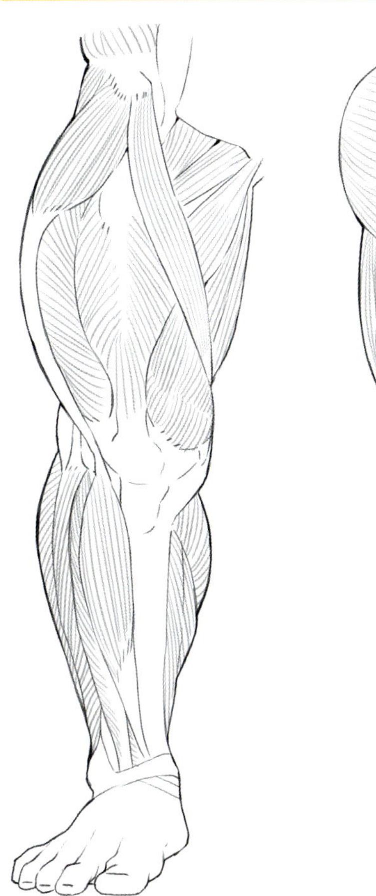

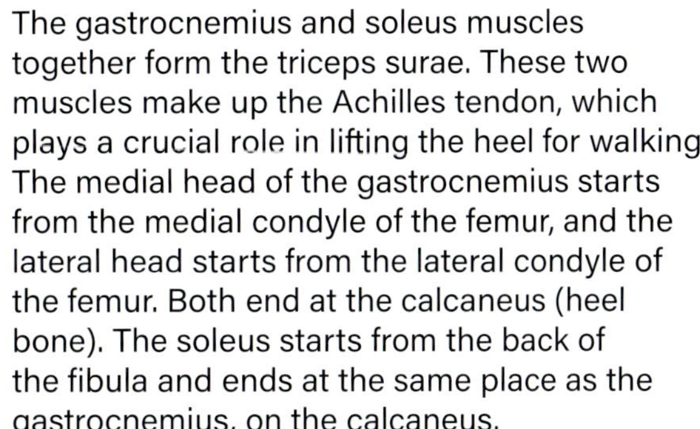

The gastrocnemius and soleus muscles together form the triceps surae. These two muscles make up the Achilles tendon, which plays a crucial role in lifting the heel for walking. The medial head of the gastrocnemius starts from the medial condyle of the femur, and the lateral head starts from the lateral condyle of the femur. Both end at the calcaneus (heel bone). The soleus starts from the back of the fibula and ends at the same place as the gastrocnemius, on the calcaneus.

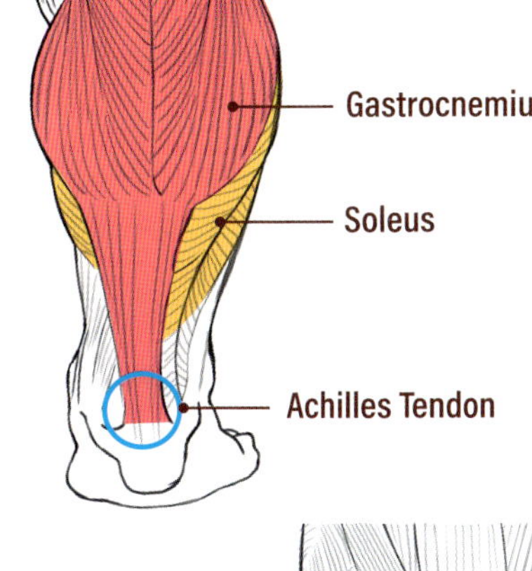

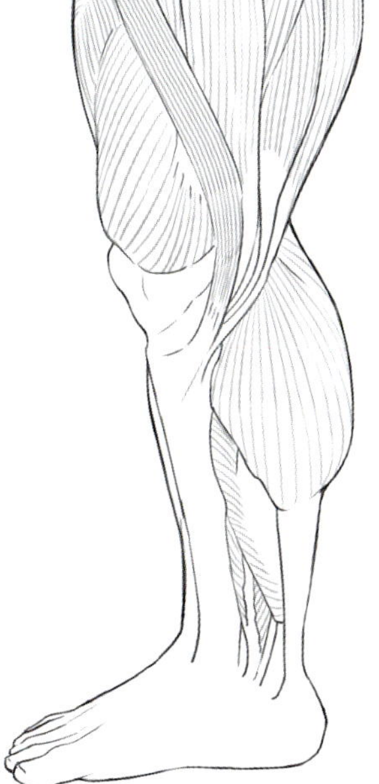

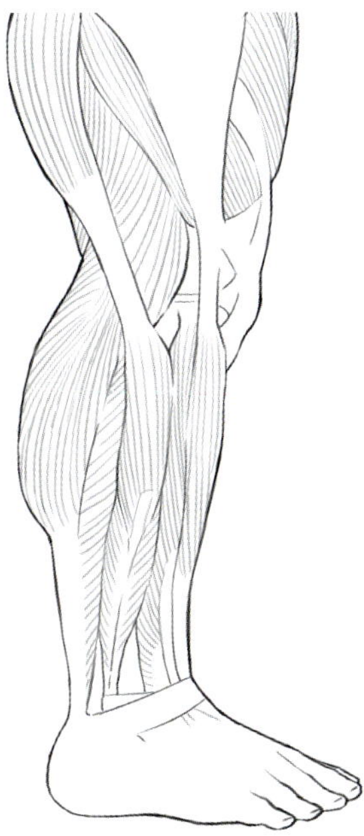

Leg Muscles (Calves)

Extensor Digitorum Longus, Tibialis Anterior

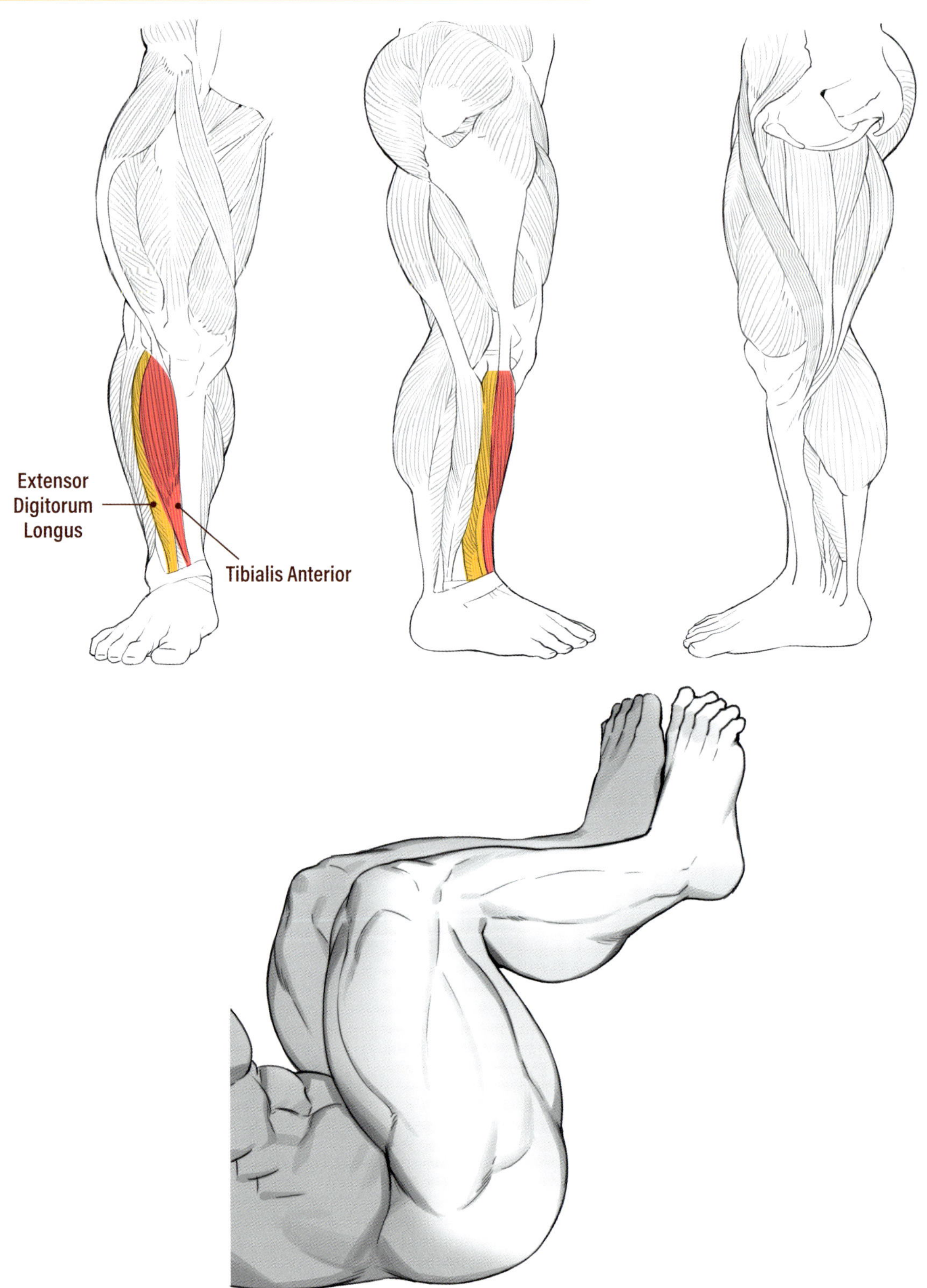

Peroneus Longus, Peroneus Brevis

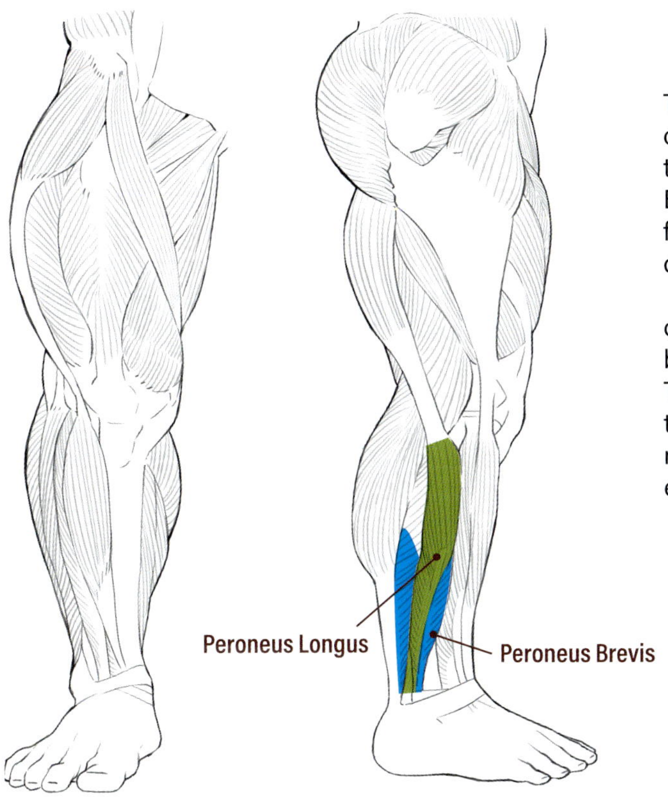

The peroneus longus runs along the outer side of the lower leg, and the peroneus brevis is the muscle covered by the peroneus longus. Both muscles help to turn the sole of the foot outward (eversion) and to point the foot downward (plantar flexion).

The peroneus longus starts from the upper outer side of the fibula, while the peroneus brevis starts from the outer side of the fibula. The peroneus longus ends at the underside of the medial cuneiform and the base of the first metatarsal bone, while the peroneus brevis ends at the base of the fifth metatarsal bone.

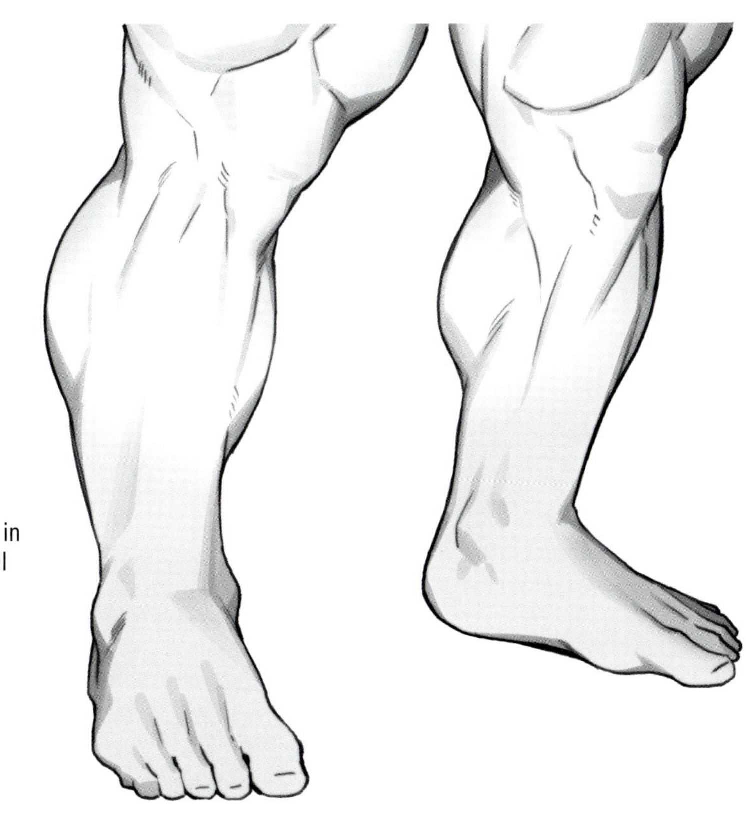

Which leg is the supporting leg in a standing pose? This factor will change the way lines appear.

Full Body Veins

Superficial Veins

Veins are categorized into deep veins and superficial veins based on their location. Superficial veins are the veins that run closer to the skin, above the muscle layer. They don't run parallel to arteries and instead run alone, often visible on the skin's surface.

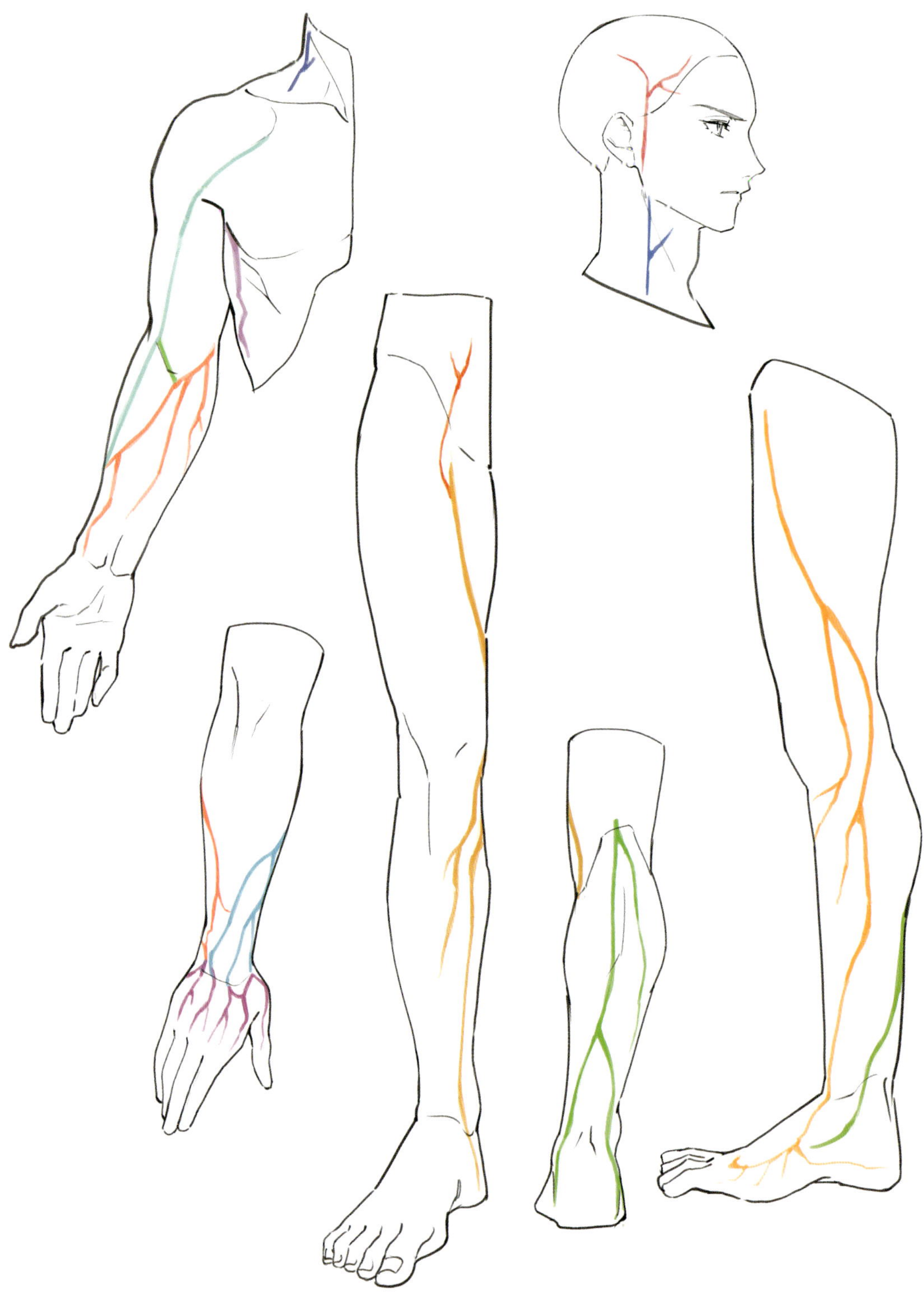

How Blood Vessels Appear from Different Angles

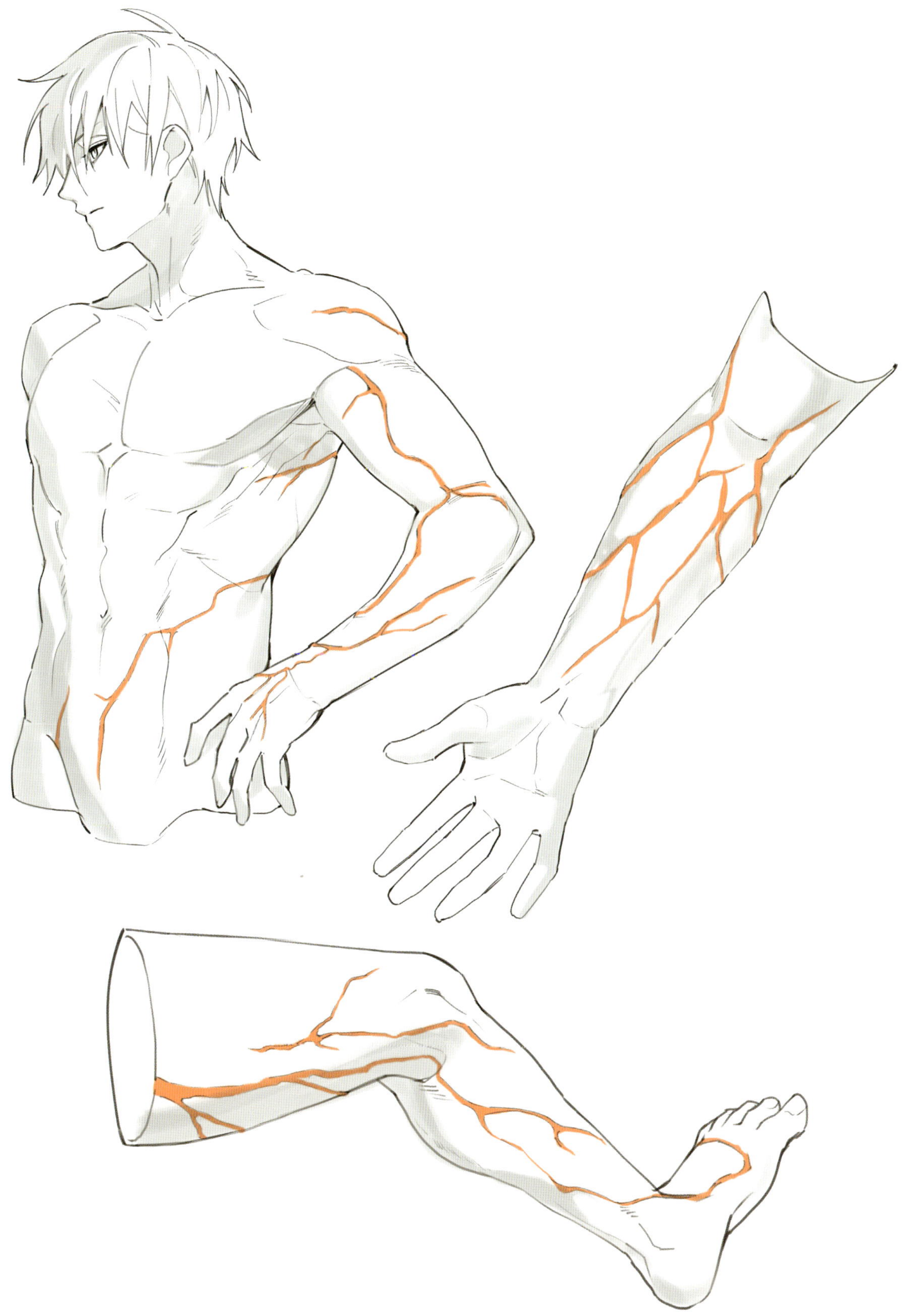

Arm Muscles

Flexor Carpi Ulnaris
Flexor Carpi Radialis
Flexor Digitorum Profundus
Flexor Carpi Radialis
Flexor Digitorum Superficialis
Flexor Pollicis Longus
Supinator
Pronator Teres
Extensor Carpi Ulnaris
Extensor Carpi Radialis Brevis
Extensor Digiti Minimi
Extensor Pollicis Brevis
Extensor Indicis
Extensor Pollicis Longus

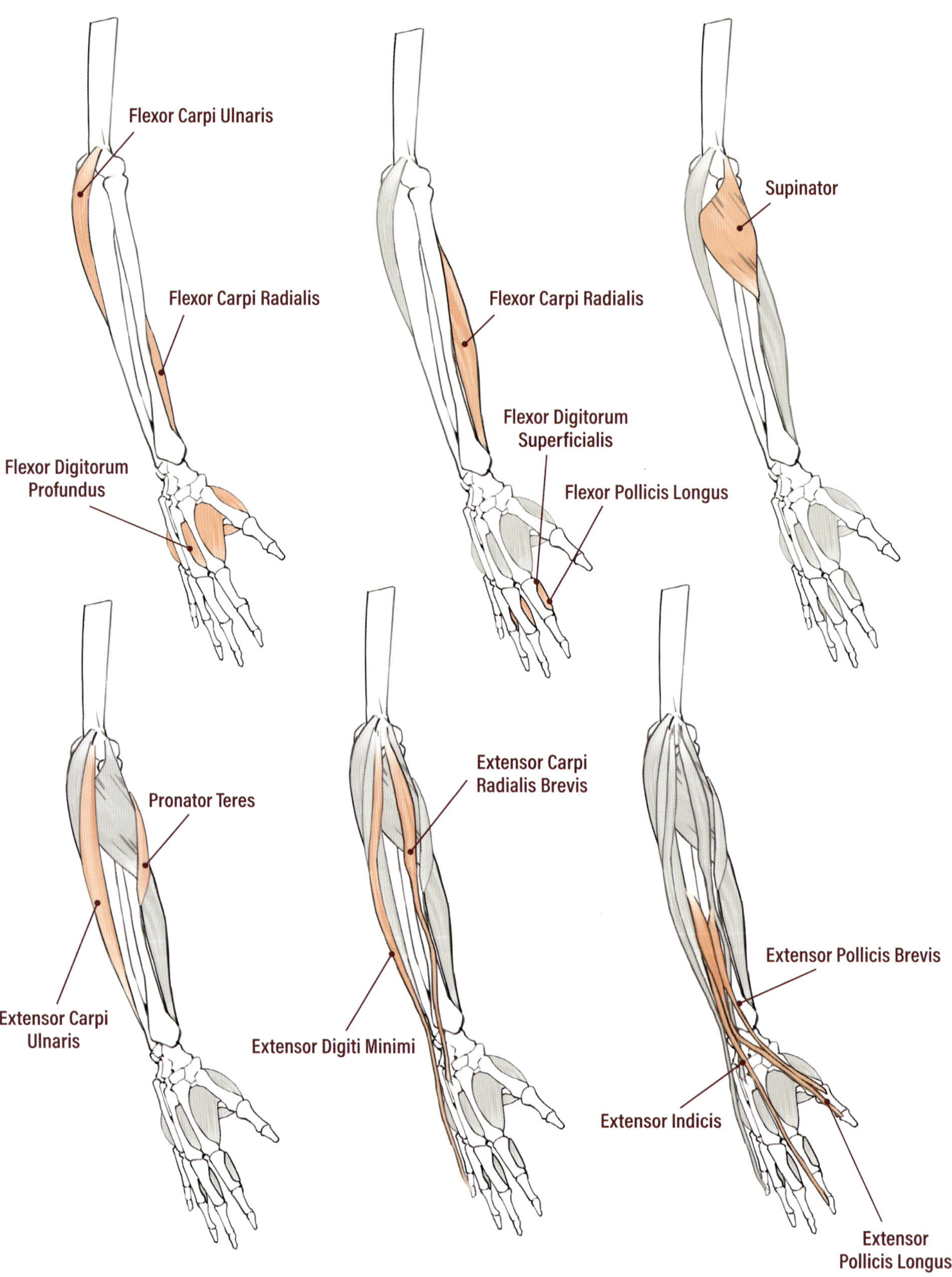

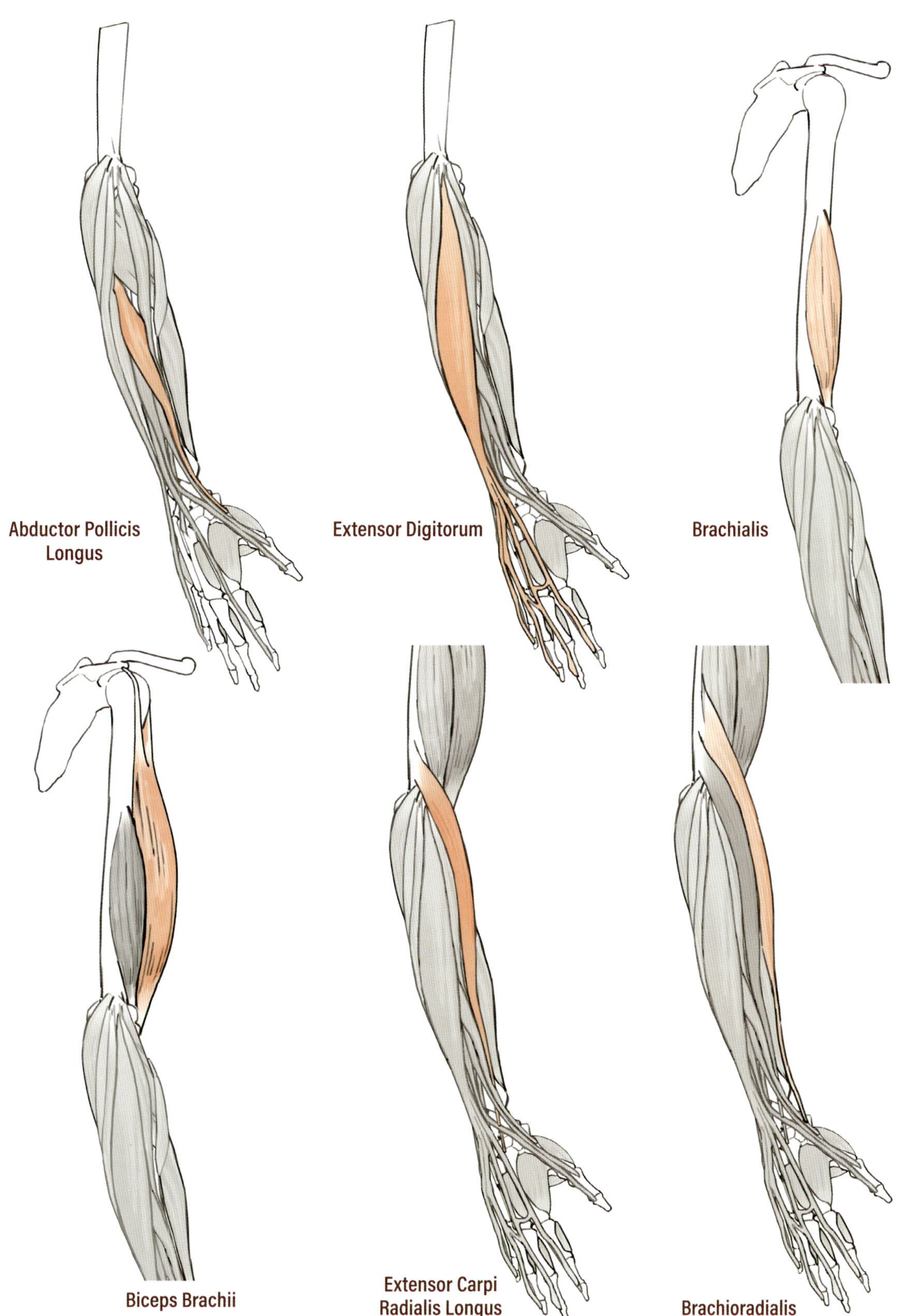

Abductor Pollicis Longus
Extensor Digitorum
Brachialis
Biceps Brachii
Extensor Carpi Radialis Longus
Brachioradialis

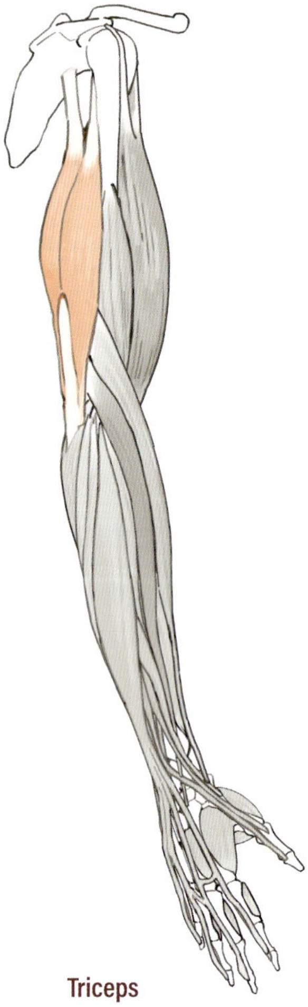

Triceps

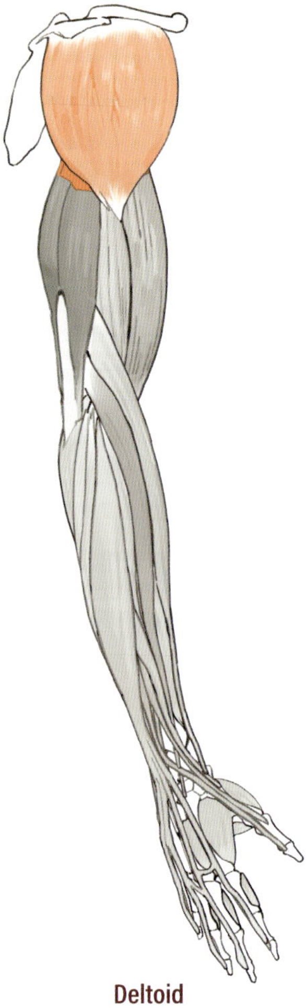

Deltoid

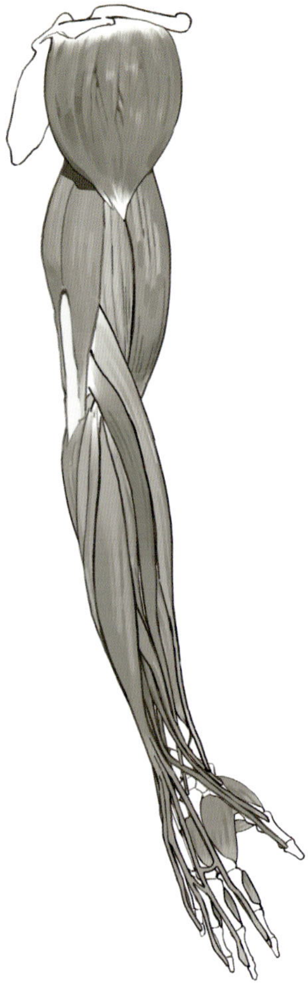

Outside Arm, Completed

Landmarks of the Arm Muscles

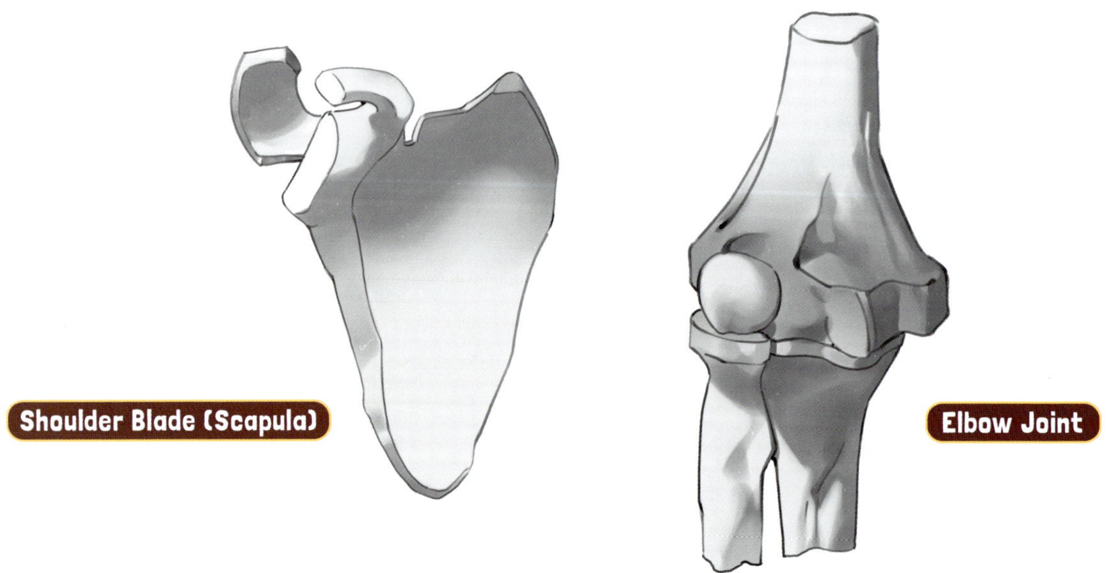

Leg Muscles

Lower Leg Bones
Viewed from the Front
Adductor Magnus
Gracilis
Adductor Brevis
Adductor Longus
Pectineus
Gluteus
Maximus
Iliotibial
Band
Vastus
Intermedius
Vastus
Lateralis
Vastus
Medialis

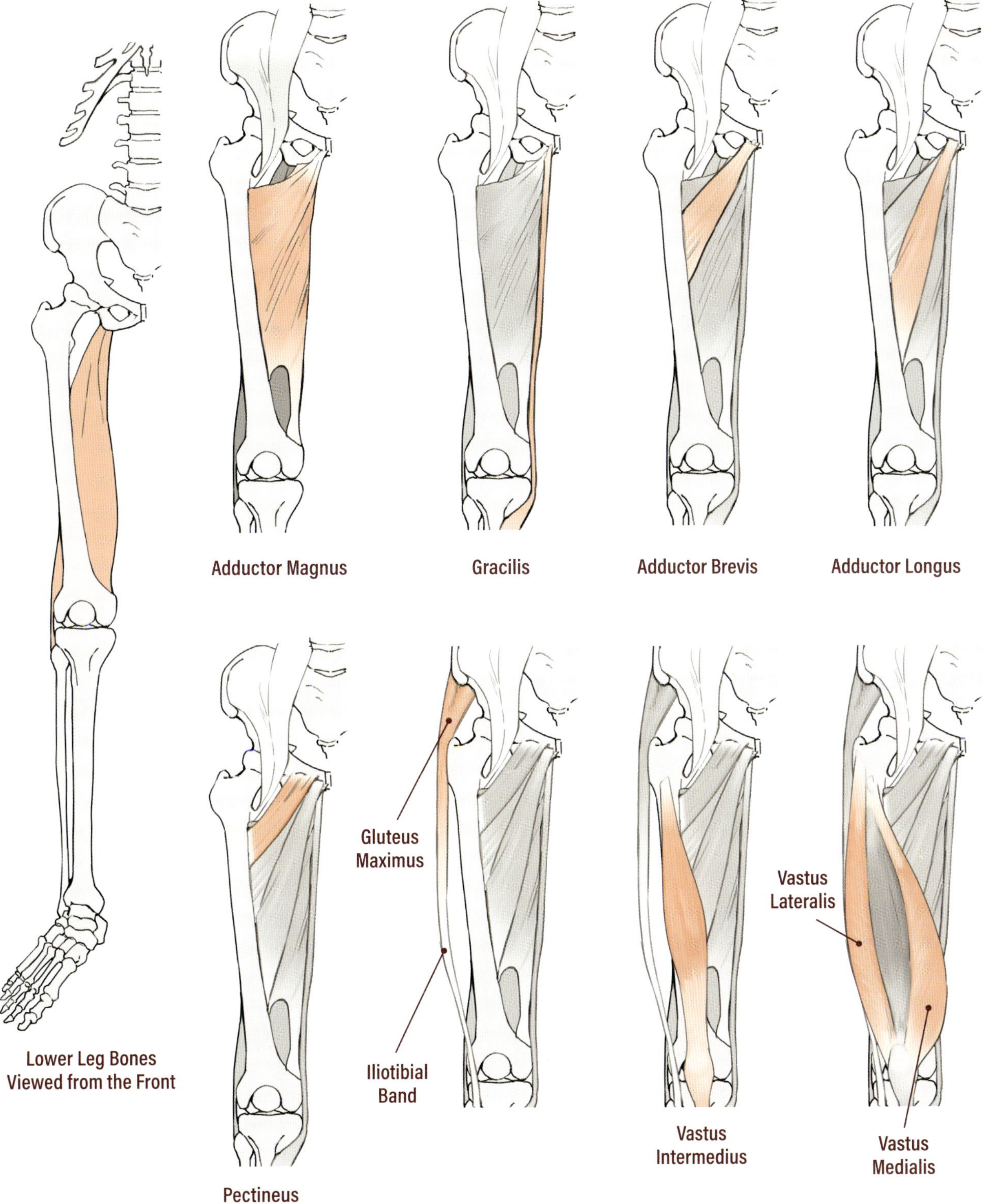

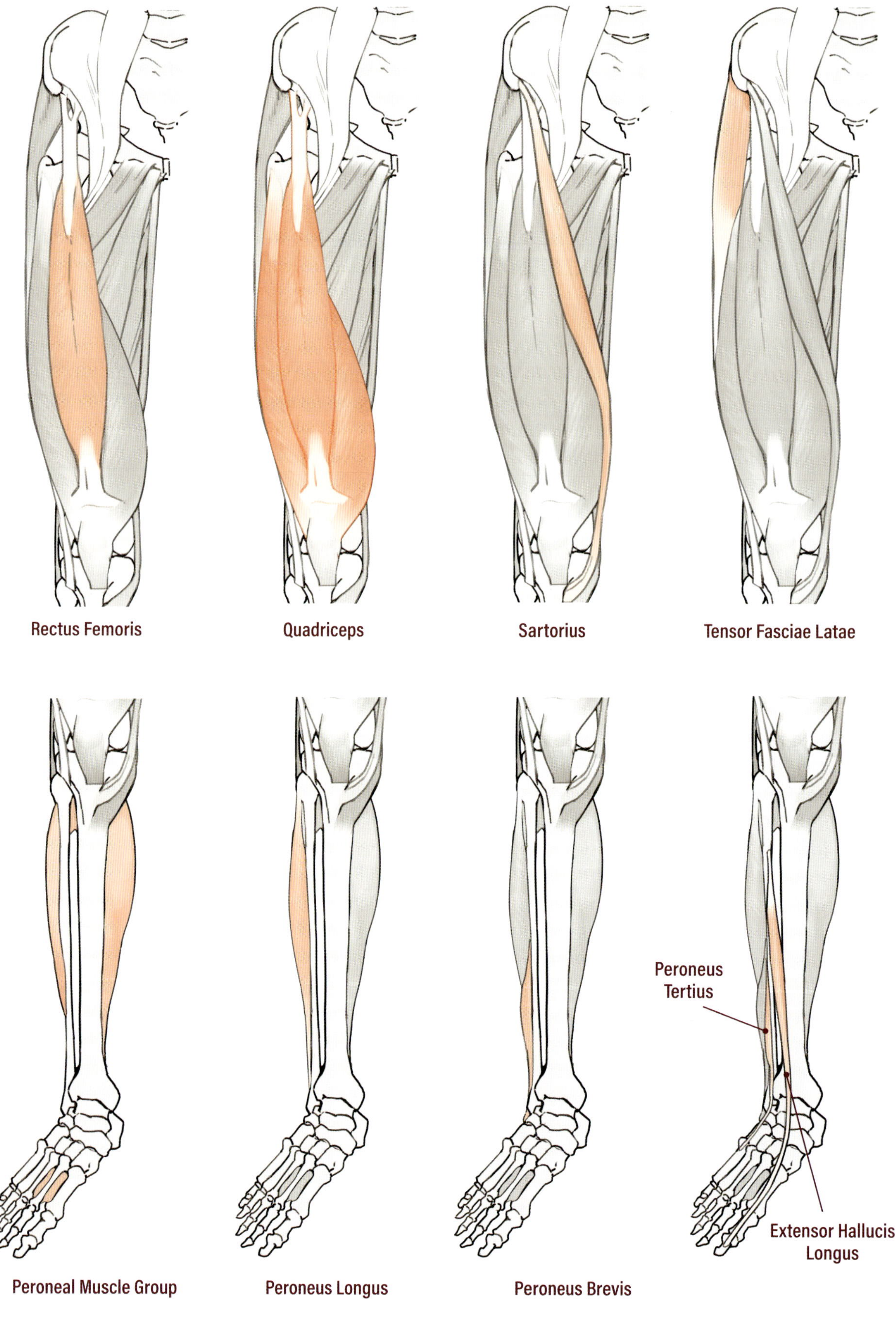
Rectus Femoris
Quadriceps
Sartorius
Tensor Fasciae Latae
Peroneus
Tertius
Extensor Hallucis
Longus
Peroneal Muscle Group
Peroneus Longus
Peroneus Brevis

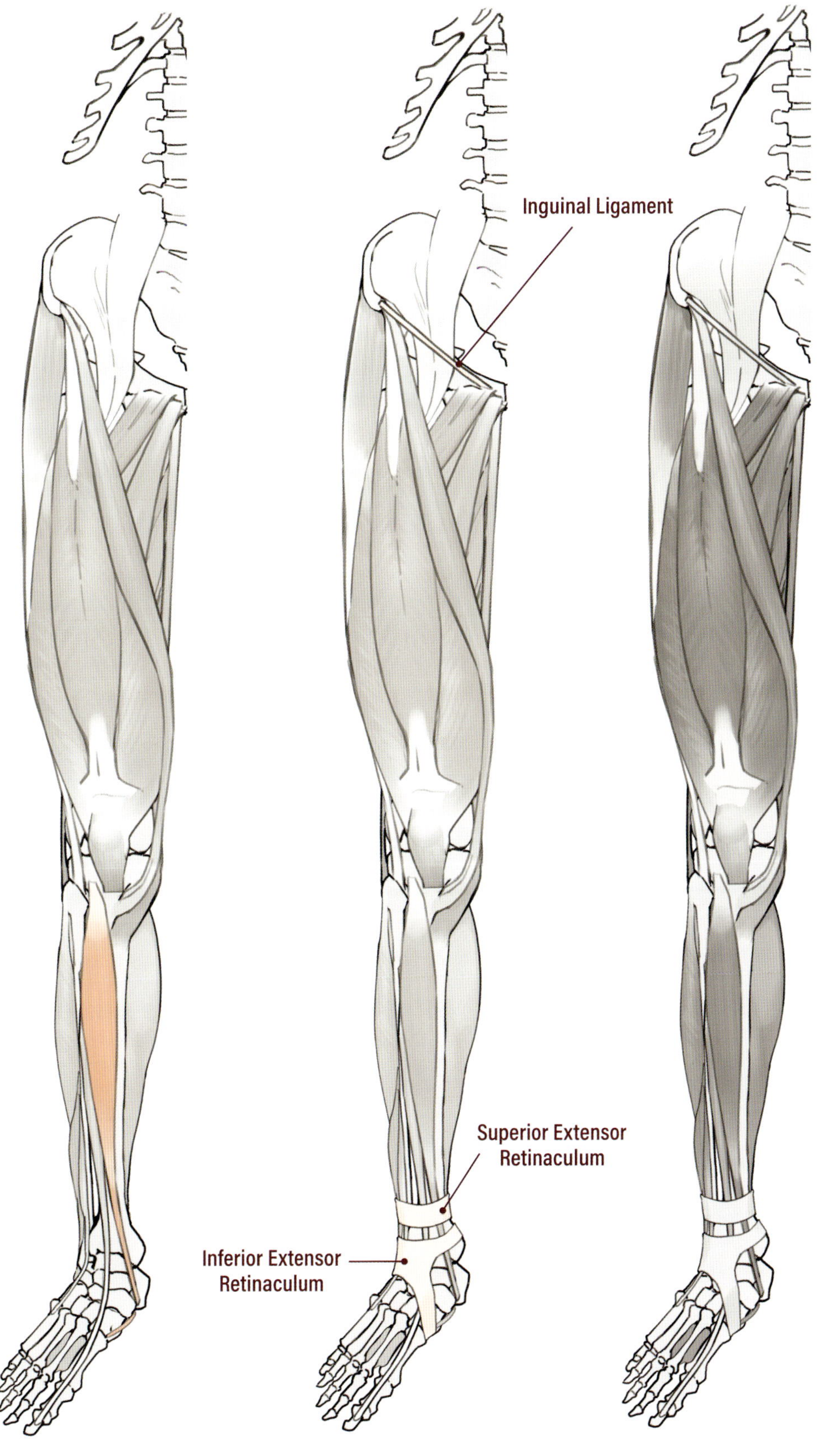

Anterior Fibular Muscle

Front of Leg, Completed

Hand and Wrist Muscles

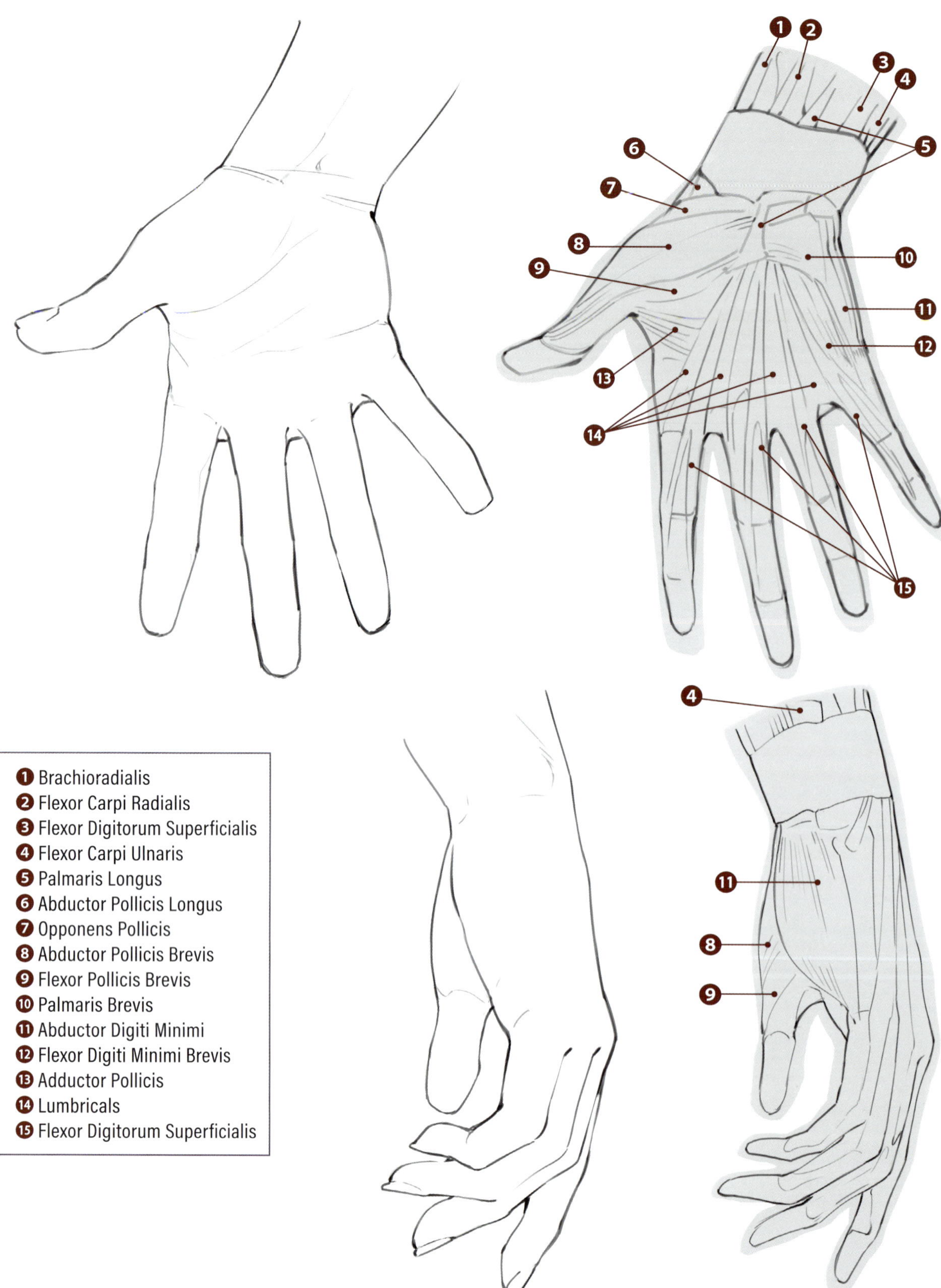

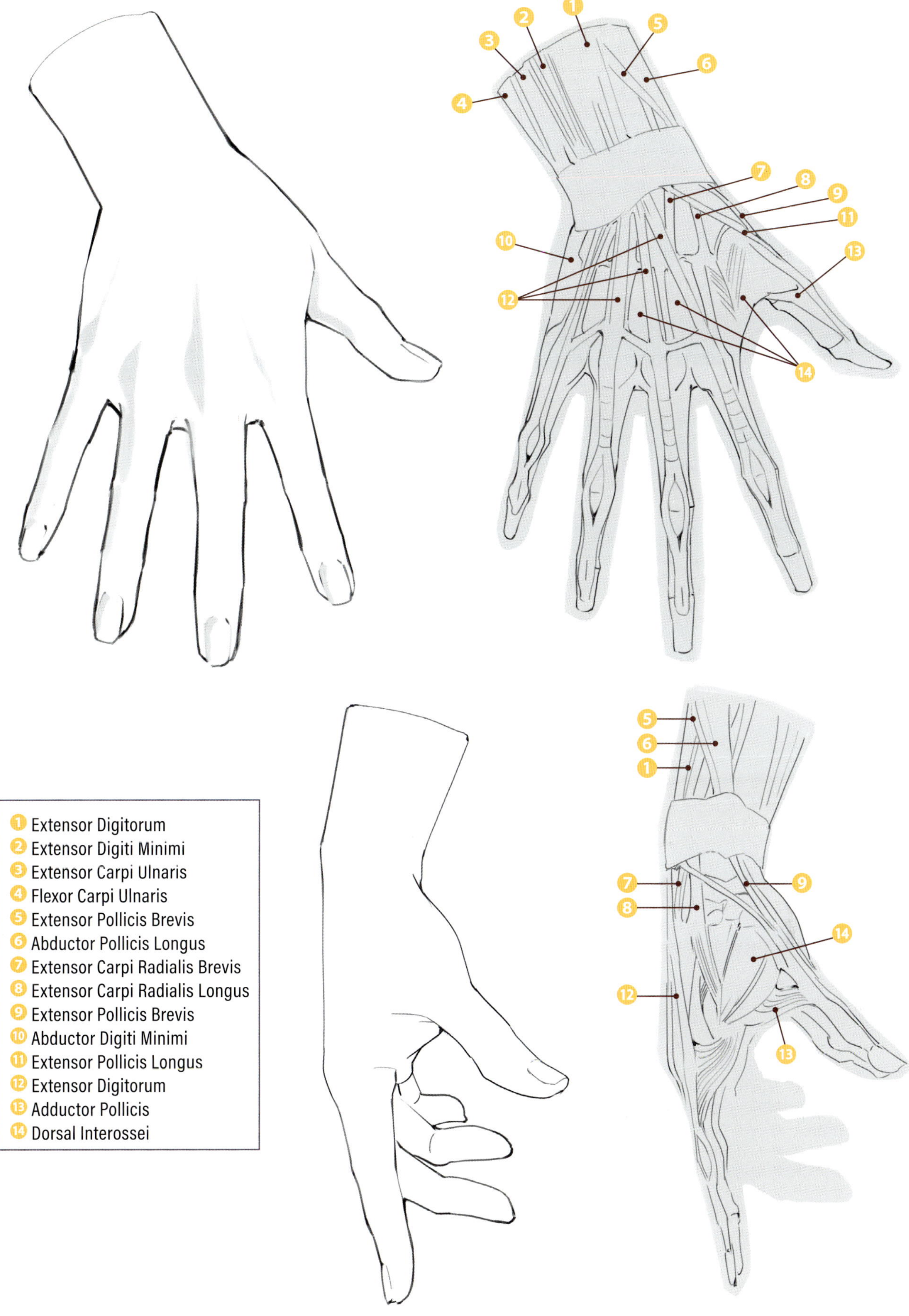
1 Extensor Digitorum
2 Extensor Digiti Minimi
3 Extensor Carpi Ulnaris
4 Flexor Carpi Ulnaris
5 Extensor Pollicis Brevis
6 Abductor Pollicis Longus
7 Extensor Carpi Radialis Brevis
8 Extensor Carpi Radialis Longus
9 Extensor Pollicis Brevis
10 Abductor Digiti Minimi
11 Extensor Pollicis Longus
12 Extensor Digitorum
13 Adductor Pollicis
14 Dorsal Interossei

Drawing Well-formed Muscles Improves Your Work

Drawing Muscles Adds Stability to the Body

In addition to the obvious muscles in the arms and legs, muscles are also present in the shoulders and neck. As shown in the leftmost image on the right, a character without muscles appears gaunt and gives a weak impression of the body.

The muscular character to the far right projects to the viewer a sense of stability and strength.

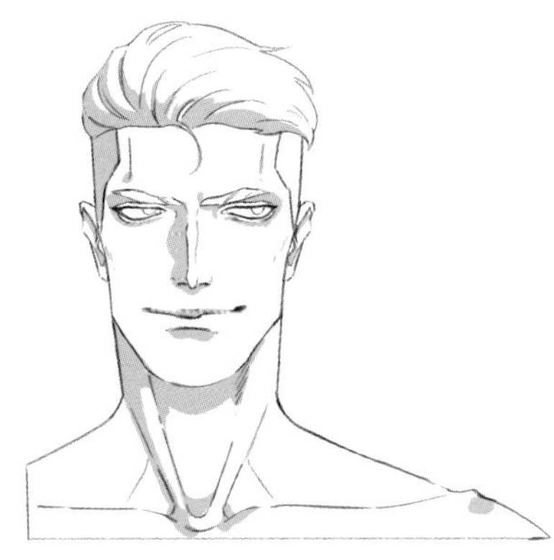

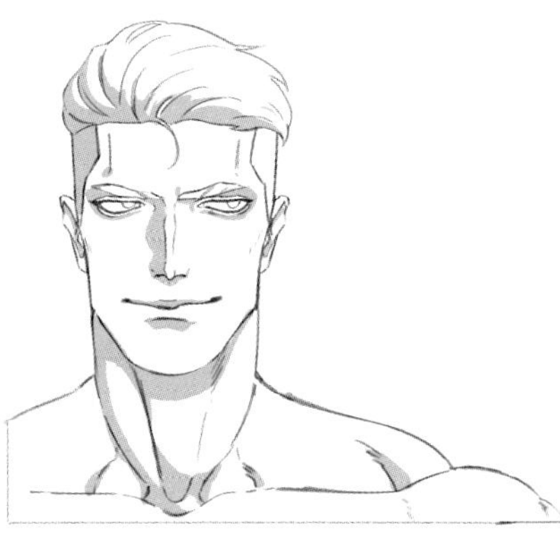

Well-defined Muscles Change the Impression

Even characters that appear slim still have muscles. Even if clothes cover certain parts, viewing the character from different angles can greatly affect the silhouette.

When drawing a well-defined character, focus on key points like the sternocleidomastoid, trapezius, deltoid and pectoral muscles. Drawing well-defined muscles is essential for creating a fully-formed character.

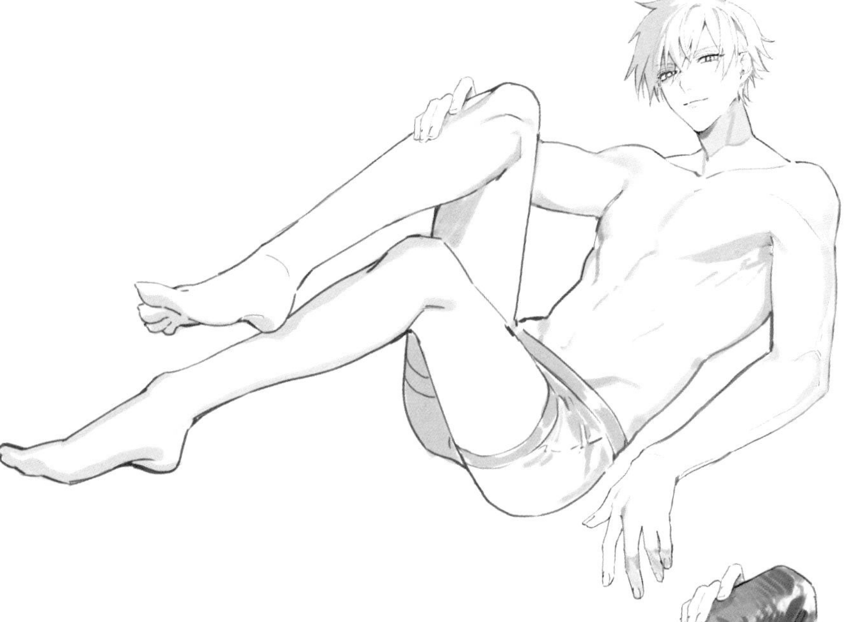

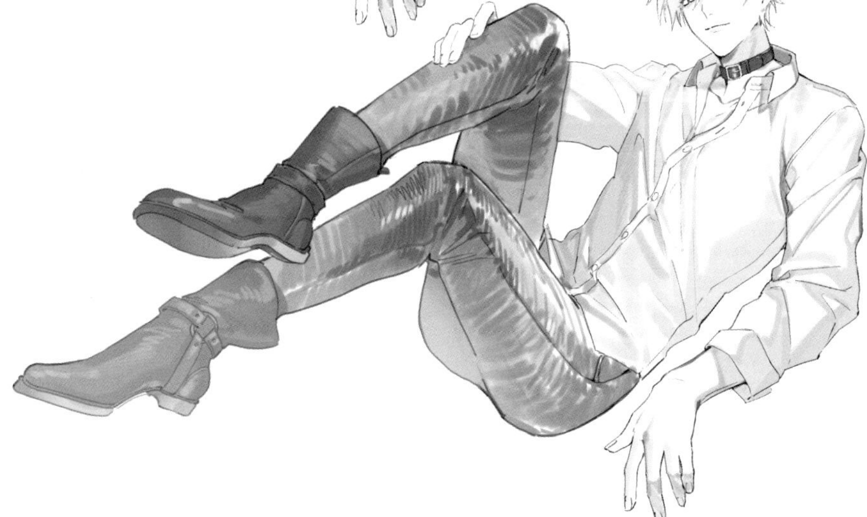

Chapter 2

Various Ways to Draw Muscles

How to Depict Each Muscle

Front View

A lean but well-balanced muscular body type. Because he's not scrawny, his muscles should be clearly portrayed.

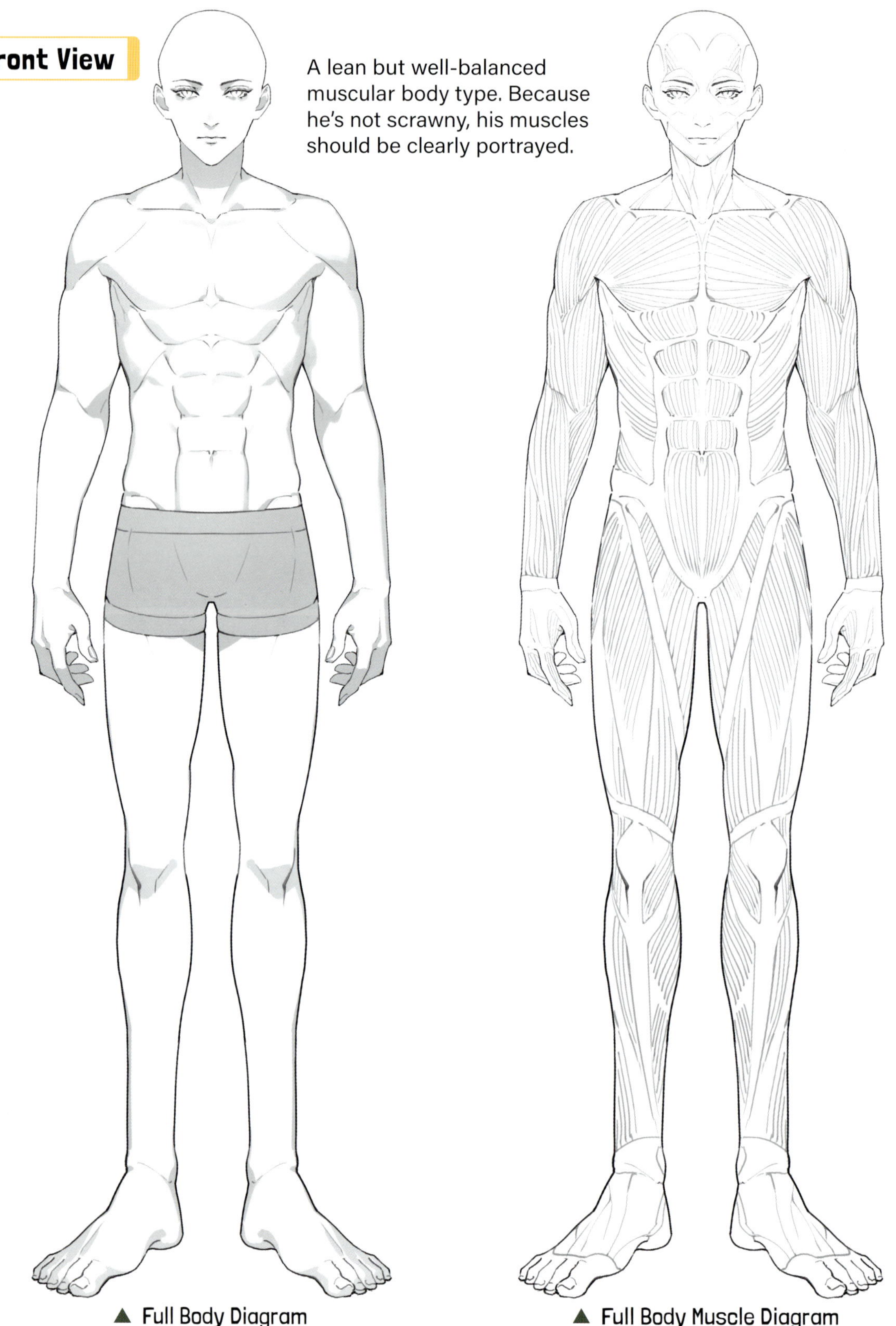

▲ Full Body Diagram

▲ Full Body Muscle Diagram

Cross Sections of the Torso

The white areas represent the ventral cavity, and the yellow areas represent muscles and fat. Because the body is well-balanced, the muscle distribution is fairly even throughout the body.

Keep in mind the overall muscle distribution while drawing.

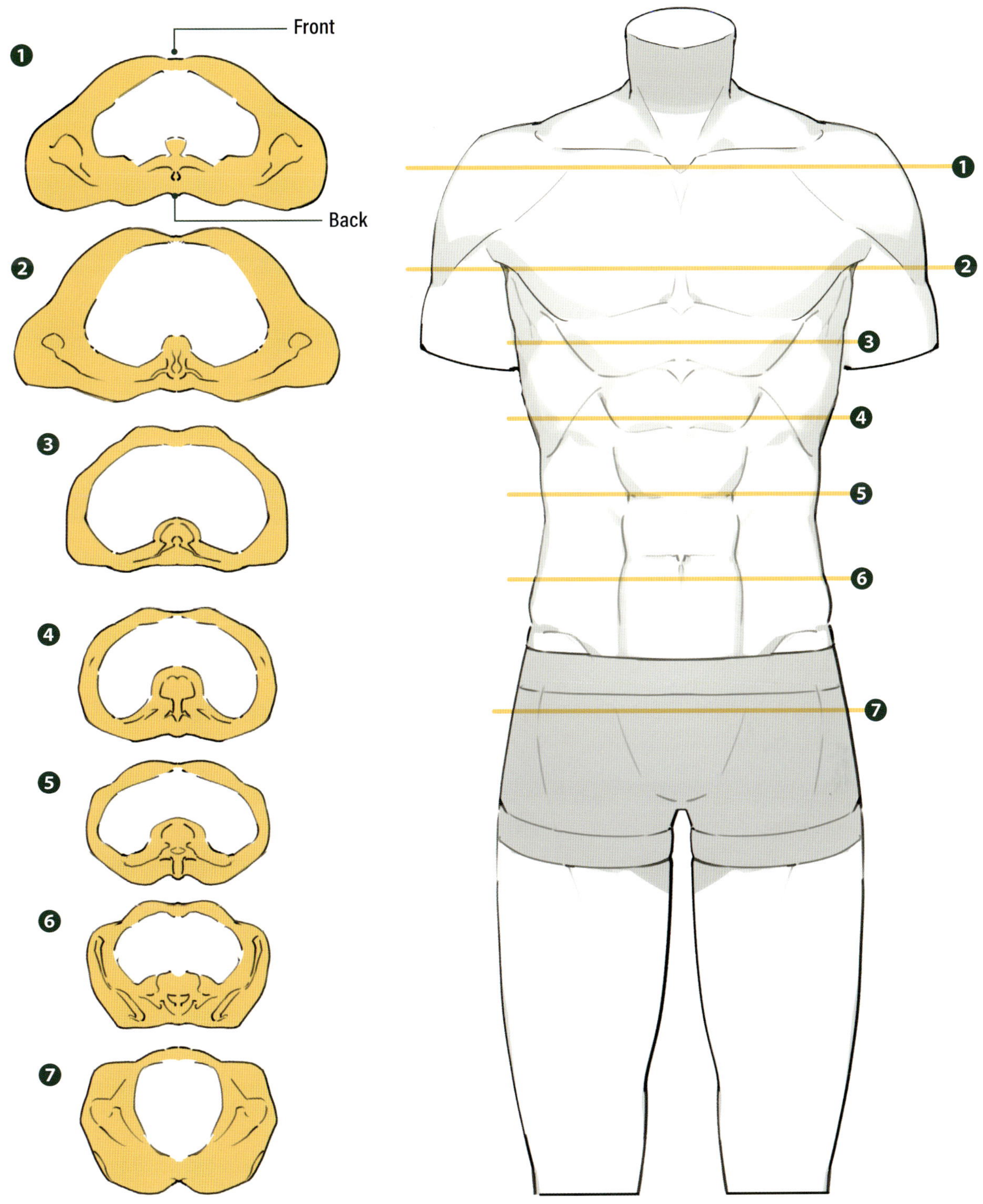

How to Depict Each Muscle

Side View

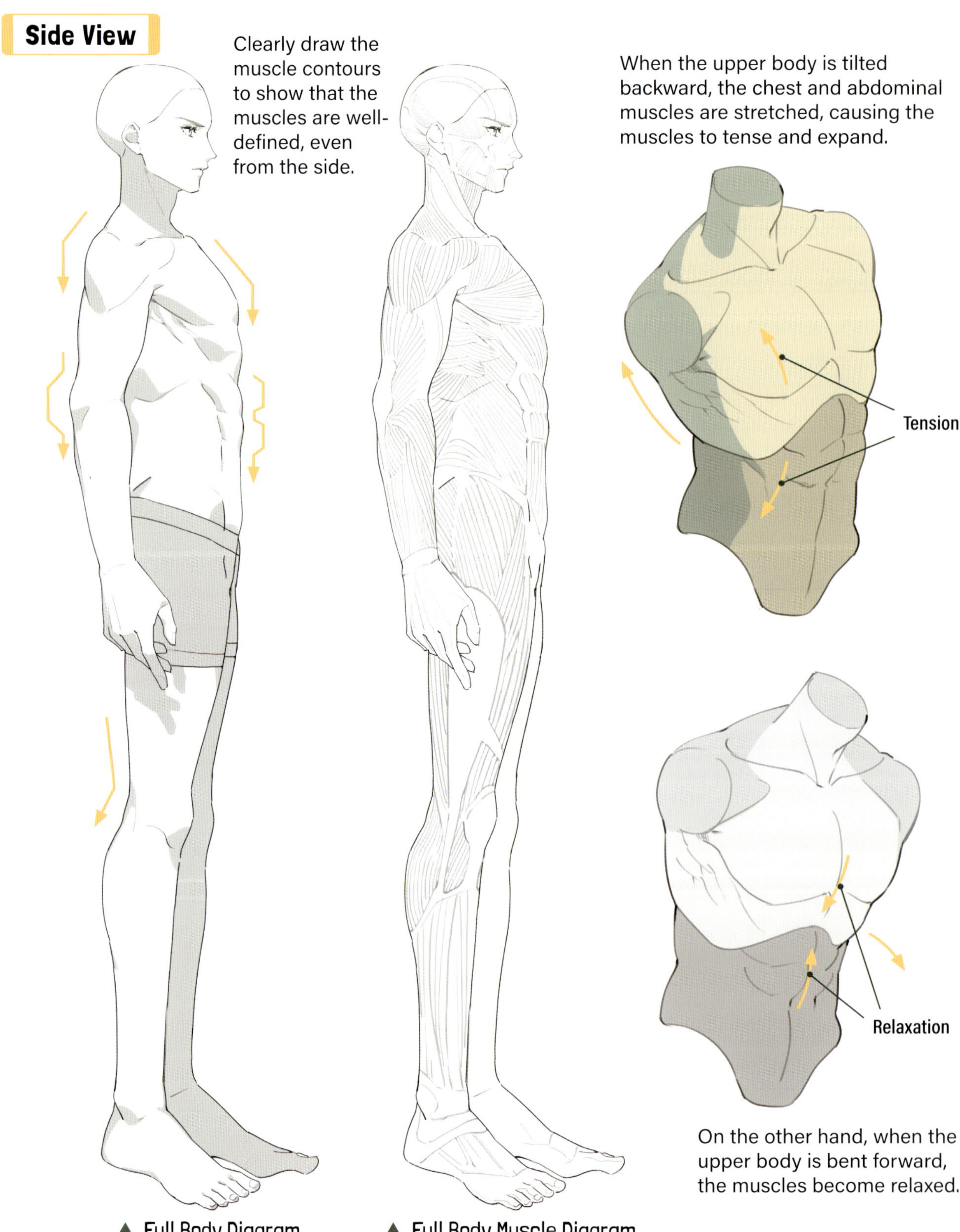

▲ Full Body Diagram

▲ Full Body Muscle Diagram

Back View

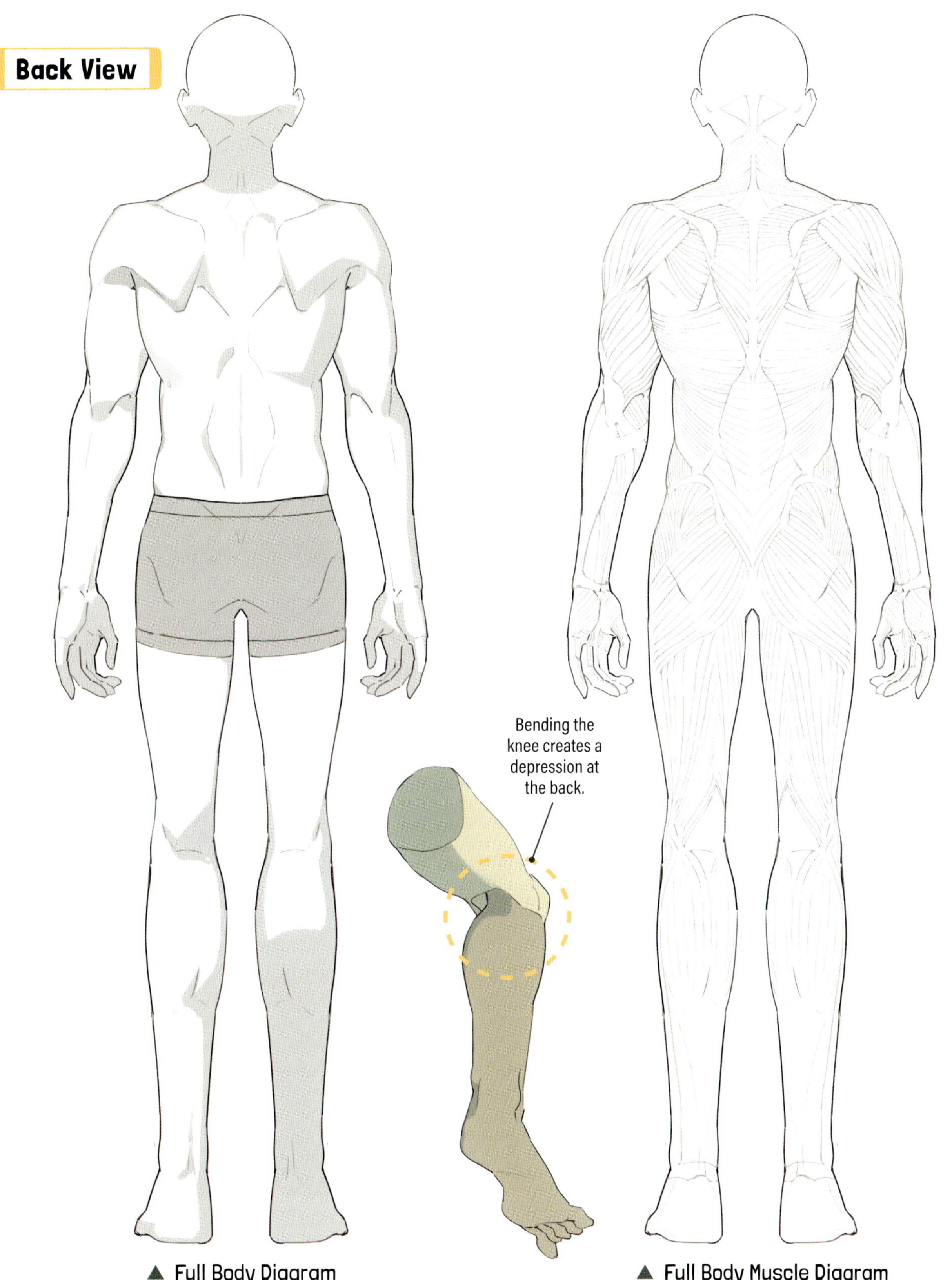

▲ Full Body Diagram

▲ Full Body Muscle Diagram

How to Draw the Figure

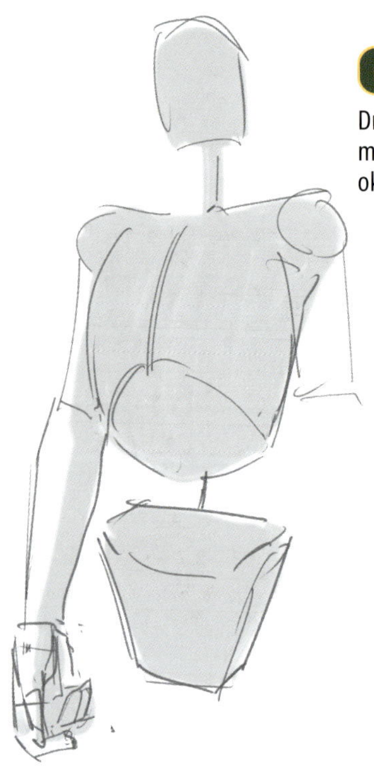

❶ Rough Outline

Draw blocky shapes to match the skeleton. It's okay to keep it simple.

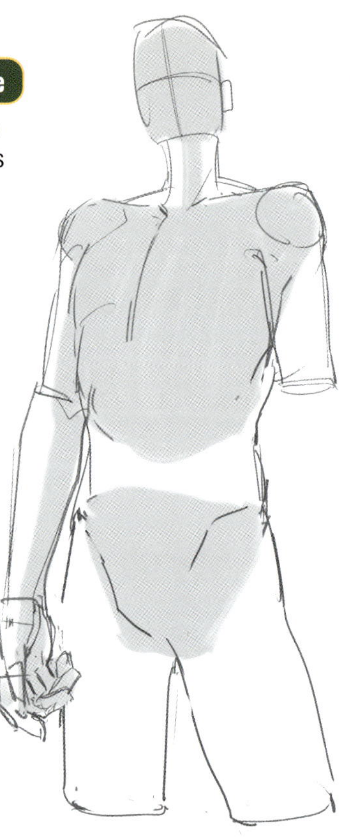

❷ Blocking In

Add flesh to the body following the rough outline. Pay attention to the body's unique curves and protrusions.

❸ Adding Muscles

Draw the outlines and boundaries of the muscles. Keep the muscles on pages 12 and 76 in mind.

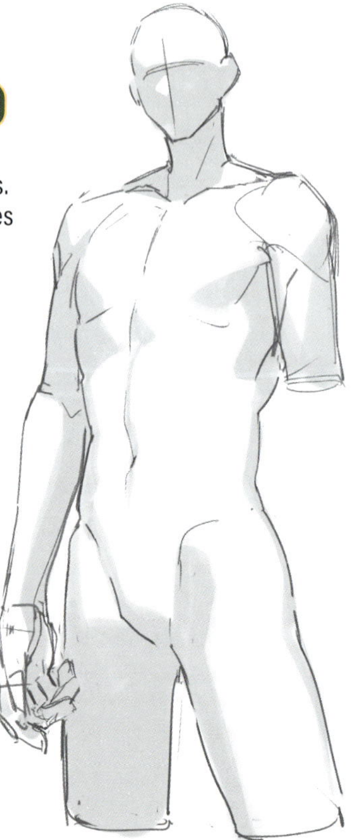

❹ Detailing

Add shadows to the muscles to give them presence. Set the light direction (in this case, from the upper right) and add shadows on the opposite sides of protrusions and curves.

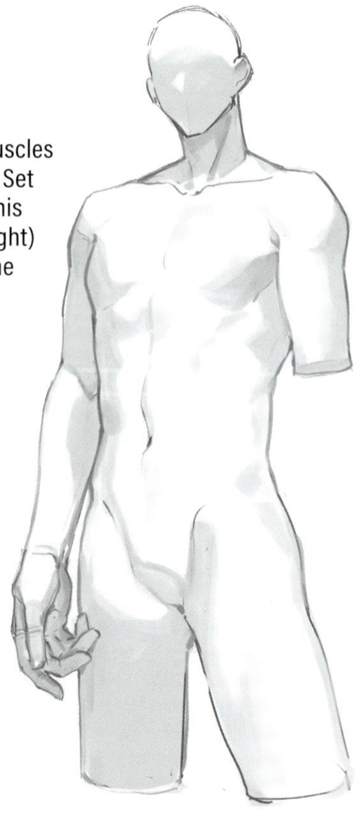

How to Apply Color

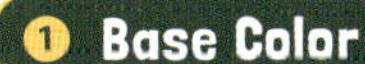

❶ Base Color

Start by applying a base color to the body.

❷ Adding Shadows

Add shadows to areas like the underarms, abs and collarbone dips.

❸ Overall Shadows

Use shadows to subtly show the muscle definition.

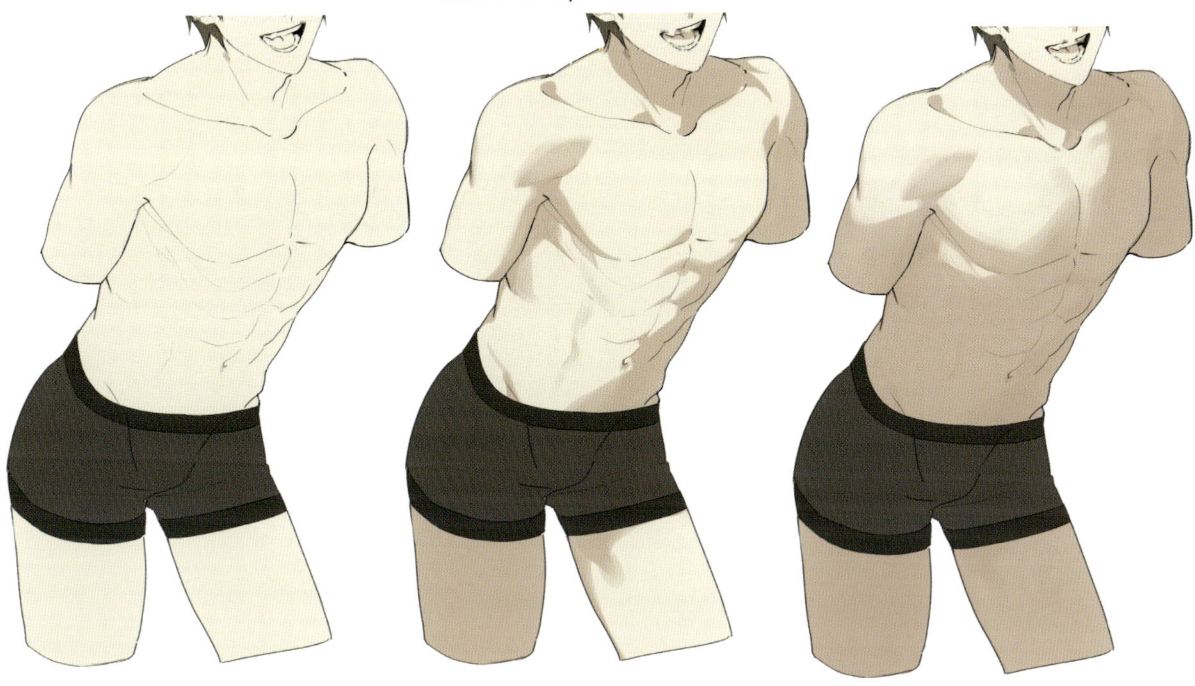

❹ Fine Shading

Differentiate between the darker and lighter parts within the shadows.

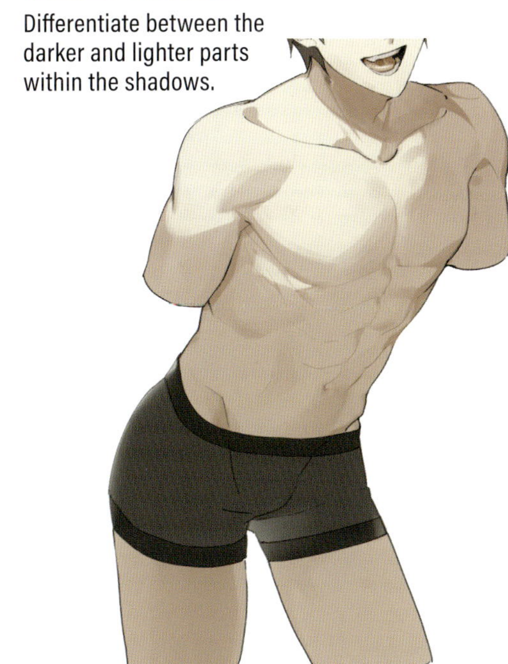

❺ Finishing Touches

Clearly show contrast with and without shading. The more detailed the light and shadow gradations, the more realistic the form will appear.

Various-angle Views of Muscles

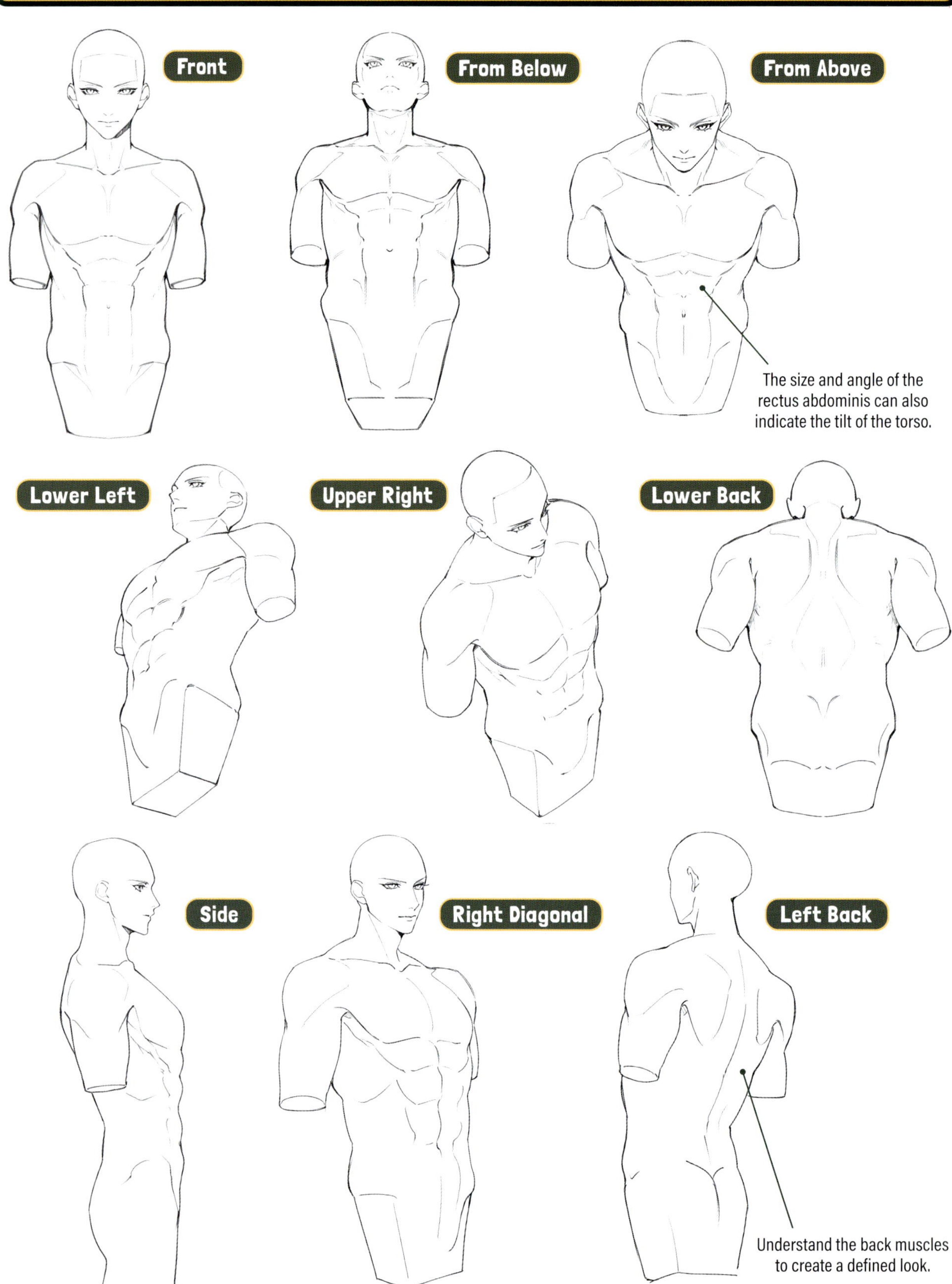

Lean Body Type Viewed from Various Angles

Because this is a lean muscular body type, it might look like there isn't much muscle at first glance, but there is clear thickness in the shoulders and chest. Accurate depiction of the six-pack abs can also express the presence of muscles.

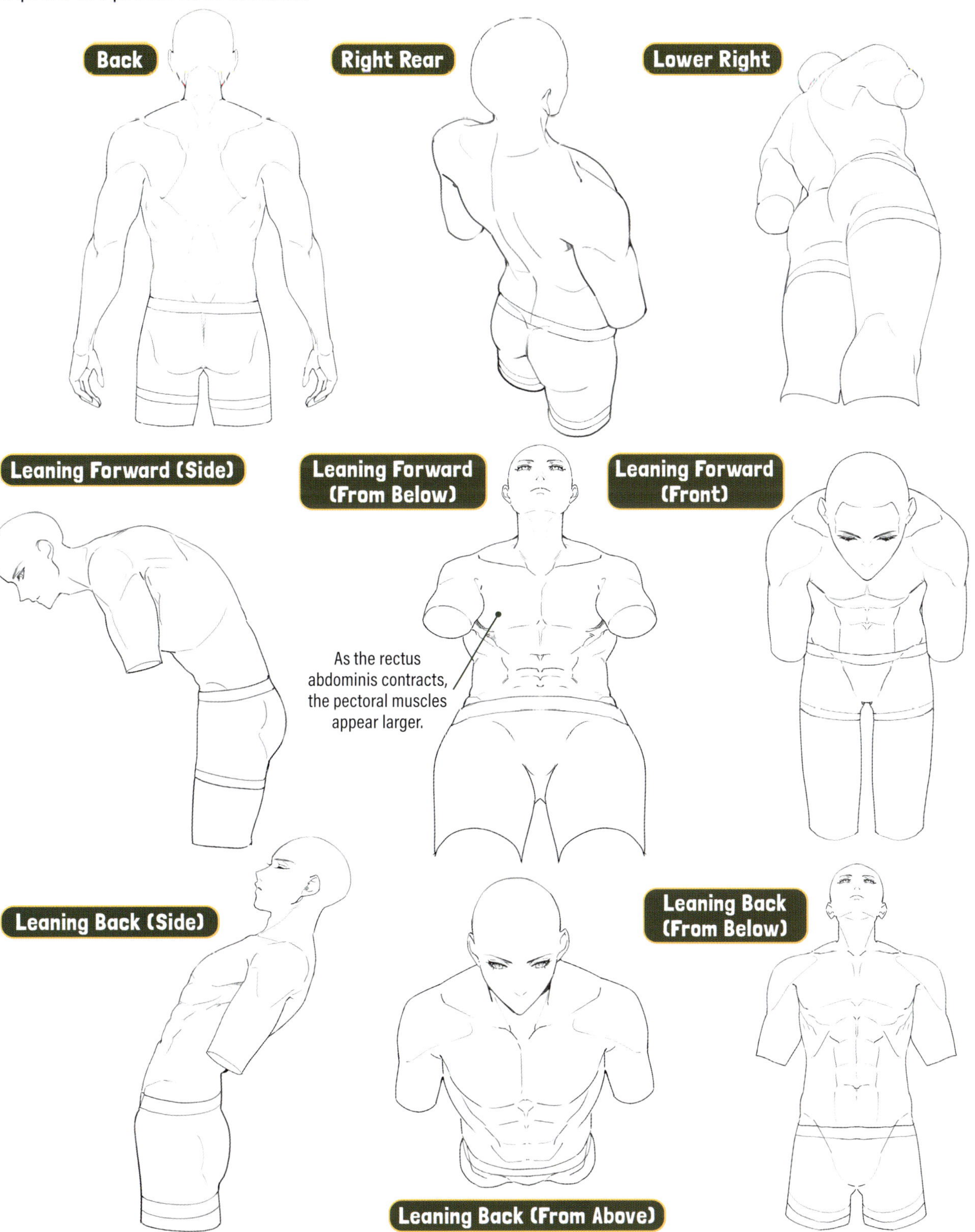

Arm Muscles

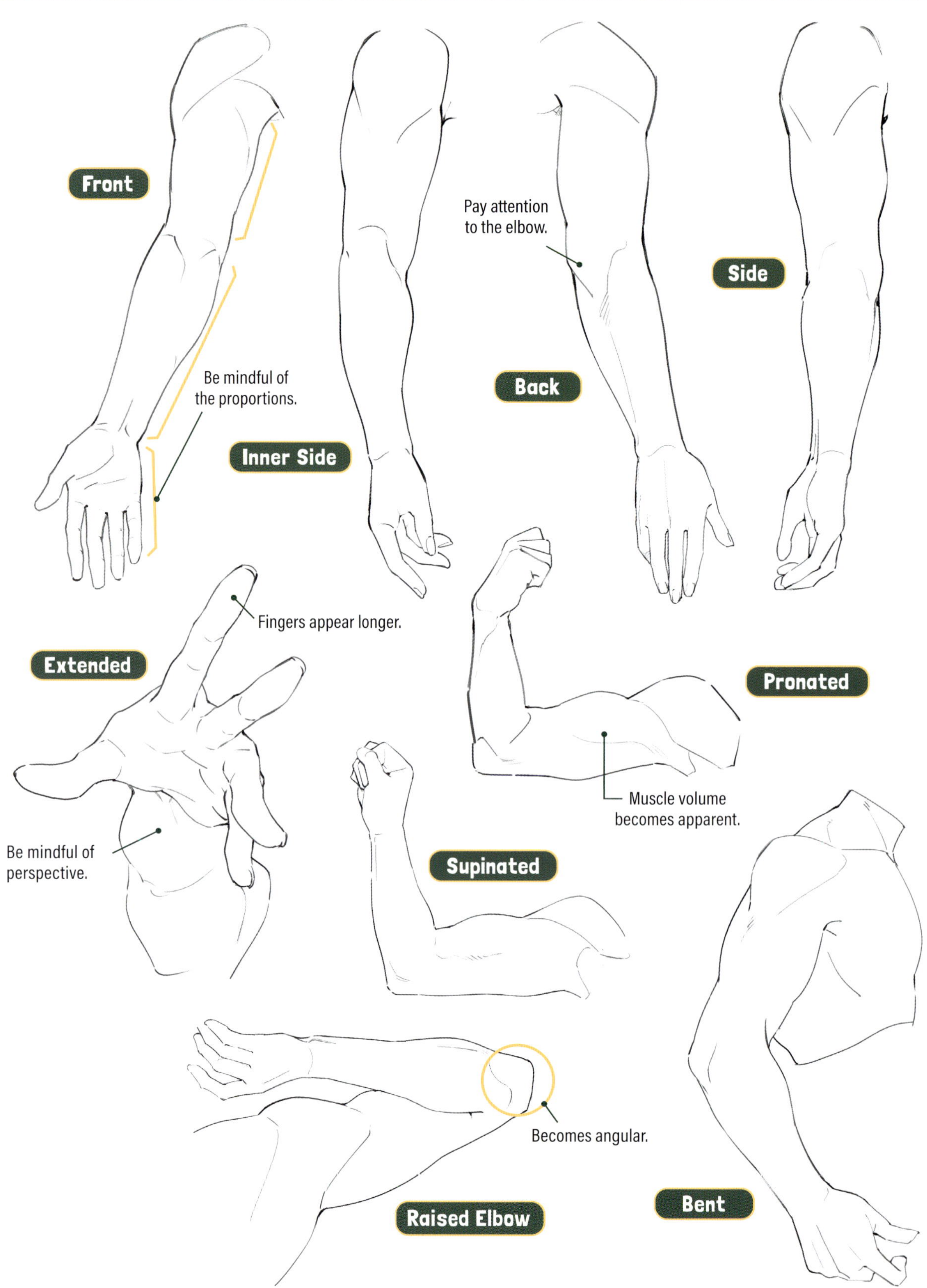
Front
Be mindful of the proportions.
Inner Side
Pay attention to the elbow.
Back
Side
Fingers appear longer.
Extended
Be mindful of perspective.
Pronated
Muscle volume becomes apparent.
Supinated
Becomes angular.
Raised Elbow
Bent

Leg Muscles

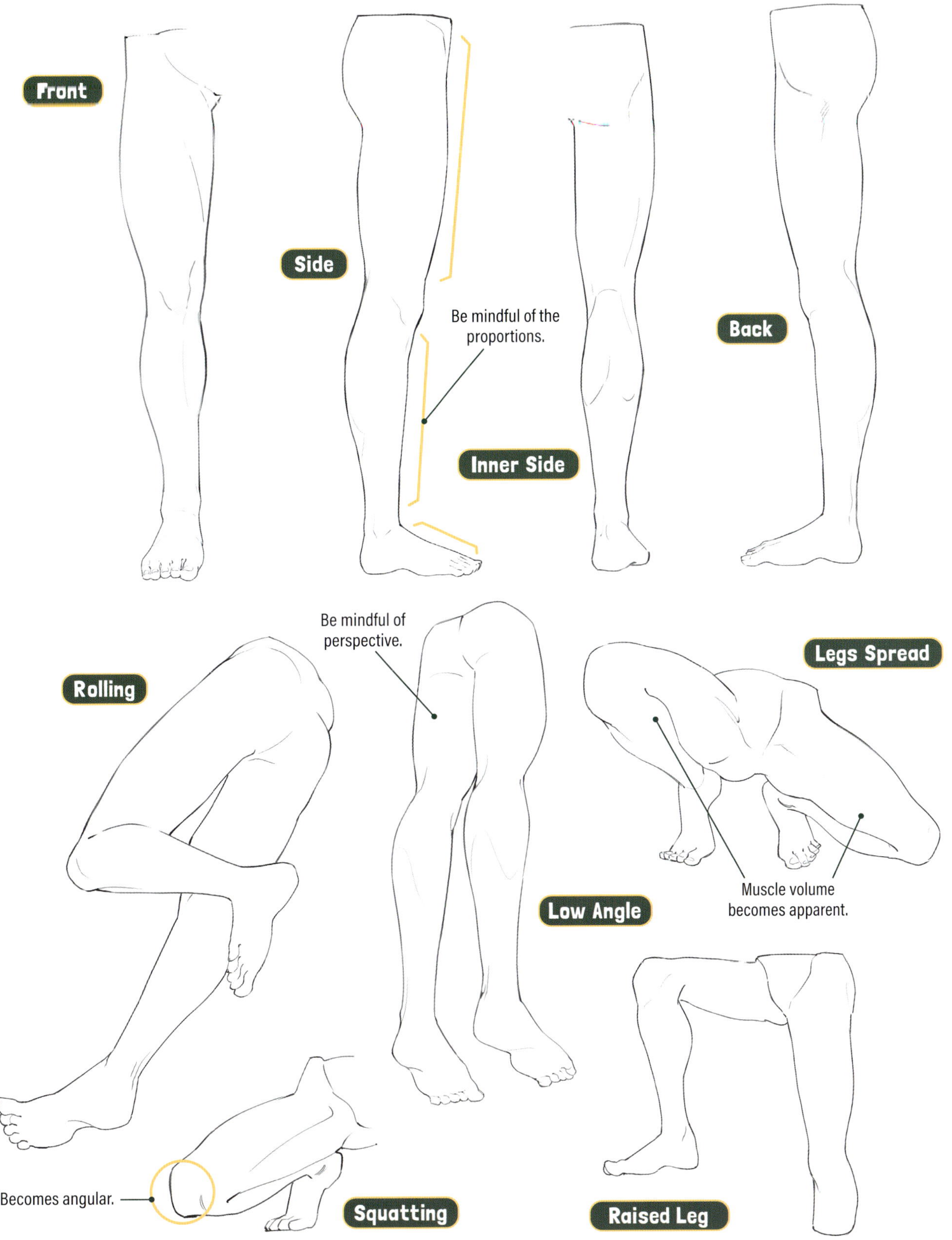

How to Depict Each Muscle

Front

This body type is close to that of a real athlete. The overall silhouette is slightly toned down, but the bumps and contours of each muscle are clearly expressed.

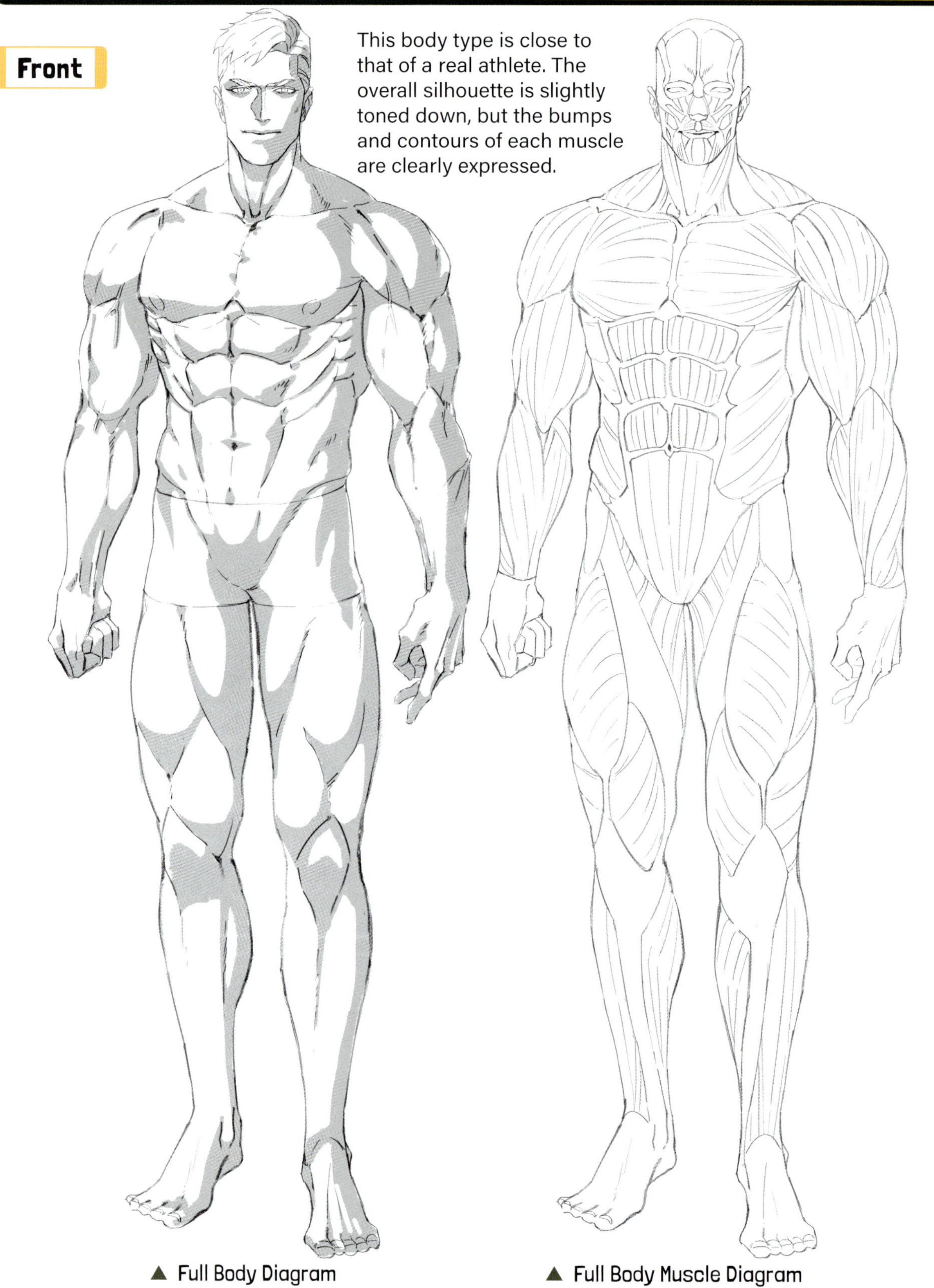

▲ Full Body Diagram

▲ Full Body Muscle Diagram

Cross Sections of the Torso

The chest becomes thick due to the pectoral muscles. The thickness of the torso from below the ribs to the pelvis is generally uniform.

Compared to the lean body type, the muscle mass is significantly increased.

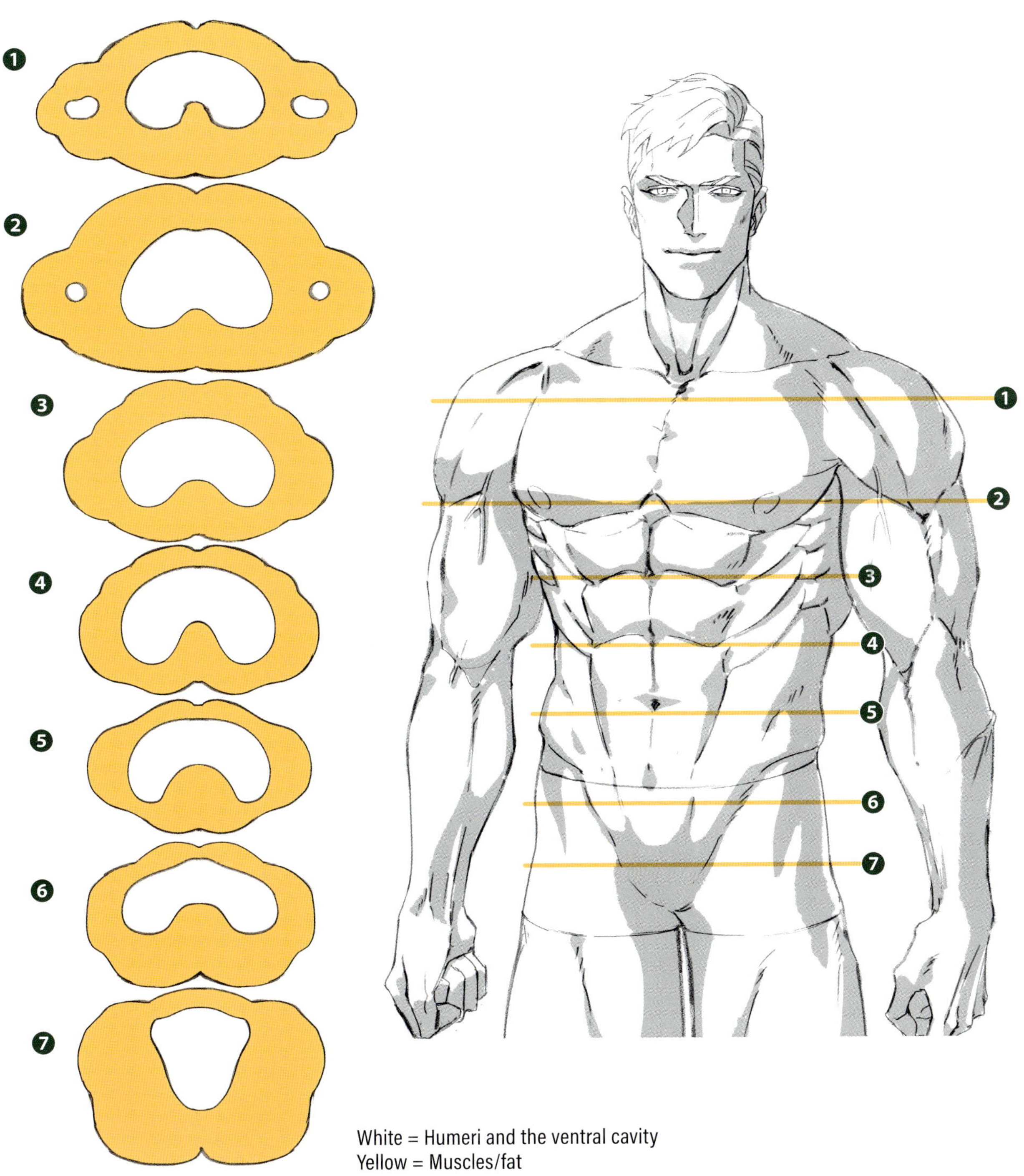

White = Humeri and the ventral cavity
Yellow = Muscles/fat

How to Depict Each Muscle

Side View

The pectoral muscles of the chest, the quadriceps of the thighs, the gluteus maximus of the buttocks, and the triceps surae of the calves create an undulating silhouette.

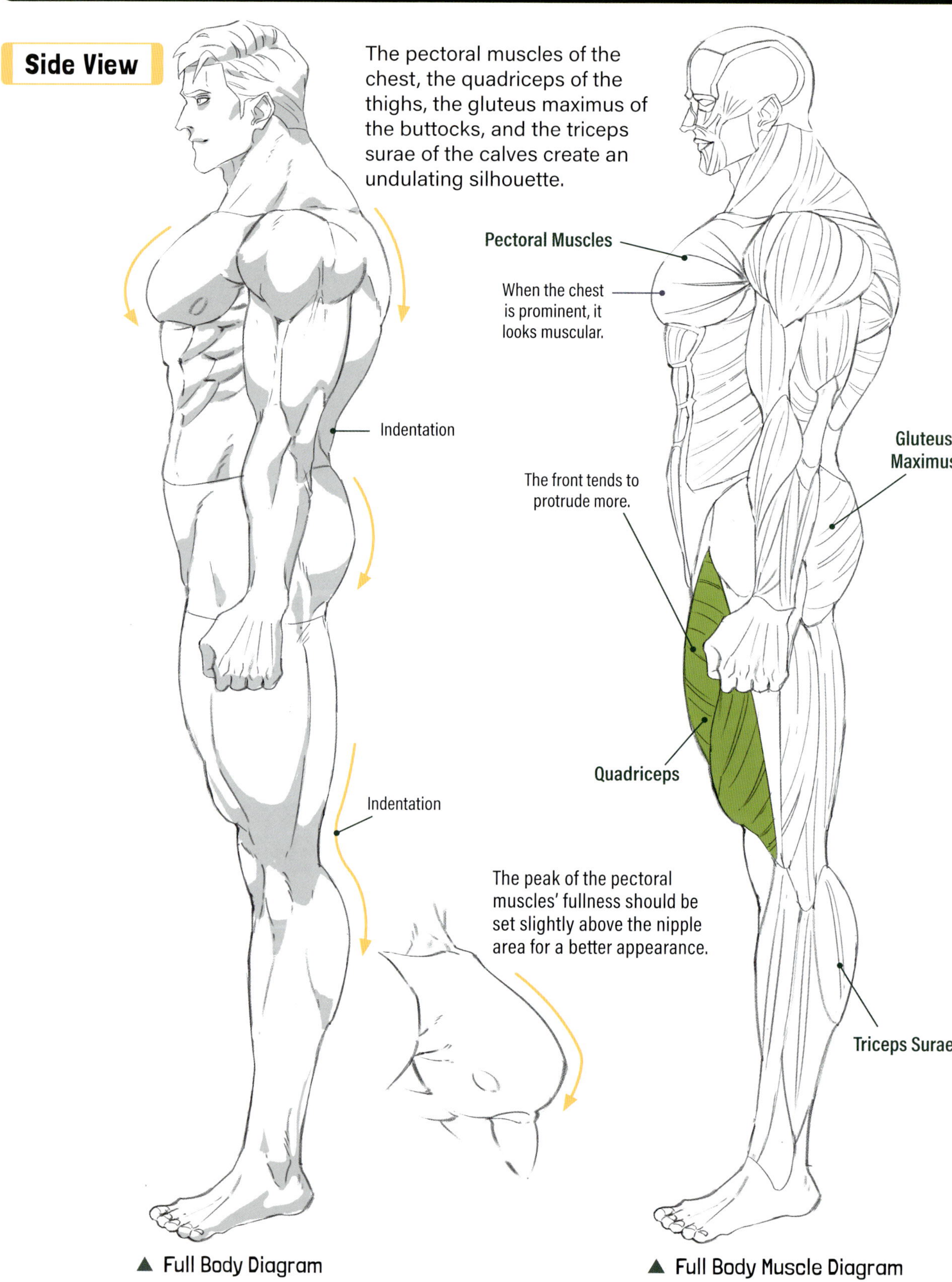

▲ Full Body Diagram

▲ Full Body Muscle Diagram

Back View

The back has many muscles. Be sure to draw even the finer muscles for a well-defined, muscular back.

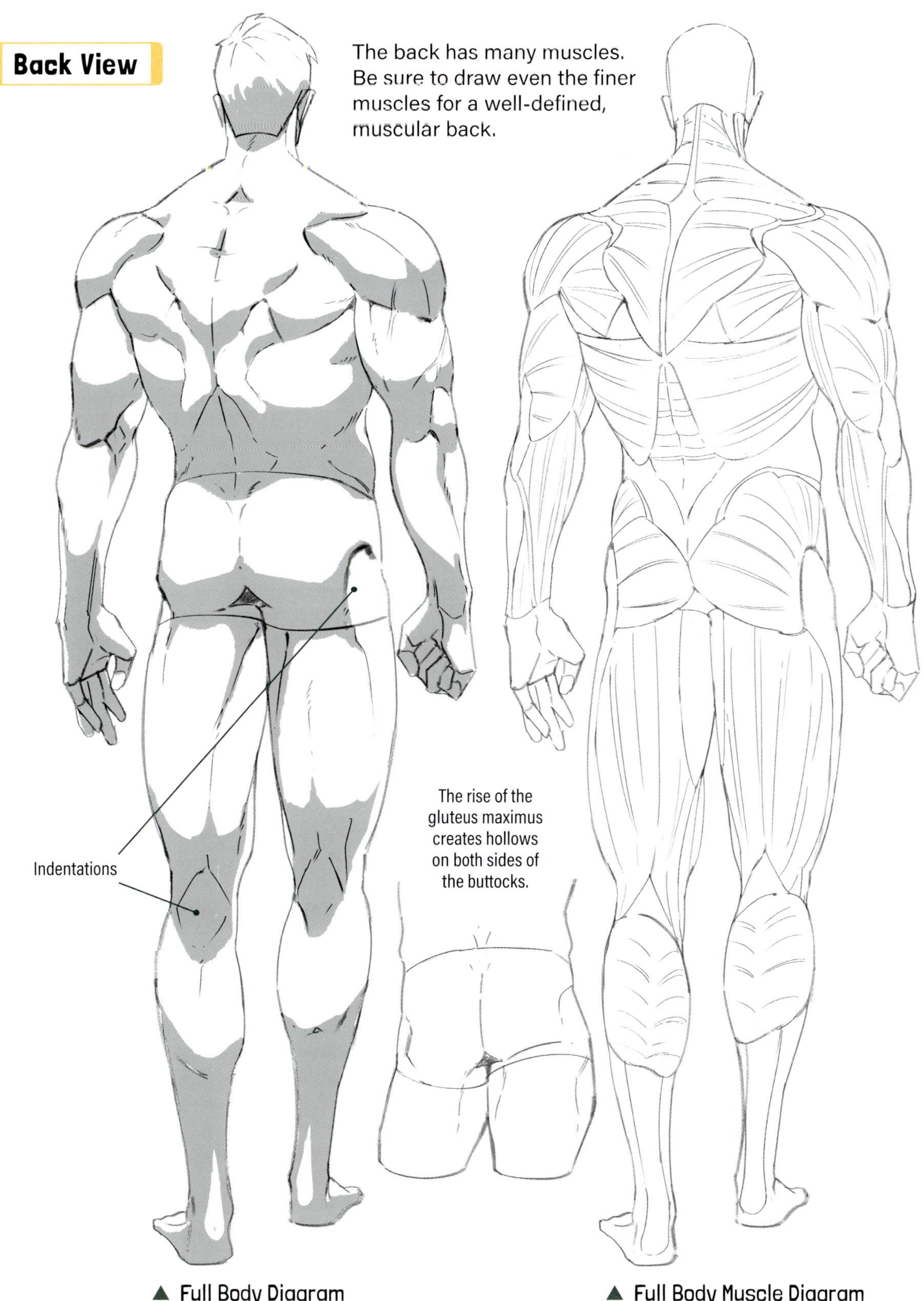

▲ Full Body Diagram

▲ Full Body Muscle Diagram

How to Draw the Figure

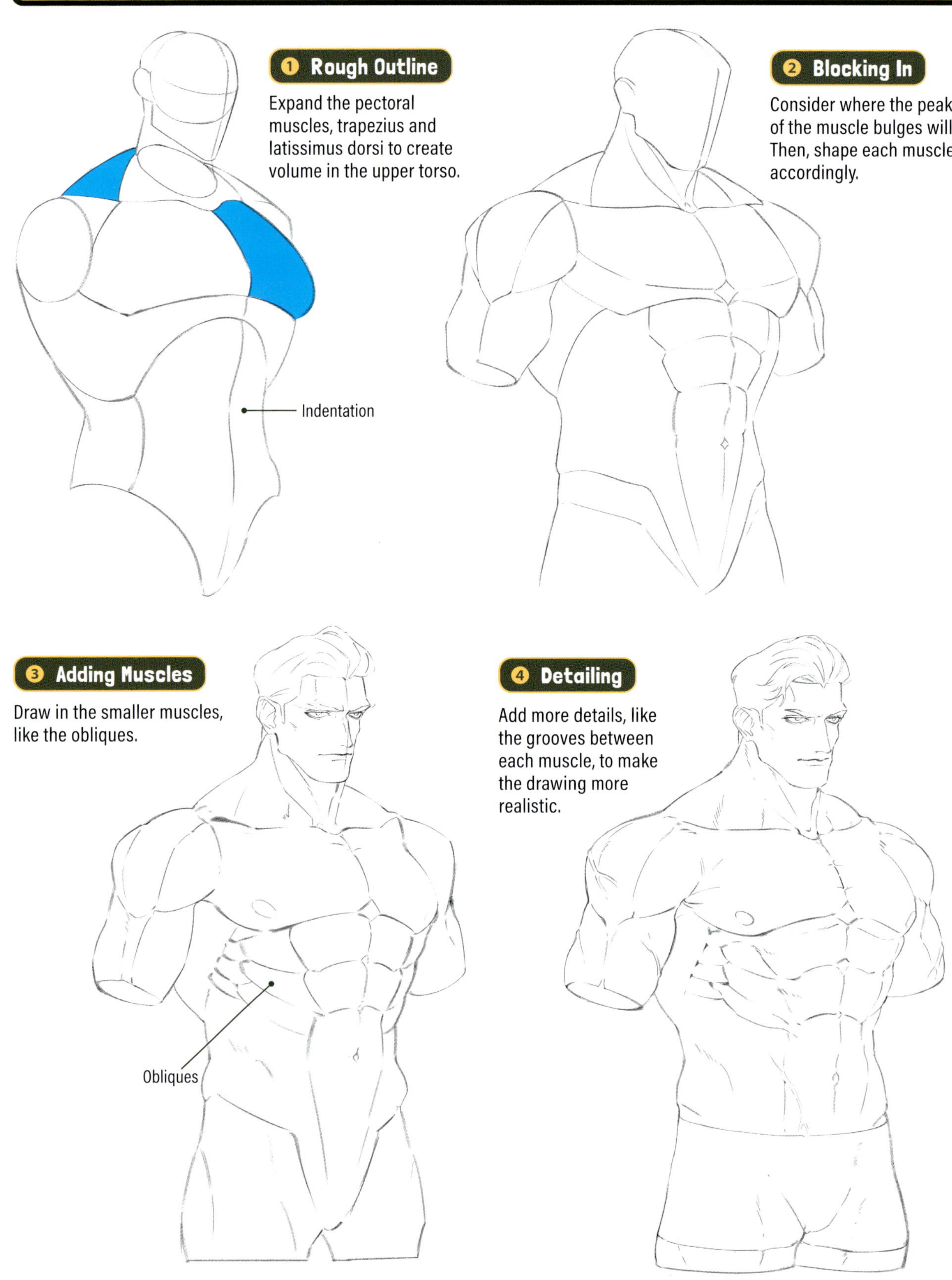

❶ Rough Outline

Expand the pectoral muscles, trapezius and latissimus dorsi to create volume in the upper torso.

❷ Blocking In

Consider where the peaks of the muscle bulges will be. Then, shape each muscle accordingly.

❸ Adding Muscles

Draw in the smaller muscles, like the obliques.

❹ Detailing

Add more details, like the grooves between each muscle, to make the drawing more realistic.

How to Apply Color

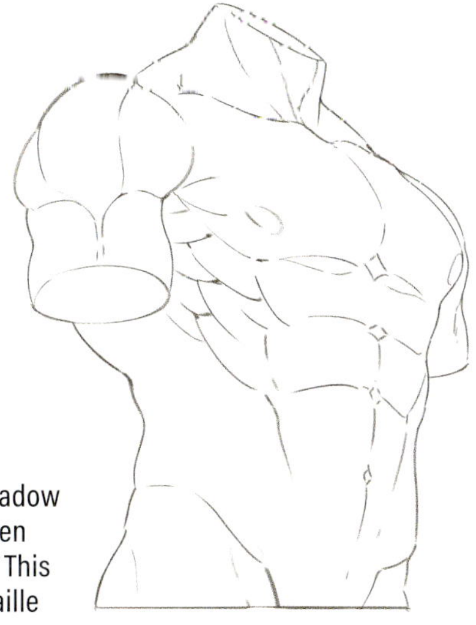

① Line Art

Start by adding the shadow color to the line art, then apply the main colors. This is done using the grisaille technique.

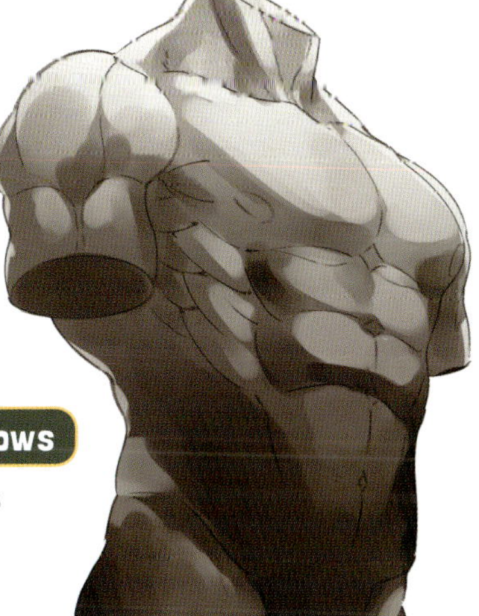

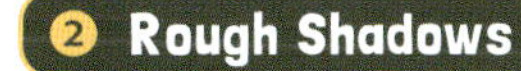

② Rough Shadows

Apply broad shadows to define the muscle shapes. Focus on the darkest areas.

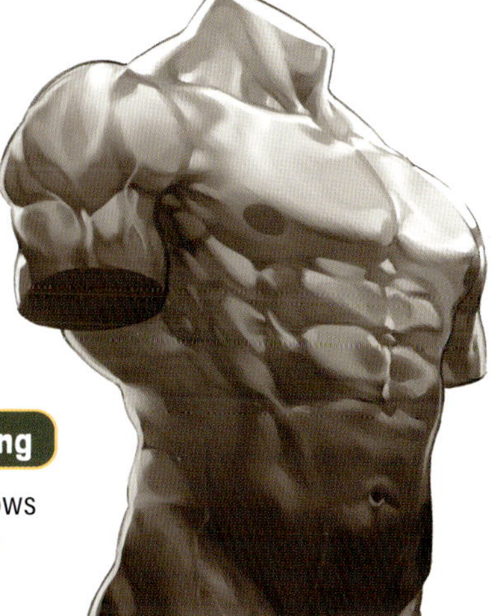

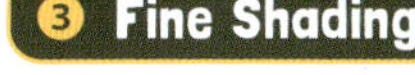

③ Fine Shading

Add detailed shadows and highlights. The more detailed the shading, the more realistic it will look.

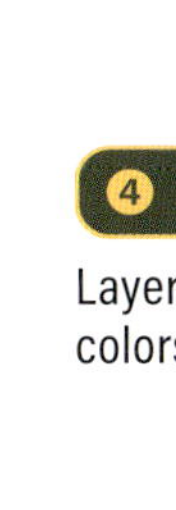

④ Coloring

Layer transparent colors over the image.

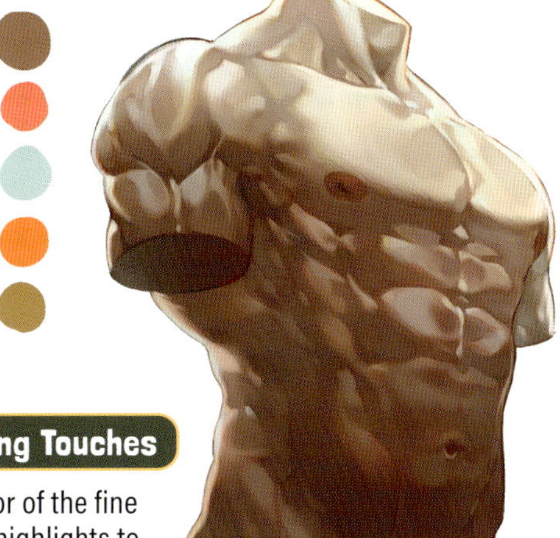

⑤ Finishing Touches

Adjust the color of the fine shadows and highlights to complete the image.

Various-angle Views of Muscles

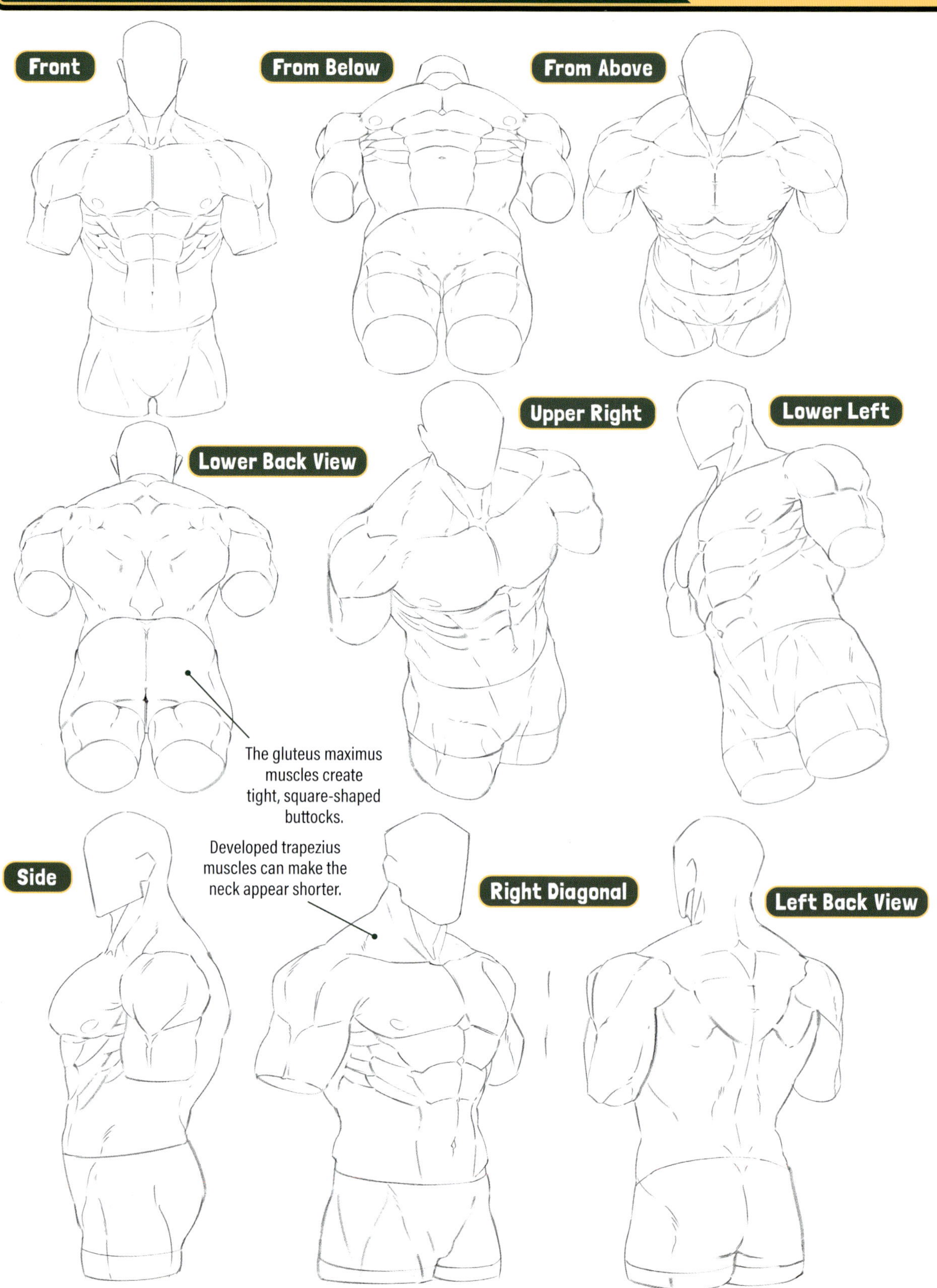

Muscular Body Type Viewed from Various Angles

When the boundaries of each muscle are clearly drawn, the muscle mass is noticeable from any angle. The chest thickness increases, and the overall body thickness also expands.

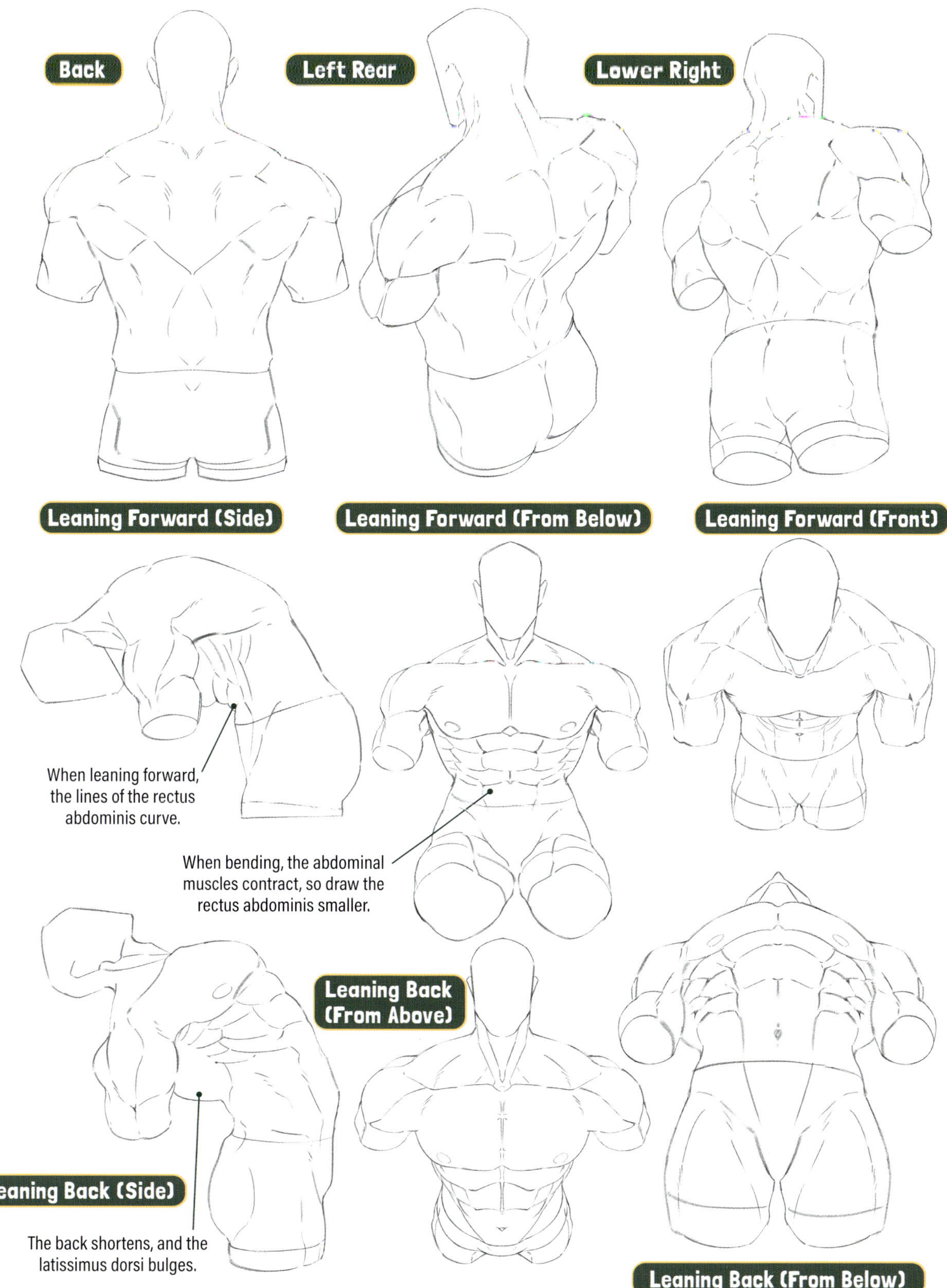

Arm Muscles

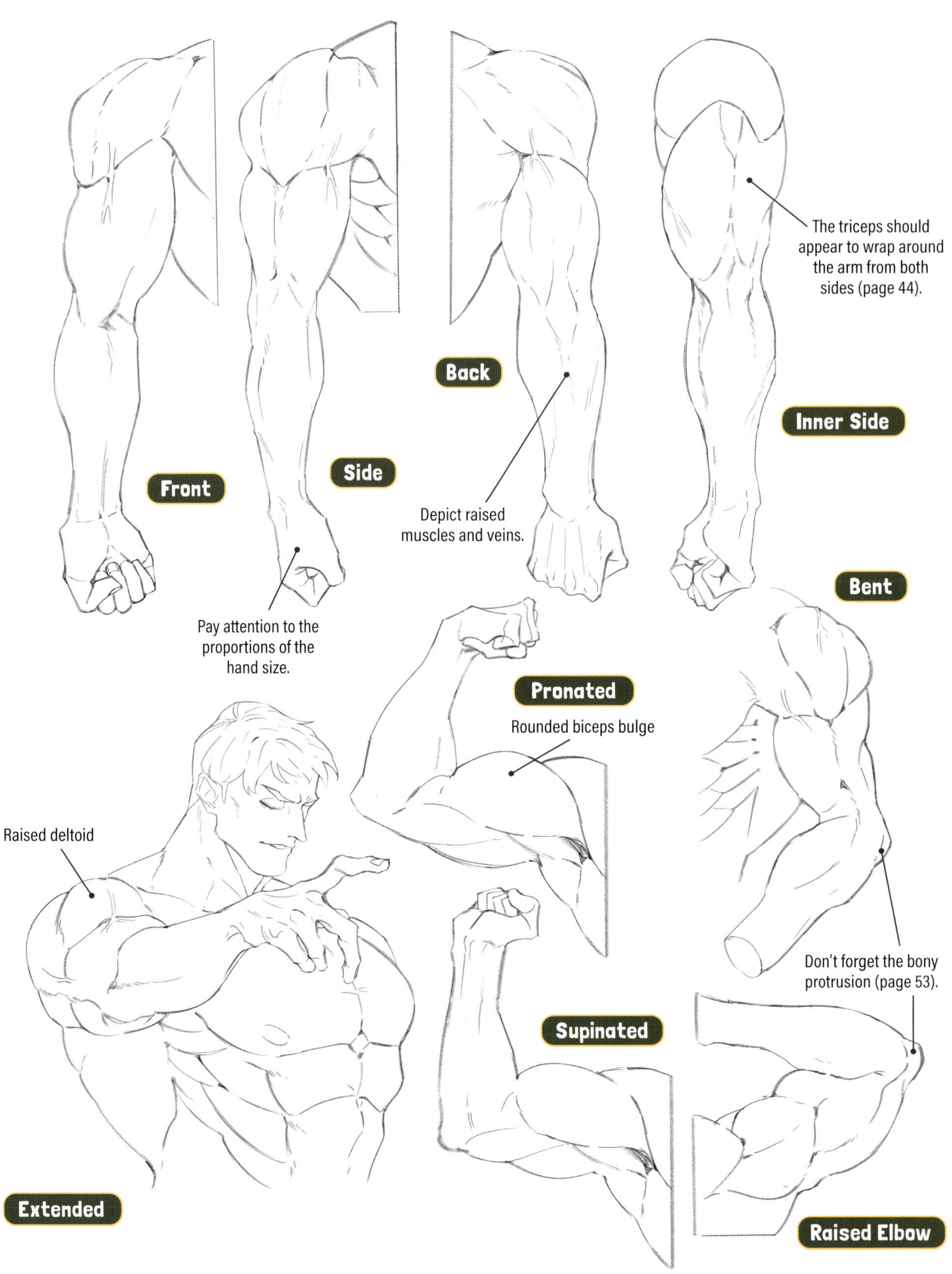
The triceps should appear to wrap around the arm from both sides (page 44).
Back
Inner Side
Side
Front
Depict raised muscles and veins.
Pay attention to the proportions of the hand size.
Bent
Pronated
Rounded biceps bulge
Raised deltoid
Don't forget the bony protrusion (page 53).
Supinated
Extended
Raised Elbow

Leg Muscles

Front
Calf bulge
Side
Back
Inner Side
Legs Spread
Thighs like tree trunks
Low Angle
Rolling
Focus on muscle tension.
Squatting
Raised Leg

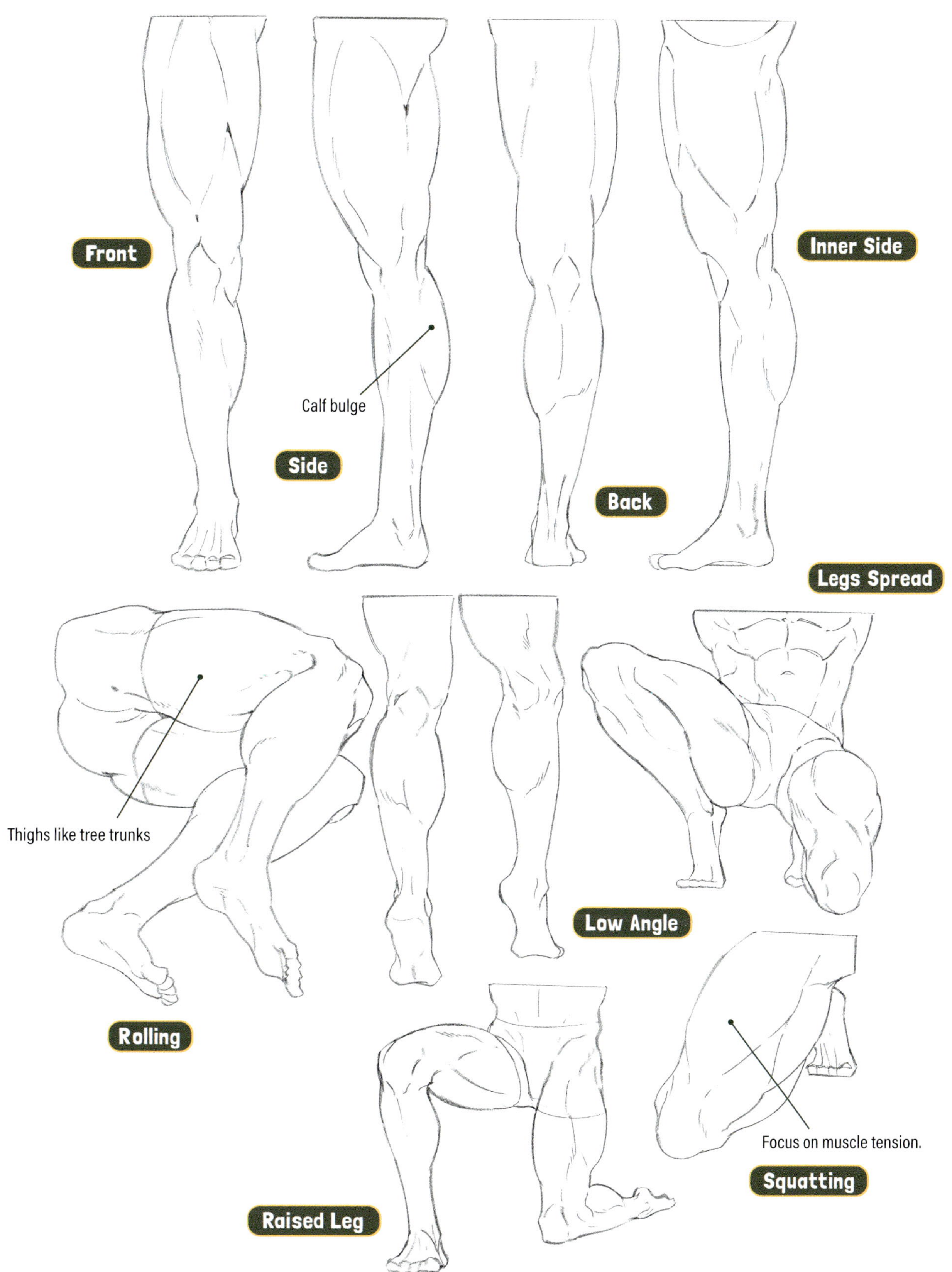

How to Depict Each Muscle

Front

This is a level of muscle mass that even bodybuilders rarely achieve, just on the edge of what humans can attain.

With shoulders so raised that they cast shadows underneath, highly developed pectoral muscles, and latissimus dorsi muscles visible even from the front, the upper body is particularly developed.

Compared to these, the head looks quite small.

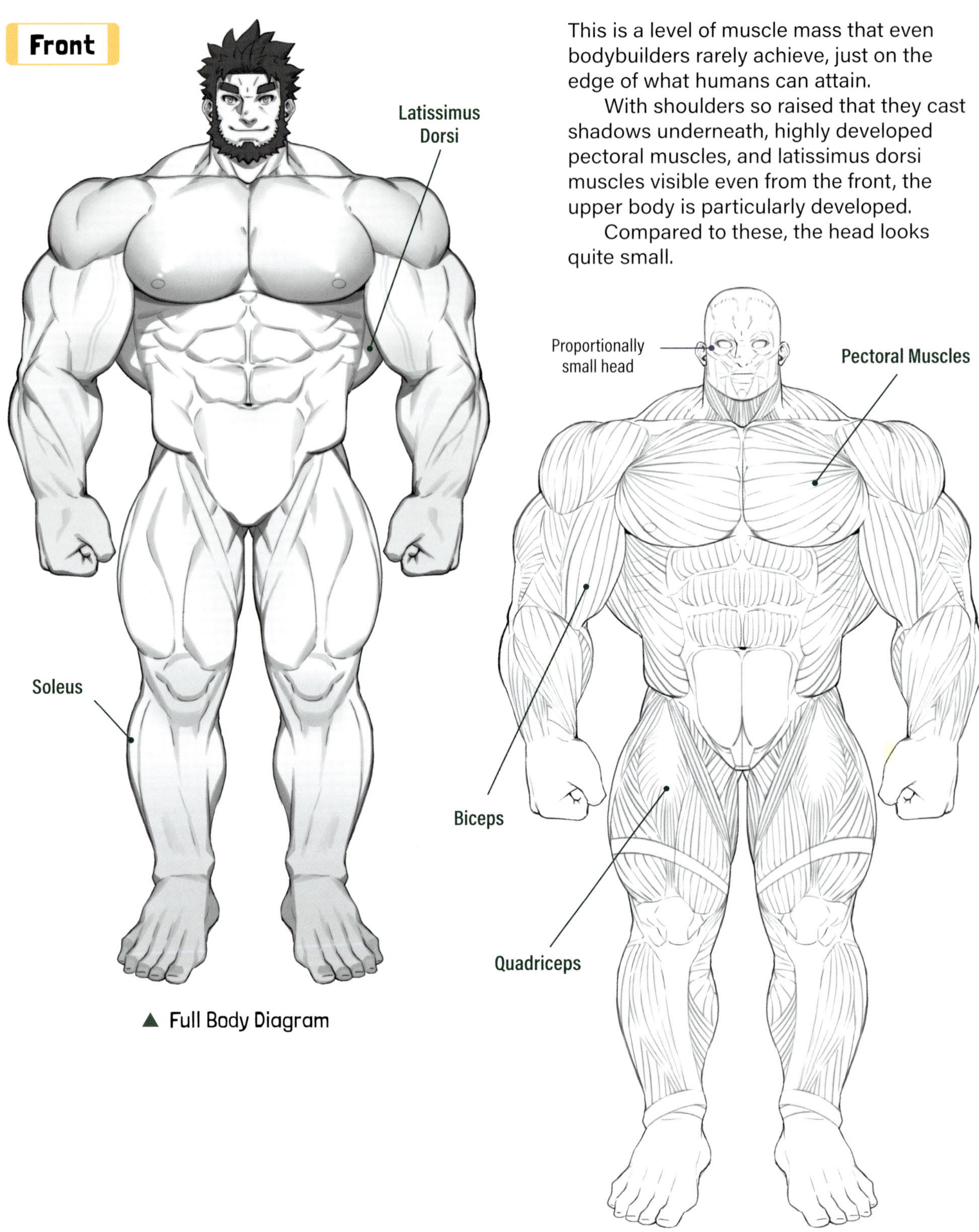

▲ Full Body Diagram

▲ Full Body Muscle Diagram

Cross Sections of the Torso

The shoulders and pectoral muscles are extremely wide, while the waist is tight and narrow, creating a clear V-shaped body.

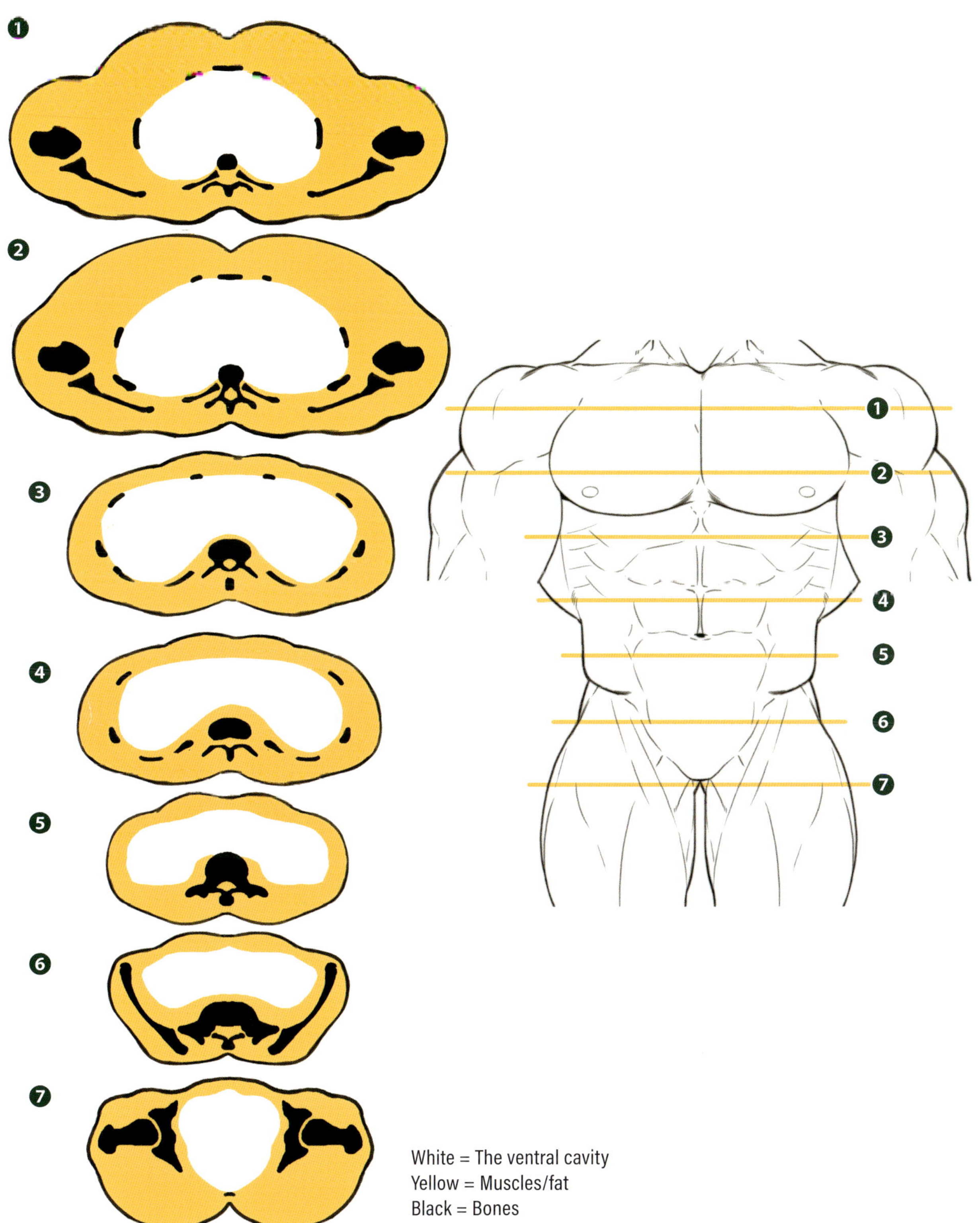

White = The ventral cavity
Yellow = Muscles/fat
Black = Bones

How to Depict Each Muscle

Side View

Trapezius

The most prominent parts are the pectoral muscles and trapezius, followed by the thighs. From the side, the enlarged shoulders and arms hide nearly half of the body.

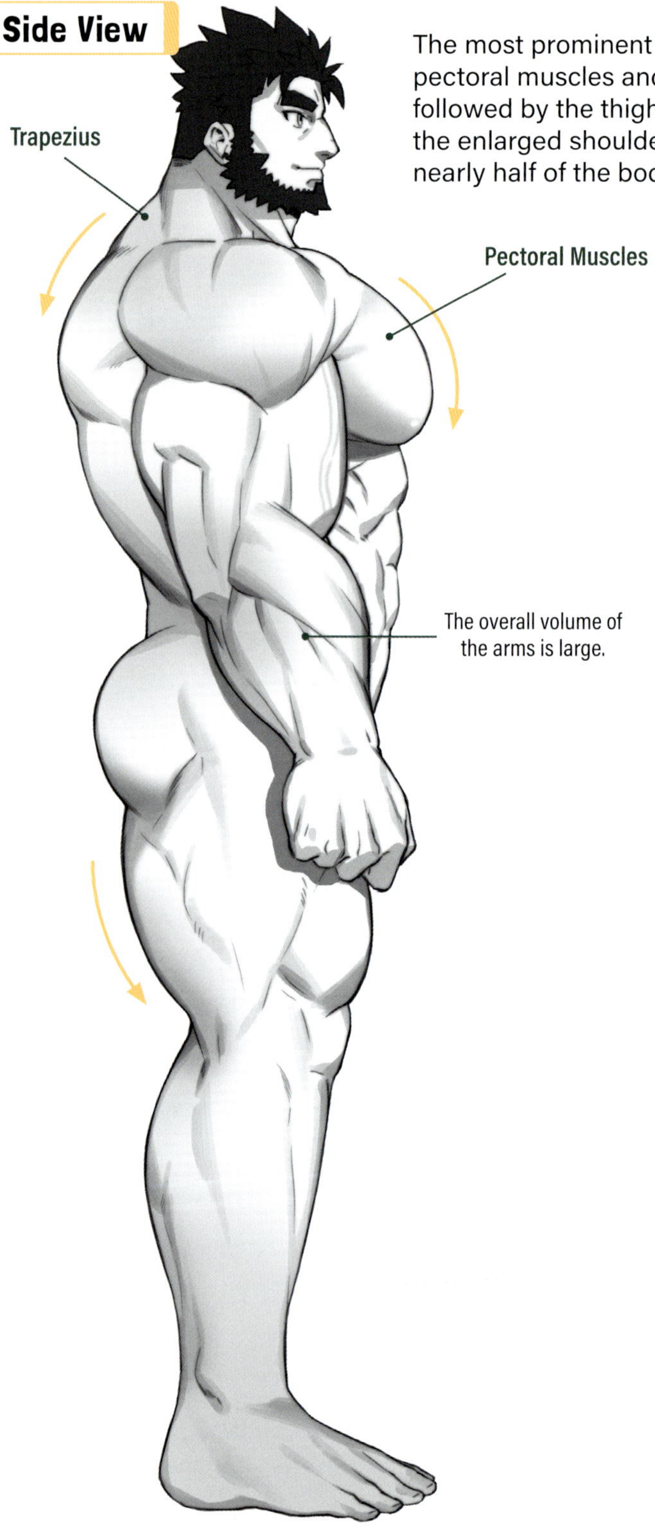

Pectoral Muscles

The overall volume of the arms is large.

▲ Full Body Diagram

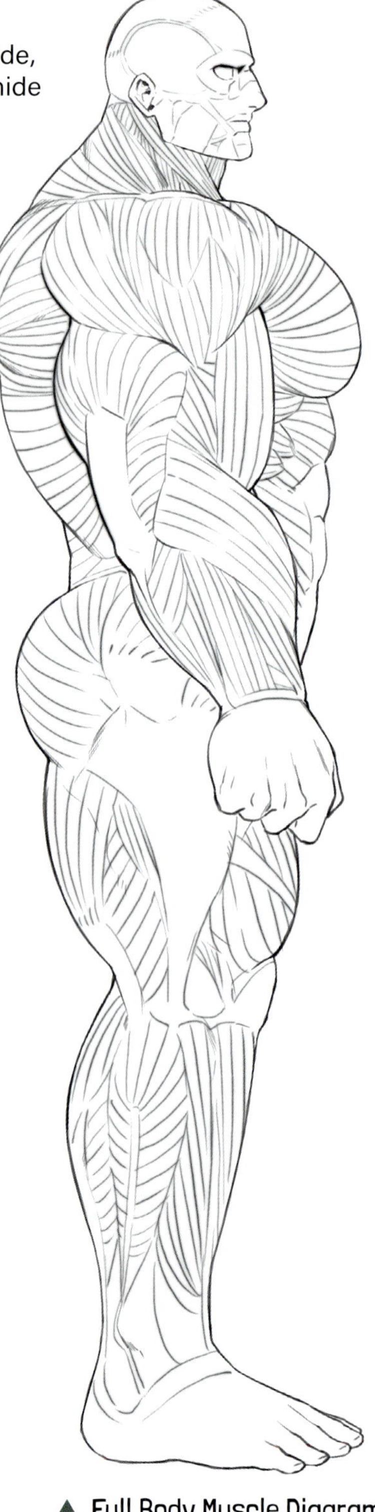

▲ Full Body Muscle Diagram

Back View

The narrow waist makes the developed latissimus dorsi stand out even more. The gluteus maximus is also firm, lifting the hip line.

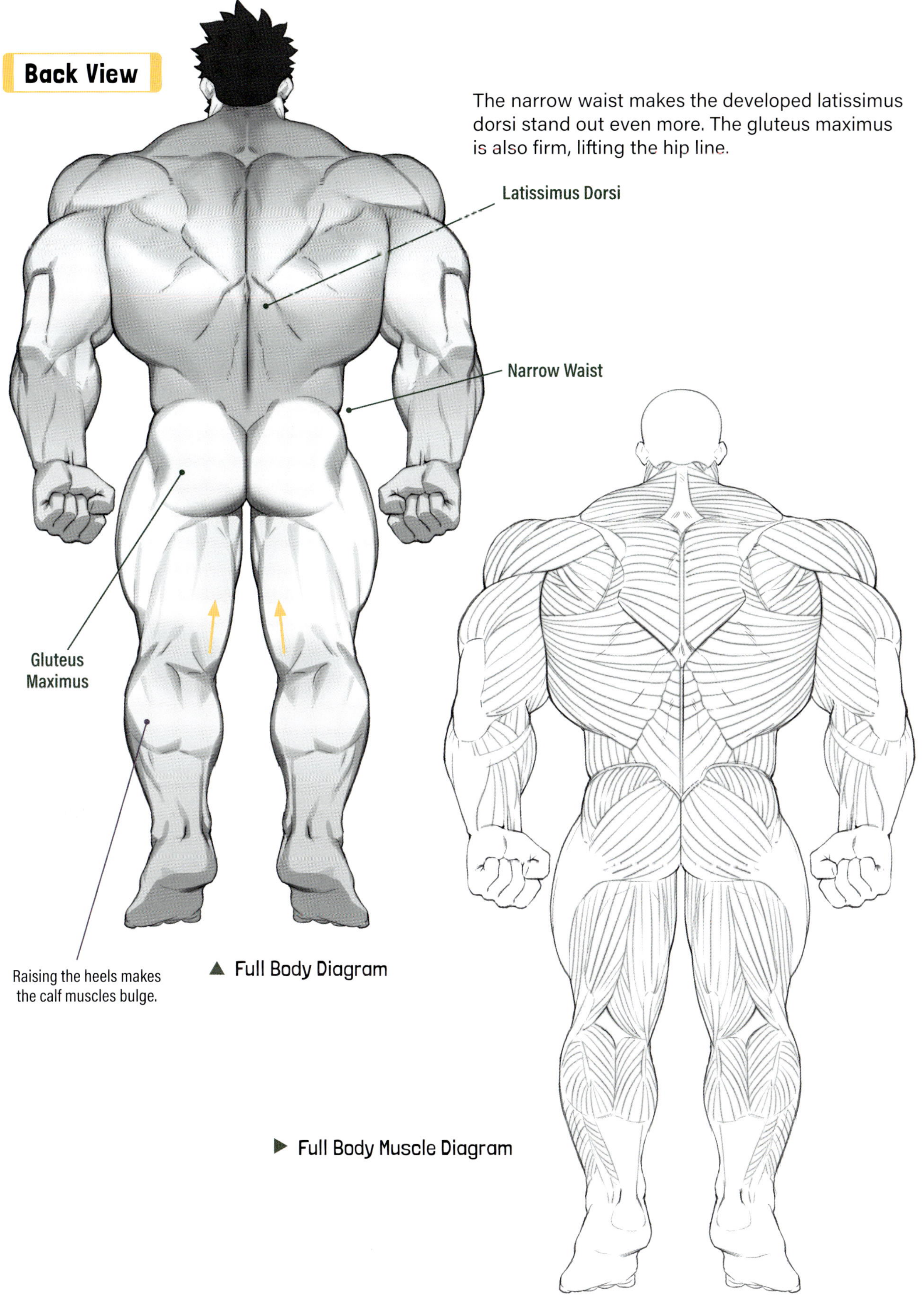

▲ Full Body Diagram

▶ Full Body Muscle Diagram

How to Draw the Figure

❶ Rough Outline

Draw the head, pectoral muscles and waist as simple shapes. Keep it rough and basic.

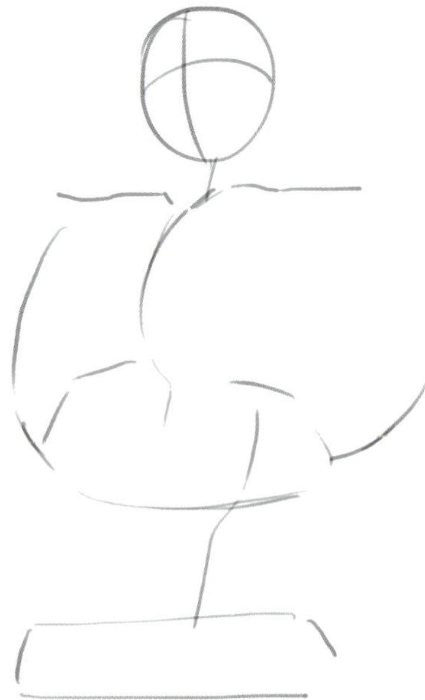

❷ Blocking In

Draw the neck and waist. Use these as the axis to connect the shapes and form the body. Draw the shoulders at this stage as well.

❸ Adding Muscles

Start to indicate the undulating muscles on top of the roughed out form. Pay attention to the size and proportion of each muscle.

❹ Detailing

Using curved lines, further define the muscles, giving them a three-dimensional look.

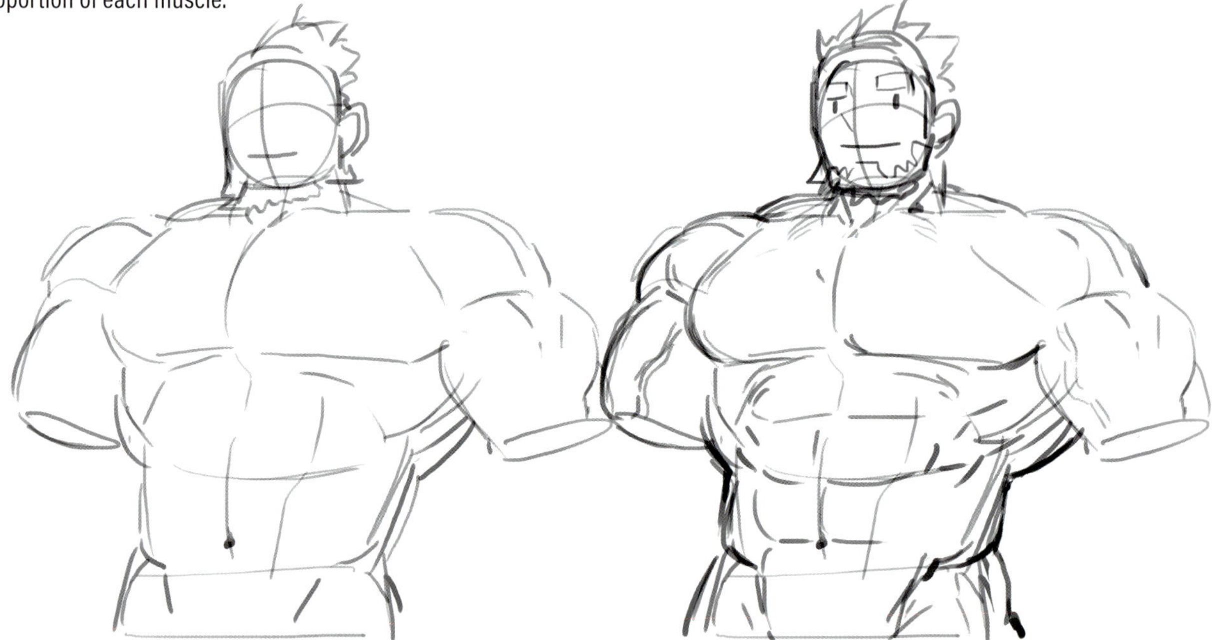

How to Apply Color

❶ Line Art

Vary the thickness of the boundary lines depending on the relative muscle thickness to create contrast.

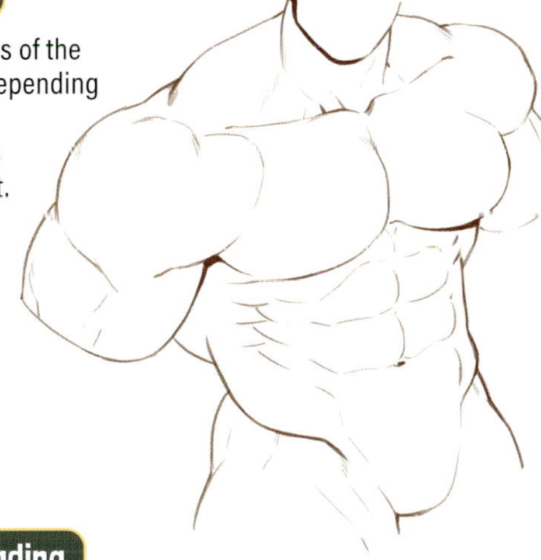

❷ Base Color

Fill in the entire body with the desired skin tone.

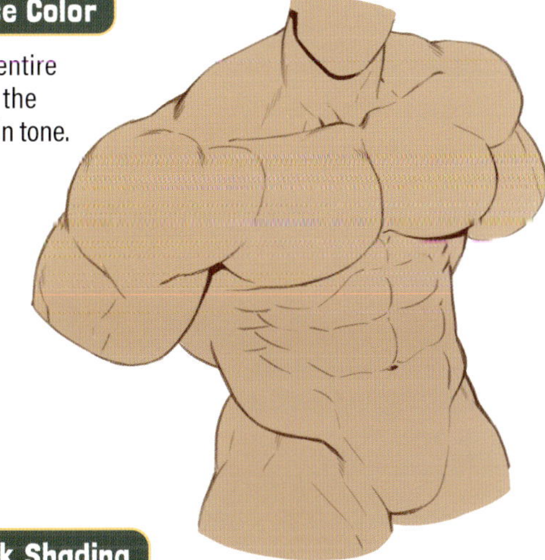

❸ Light Shading

Apply rough shadows to the edges of areas where muscles bulge. This helps establish the three-dimensional shape.

❹ Dark Shading

Add another layer of darker shadows, keeping reflective light in mind. This makes the shapes stand out even more.

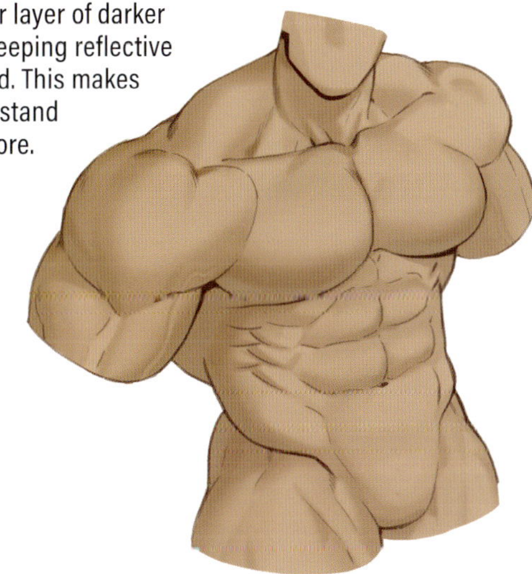

❺ Highlights

Paint the peaks of the bulging muscles with a color lighter than the base. The light source is coming from the upper right.

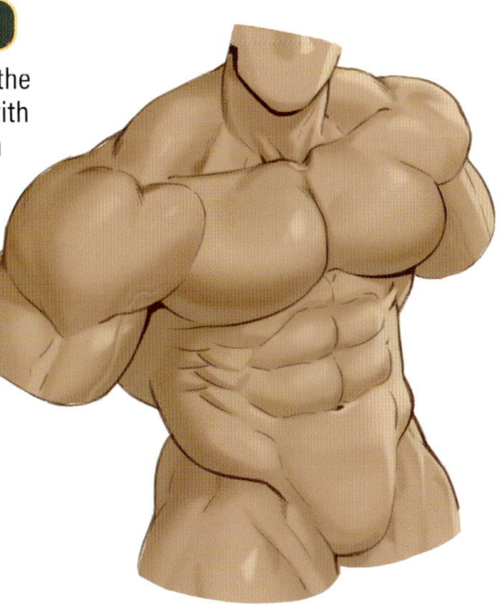

❻ Finishing Touches

Increase the contrast through color adjustment to create a shiny, polished look.

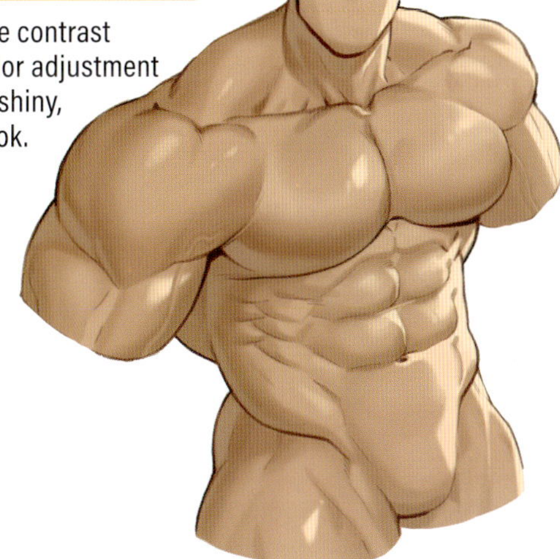

Various-angle Views of Muscles

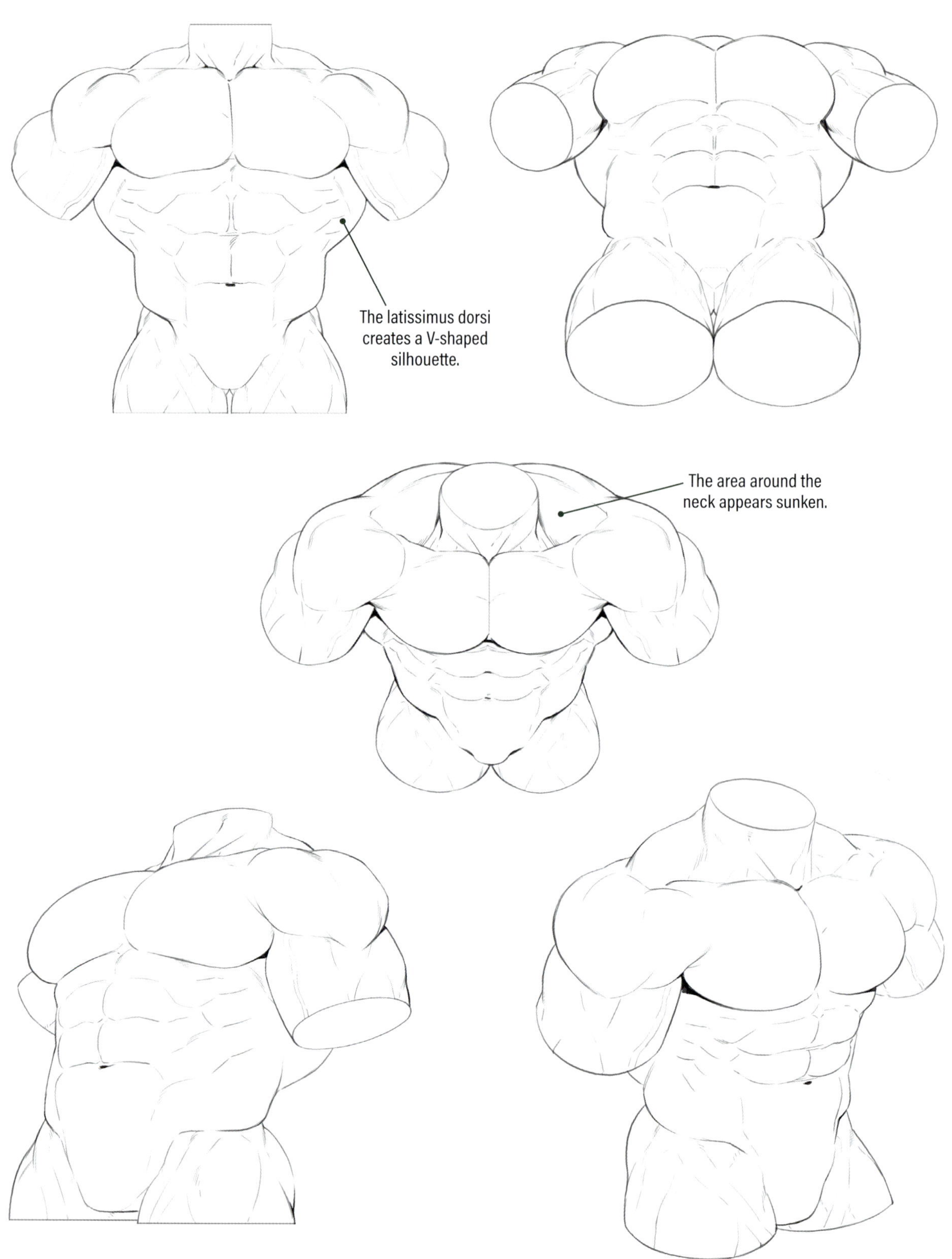

In an extremely muscular body type, the rounded, bulging pectoral muscles stand out the most. Using curved lines for the muscle outlines gives a sense of volume and a softer, less rigid appearance.

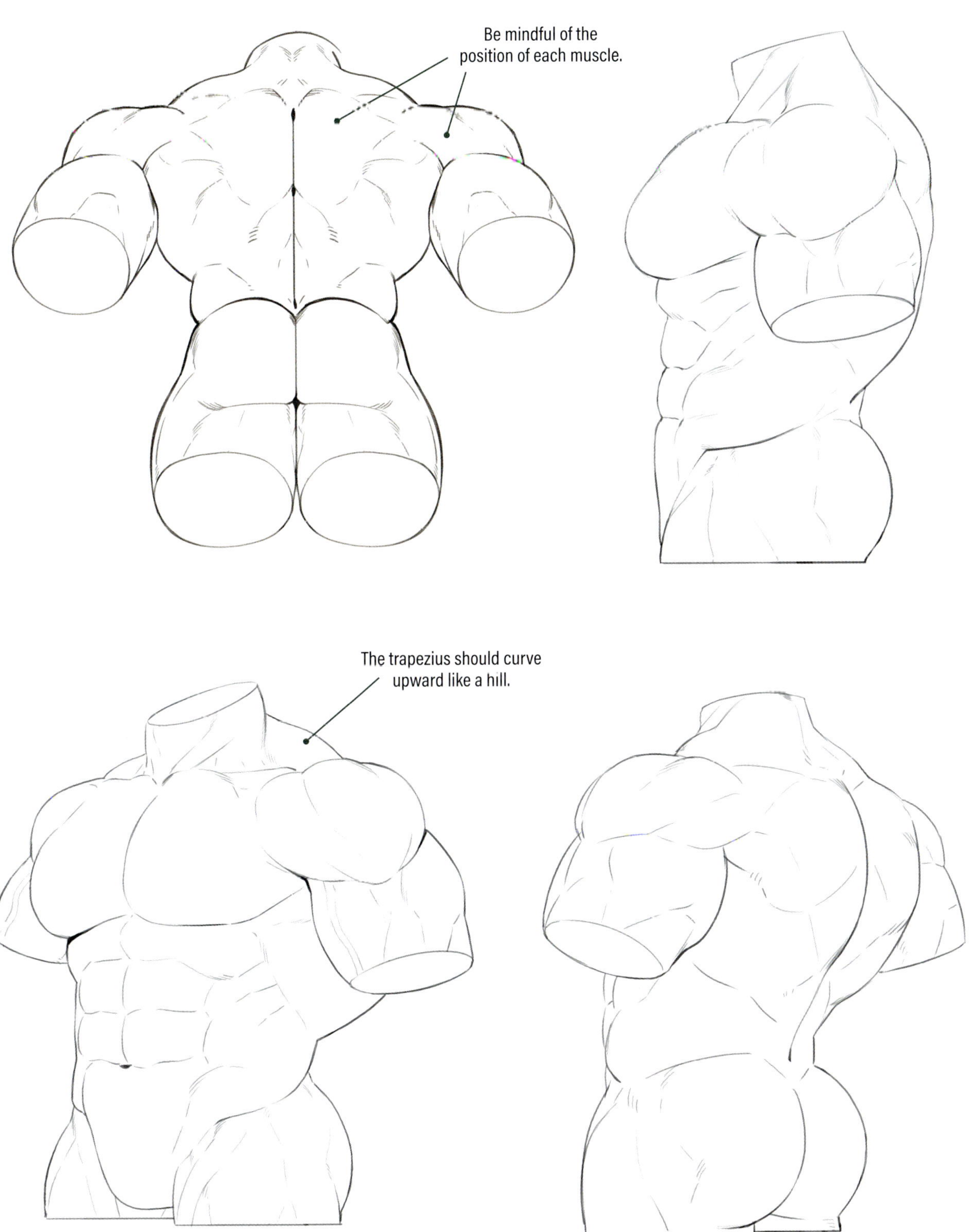

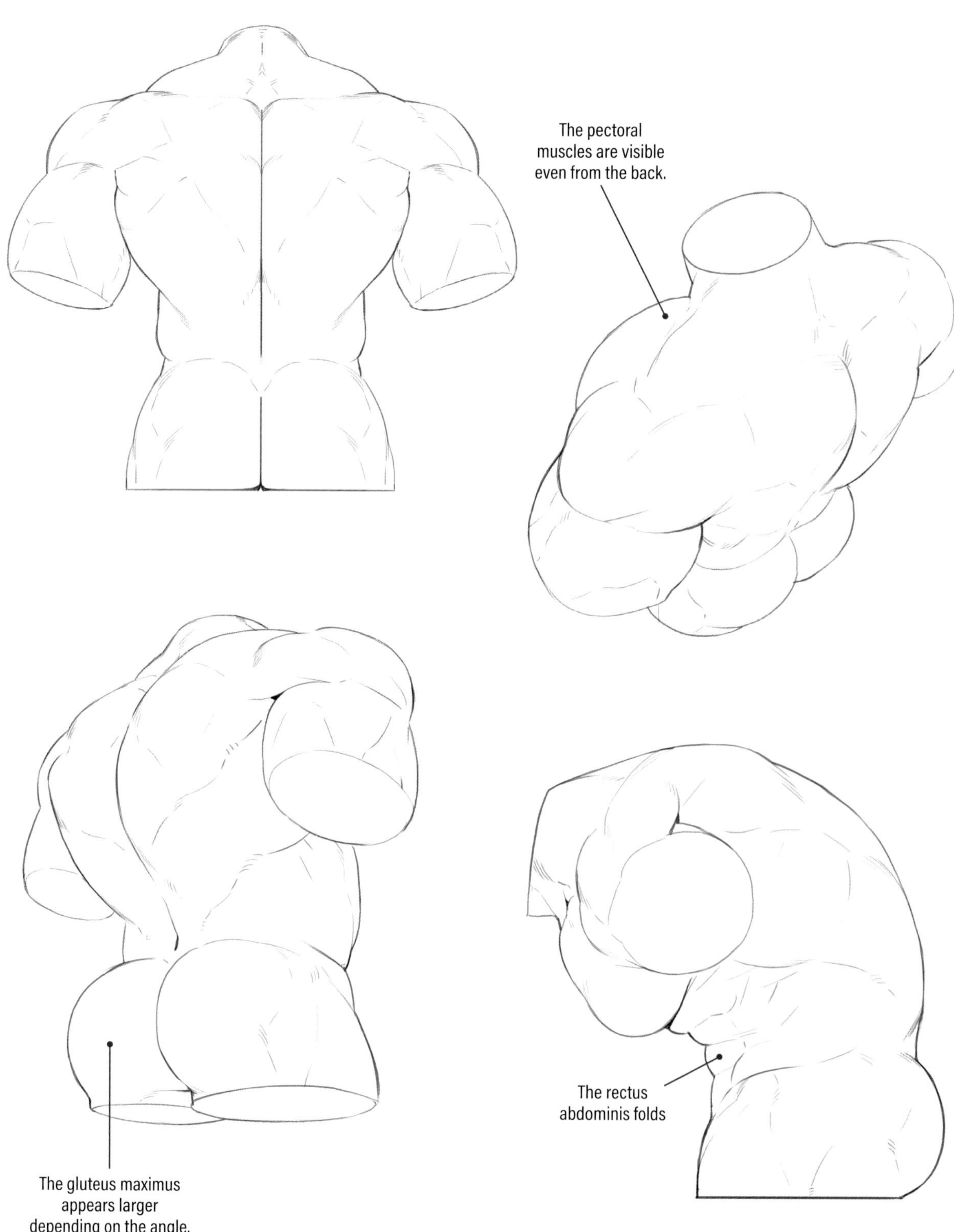
The pectoral
muscles are visible
even from the back.
The gluteus maximus
appears larger
depending on the angle.
The rectus
abdominis folds

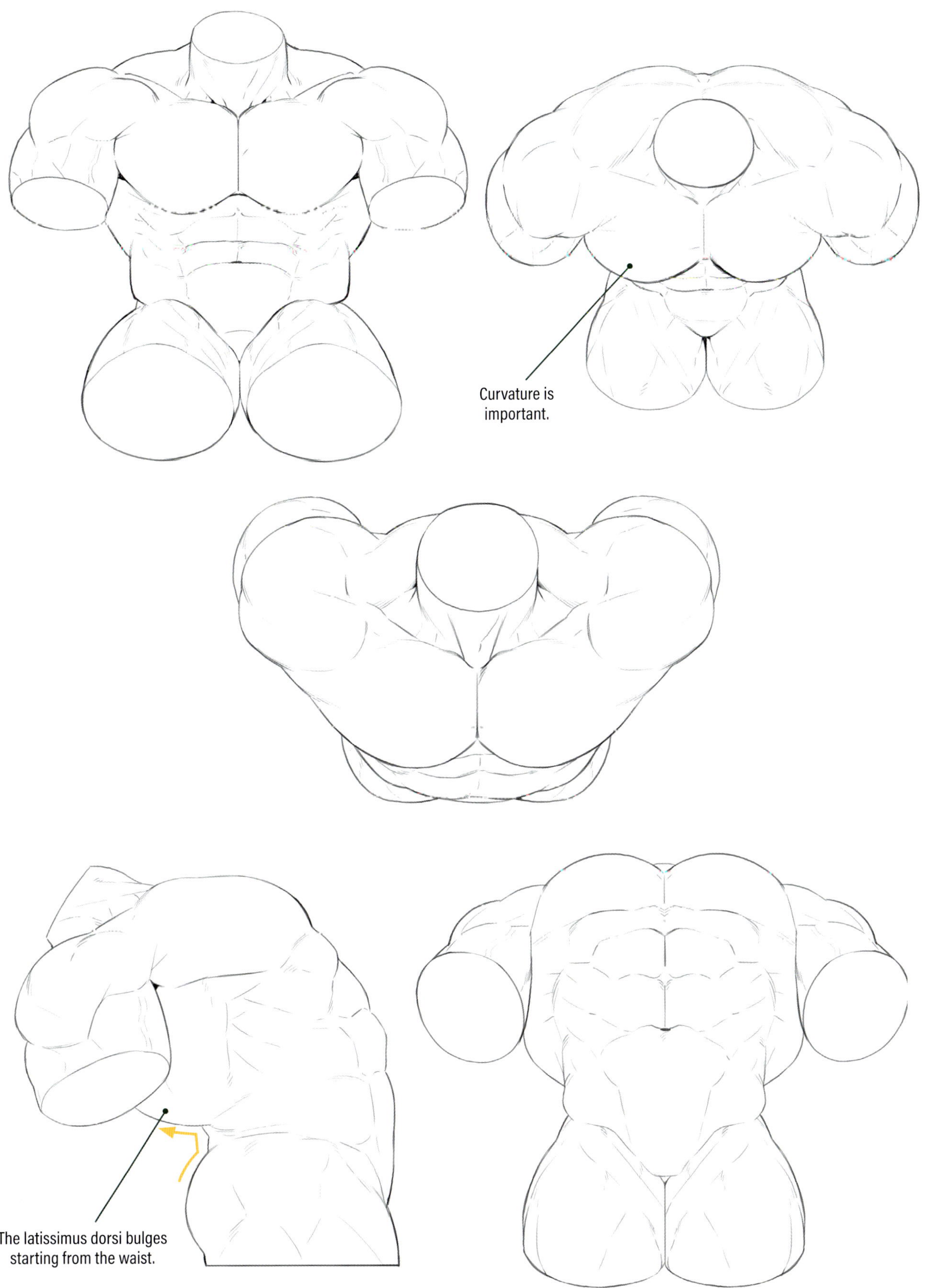
Curvature is
important.
The latissimus dorsi bulges
starting from the waist.

Arm Muscles

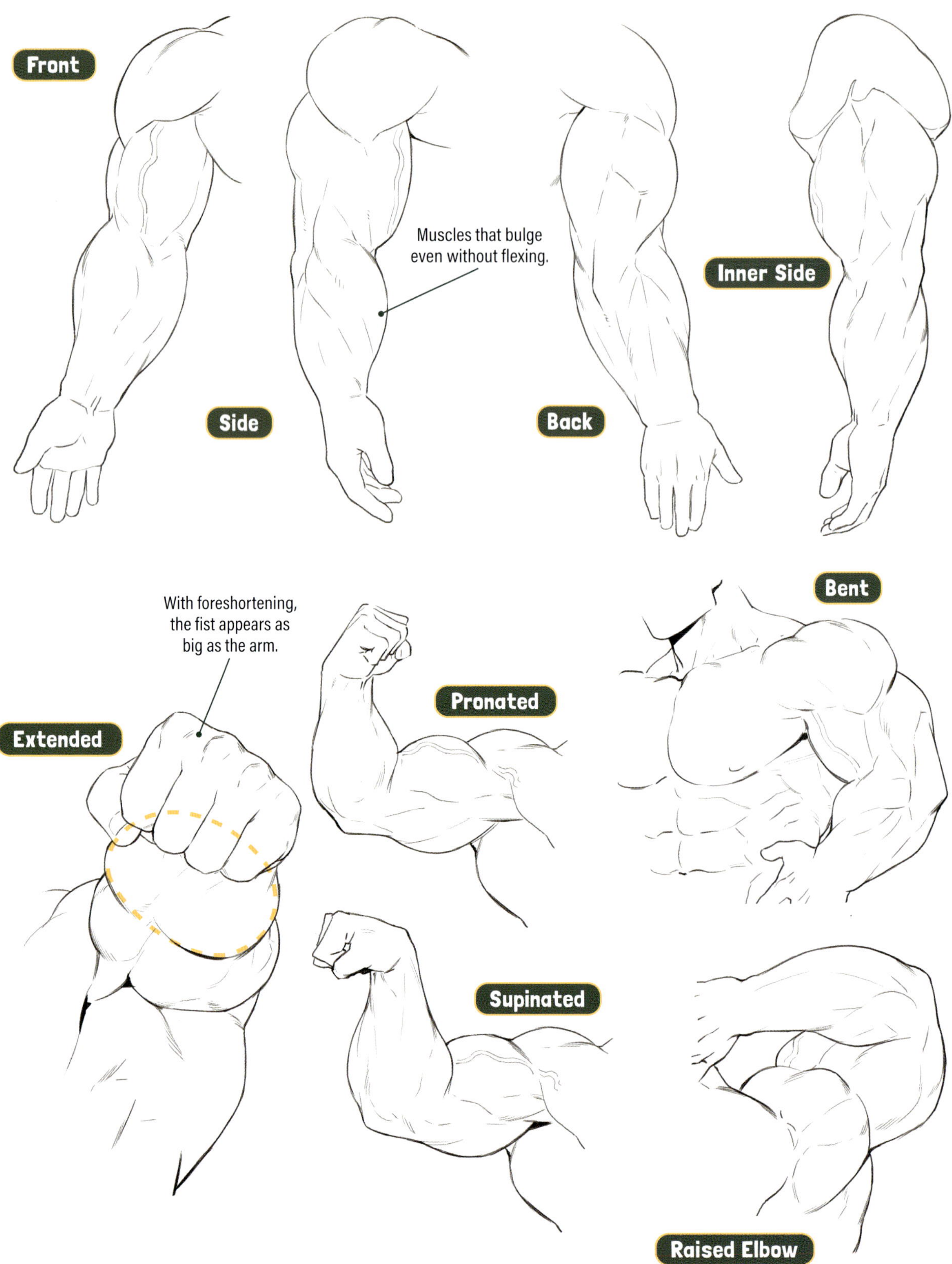
Front
Side
Muscles that bulge even without flexing.
Back
Inner Side
With foreshortening, the fist appears as big as the arm.
Extended
Pronated
Bent
Supinated
Raised Elbow

Leg Muscles

Back
Gastrocnemius that appears heart-shaped.
Side
Inner Side
Front
Legs Spread
Rolling
Low Angle
Adding contrast gives a powerful impression.
Raised Leg

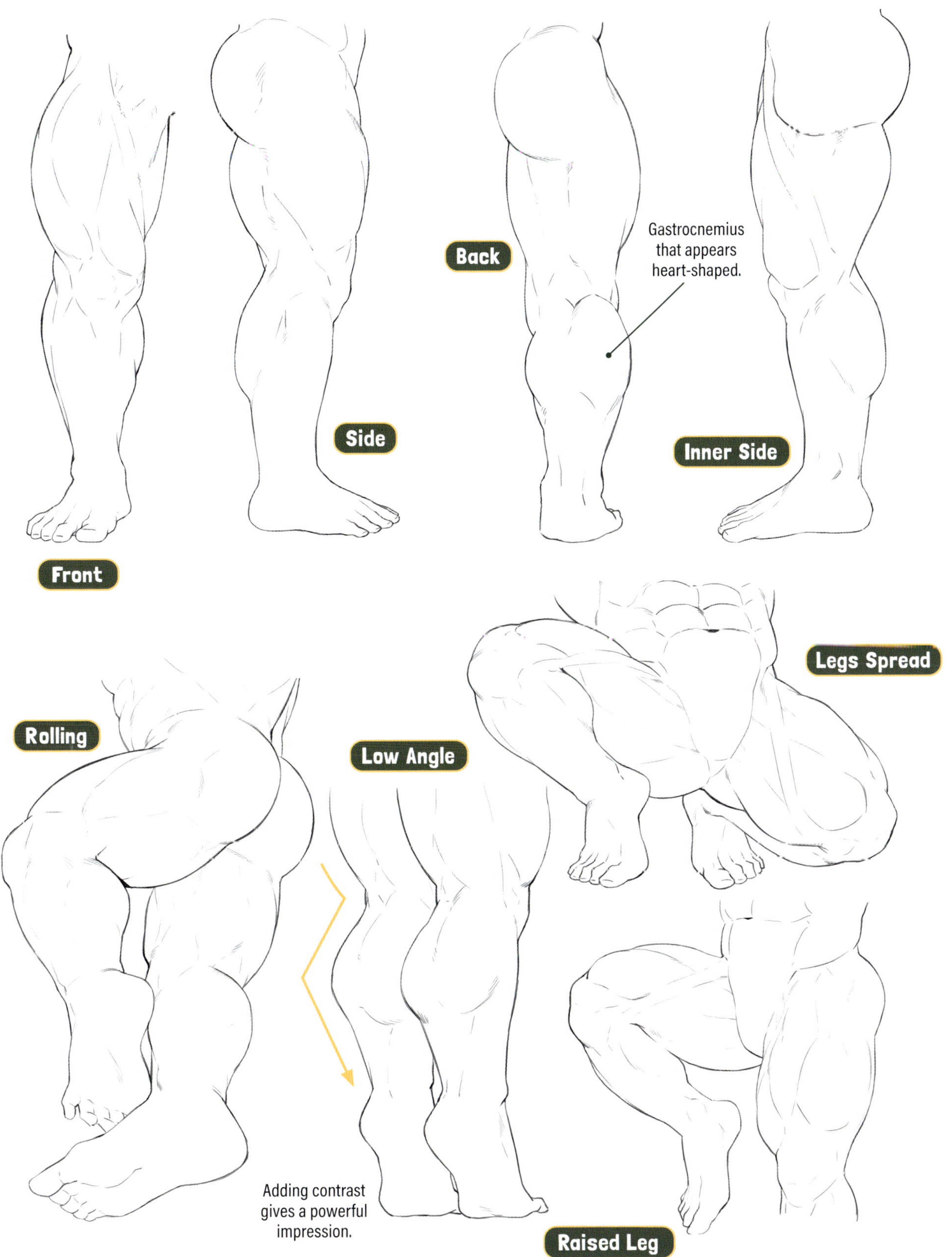

How to Depict Each Muscle

Front

This character has muscles beyond human comprehension, resembling a resident of a fantasy world with an impossible physique. The overwhelming trapezius muscles cover the neck, connecting the line between the shoulders and the head. To balance the oversized arm and leg muscles, the extremities of the hands and feet are also significantly enlarged. However, no matter how much they are exaggerated, the muscle groups themselves are still organized in the same way as for a normal human body. This is something to be mindful of.

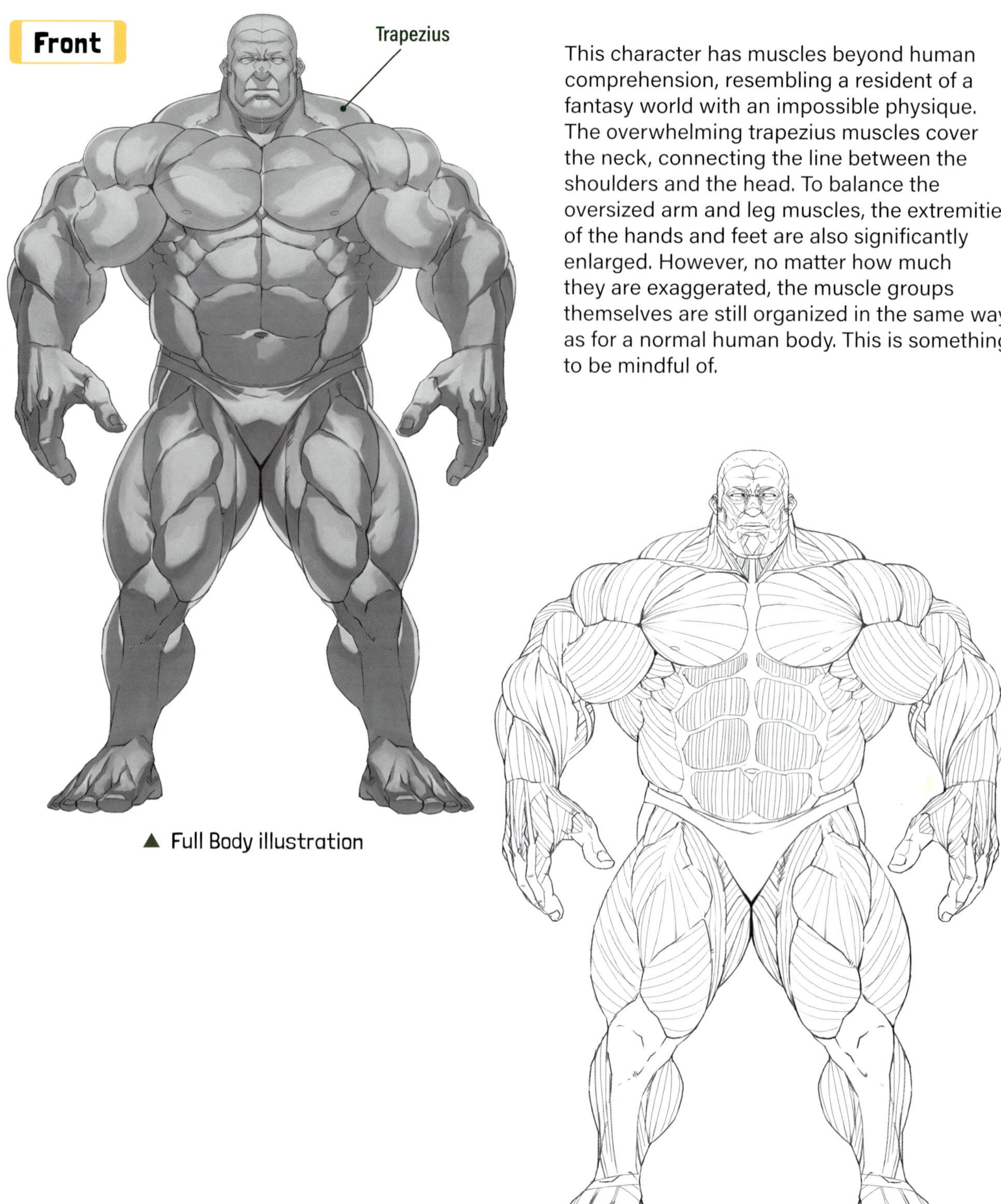

▲ Full Body illustration

▲ Full Body Muscle Illustration

Cross Sections of the Torso

While the muscles are exaggerated, the positions of the bones and organs are not much different from those in a regular human body. The ventral cavity and skeletal framework are also significantly larger compared to a lean physique.

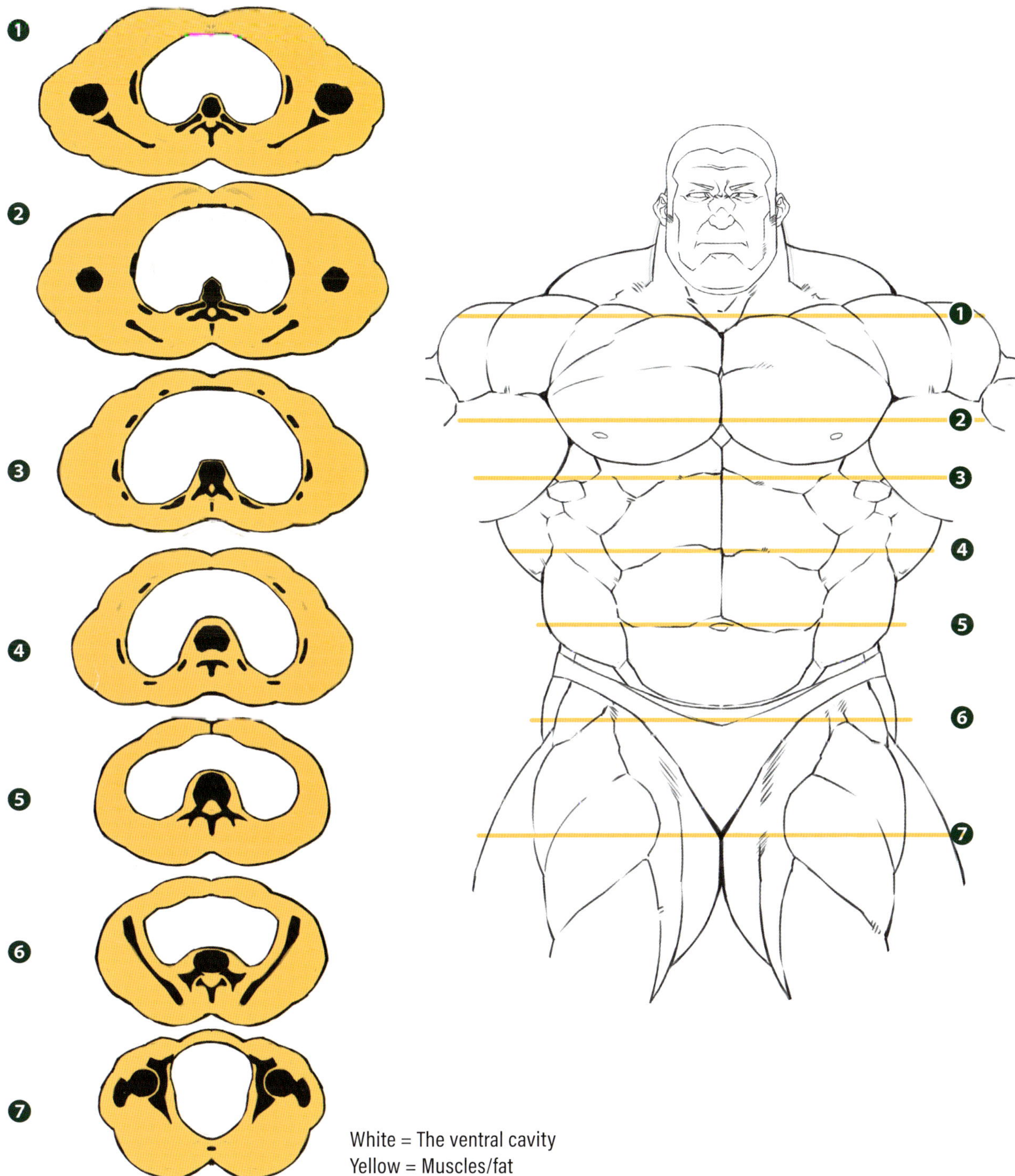

White = The ventral cavity
Yellow = Muscles/fat
Black = Bones

How to Depict Each Muscle

Side View

The pectoral muscles project forward. The rectus abdominis muscles make the abdomen look bigger.

The enlarged trapezius muscles practically connect the back of the head to the back.

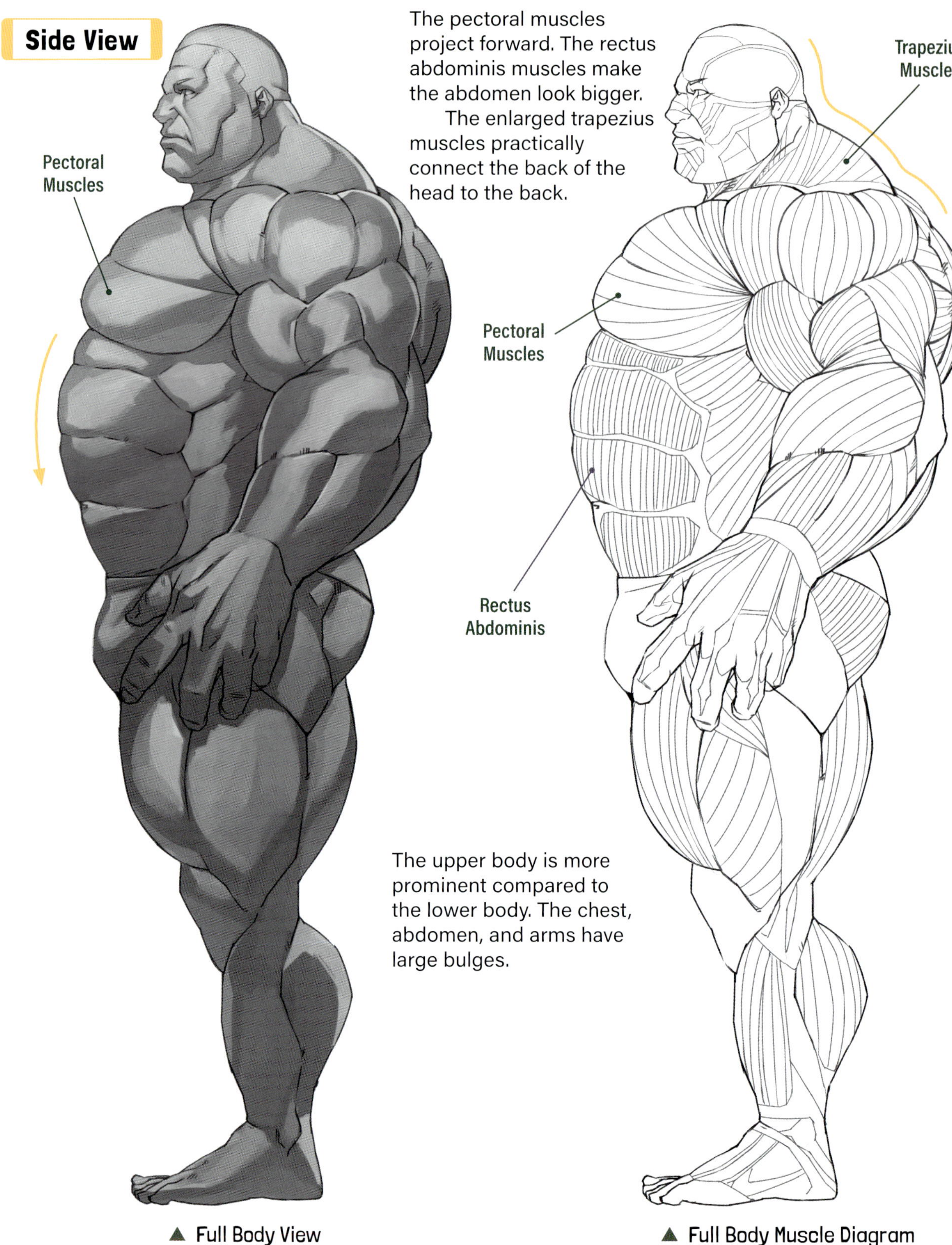

The upper body is more prominent compared to the lower body. The chest, abdomen, and arms have large bulges.

▲ Full Body View

▲ Full Body Muscle Diagram

Back View

From the back, the development of the trapezius muscles is clear. The latissimus dorsi muscles are boldly extended downward.

By slightly tapering the waist and hips, the large thighs are emphasized. The key is how much to exaggerate the position and shape of each muscle.

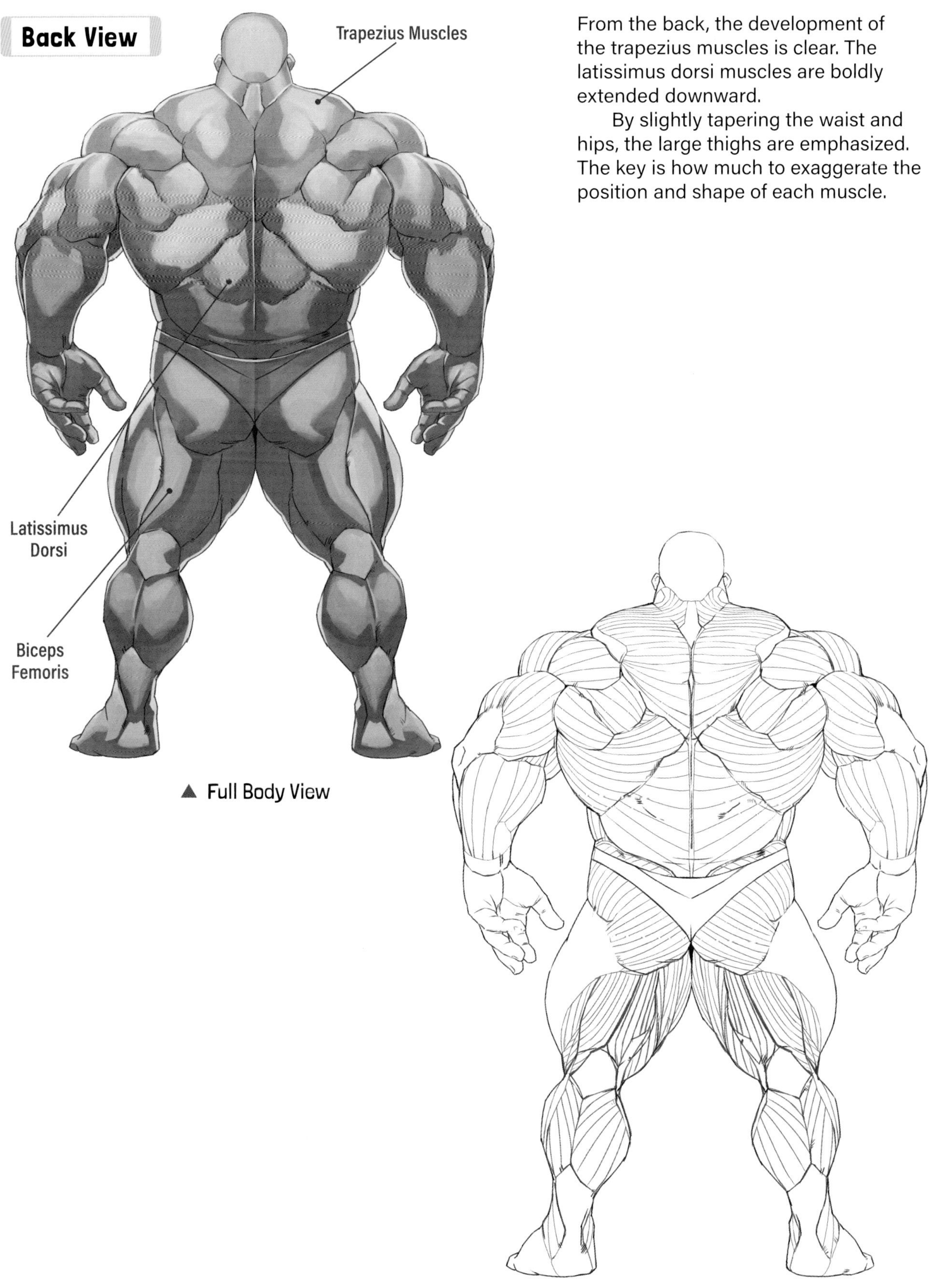

▲ Full Body View

▲ Full Body Muscle Diagram

How to Draw the Figure

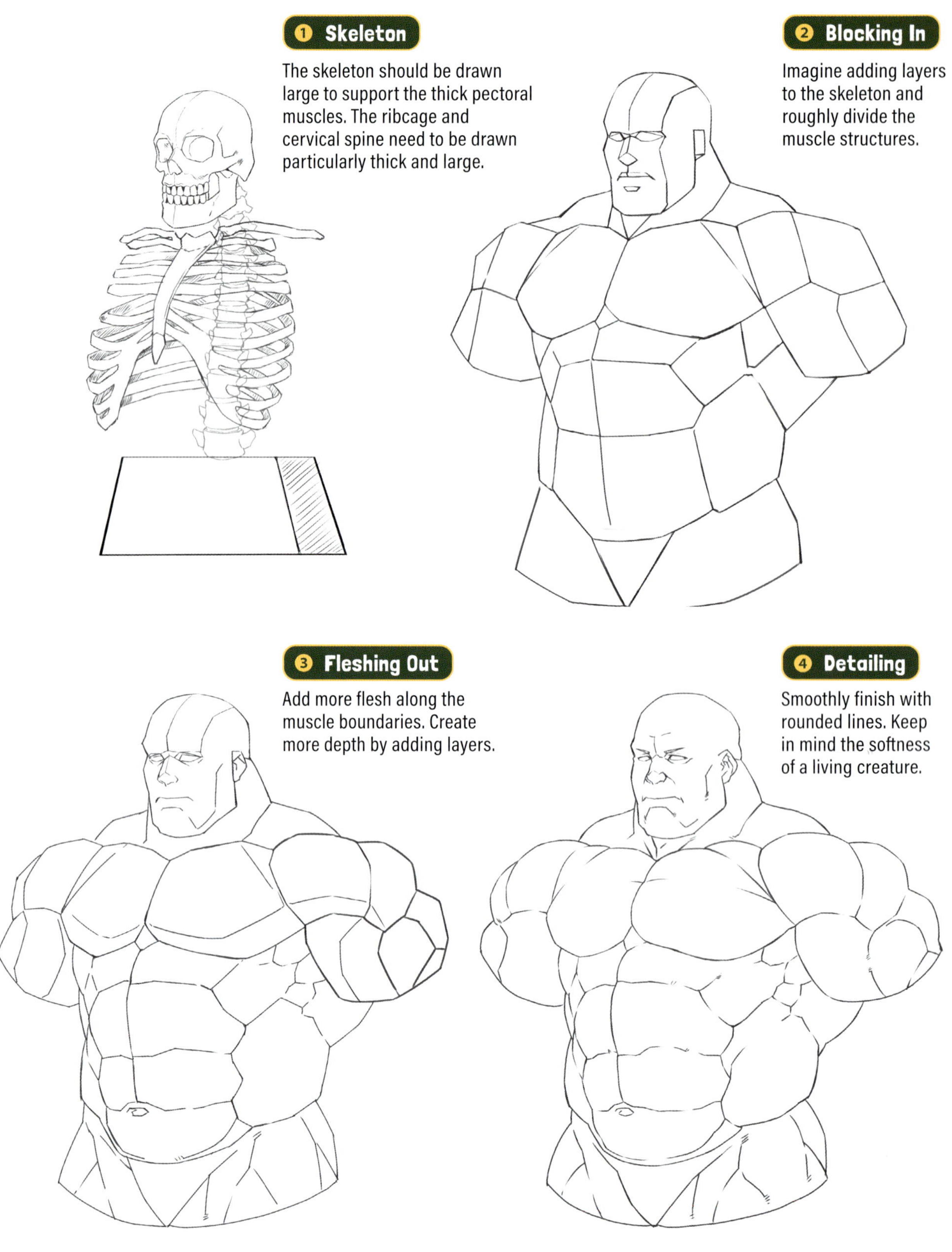

How to Apply Color

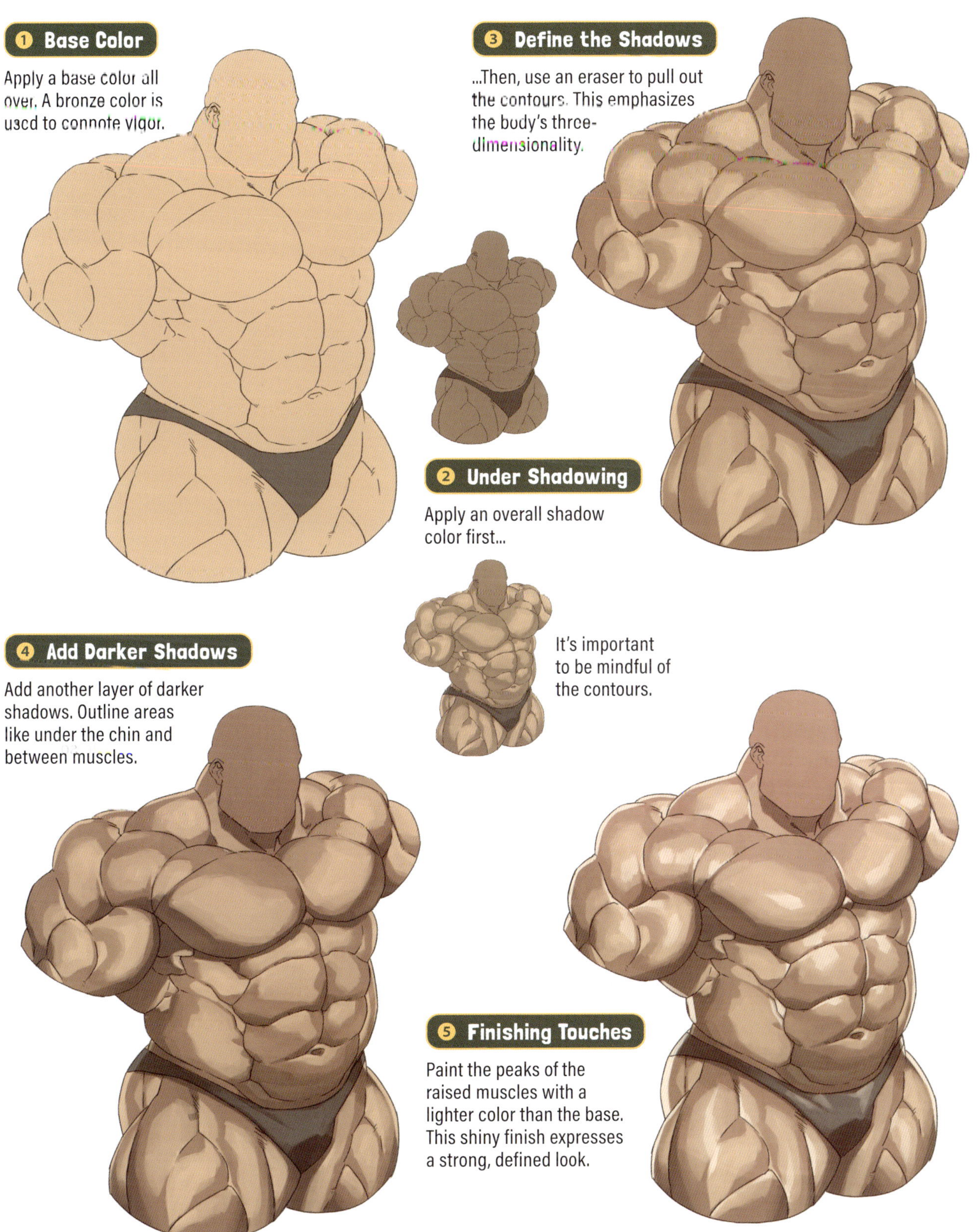

1 Base Color

Apply a base color all over. A bronze color is used to connote vigor.

2 Under Shadowing

Apply an overall shadow color first...

3 Define the Shadows

...Then, use an eraser to pull out the contours. This emphasizes the body's three-dimensionality.

It's important to be mindful of the contours.

4 Add Darker Shadows

Add another layer of darker shadows. Outline areas like under the chin and between muscles.

5 Finishing Touches

Paint the peaks of the raised muscles with a lighter color than the base. This shiny finish expresses a strong, defined look.

Various-angle Views of Muscles

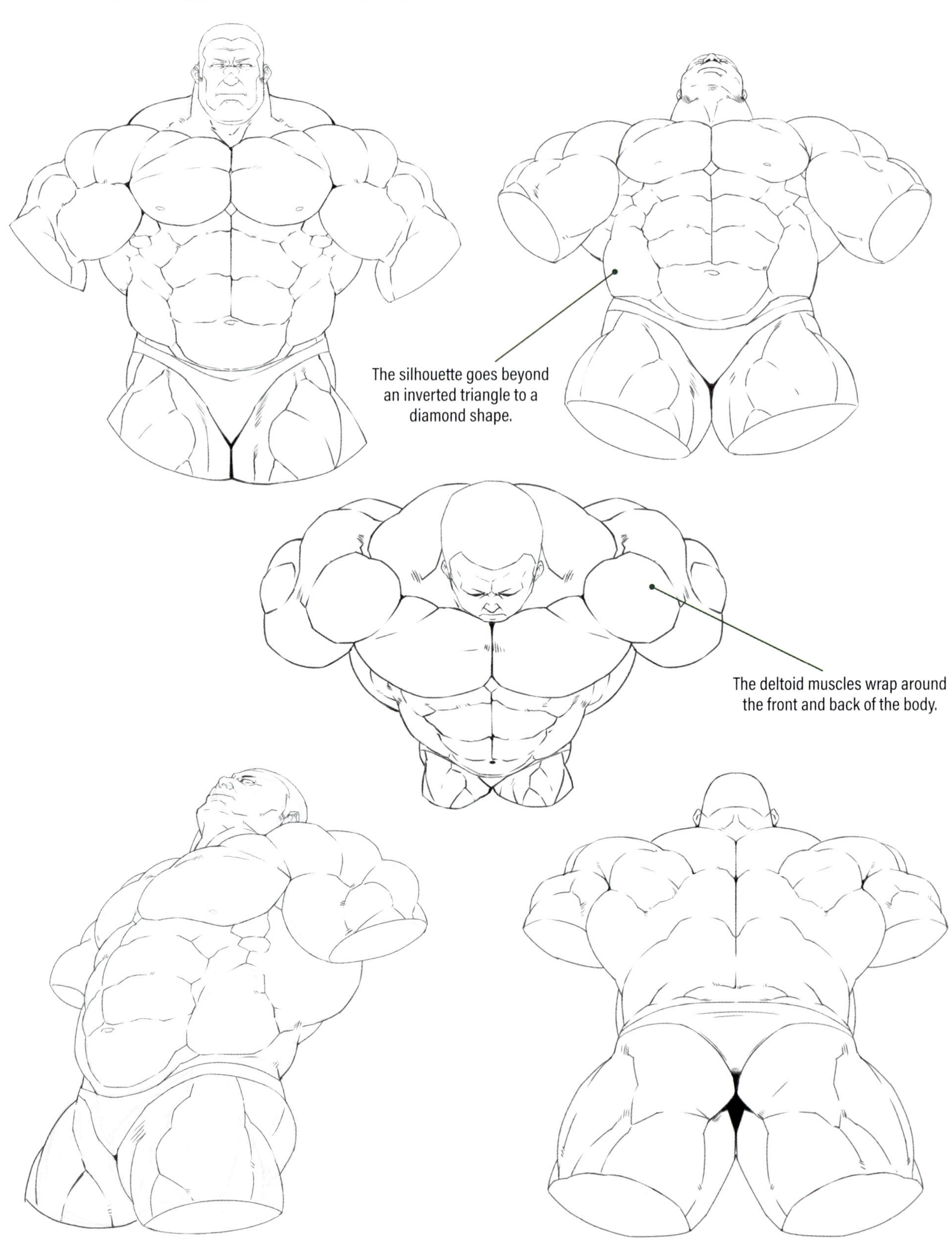

The exaggerated muscles push against each other as they swell. Each muscle is huge. Moreover, they are clearly divided, and you can see the size of the muscles from any angle.

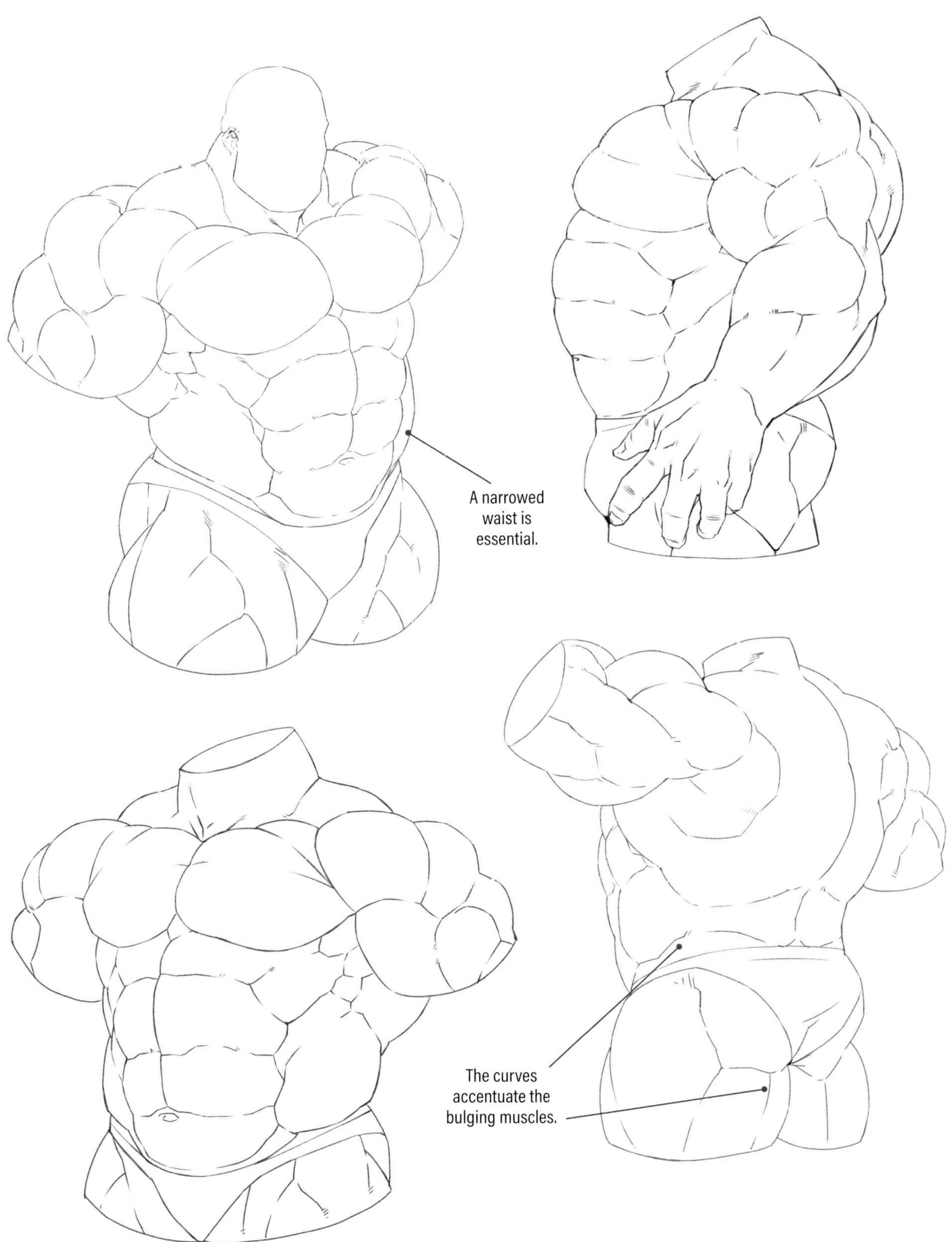

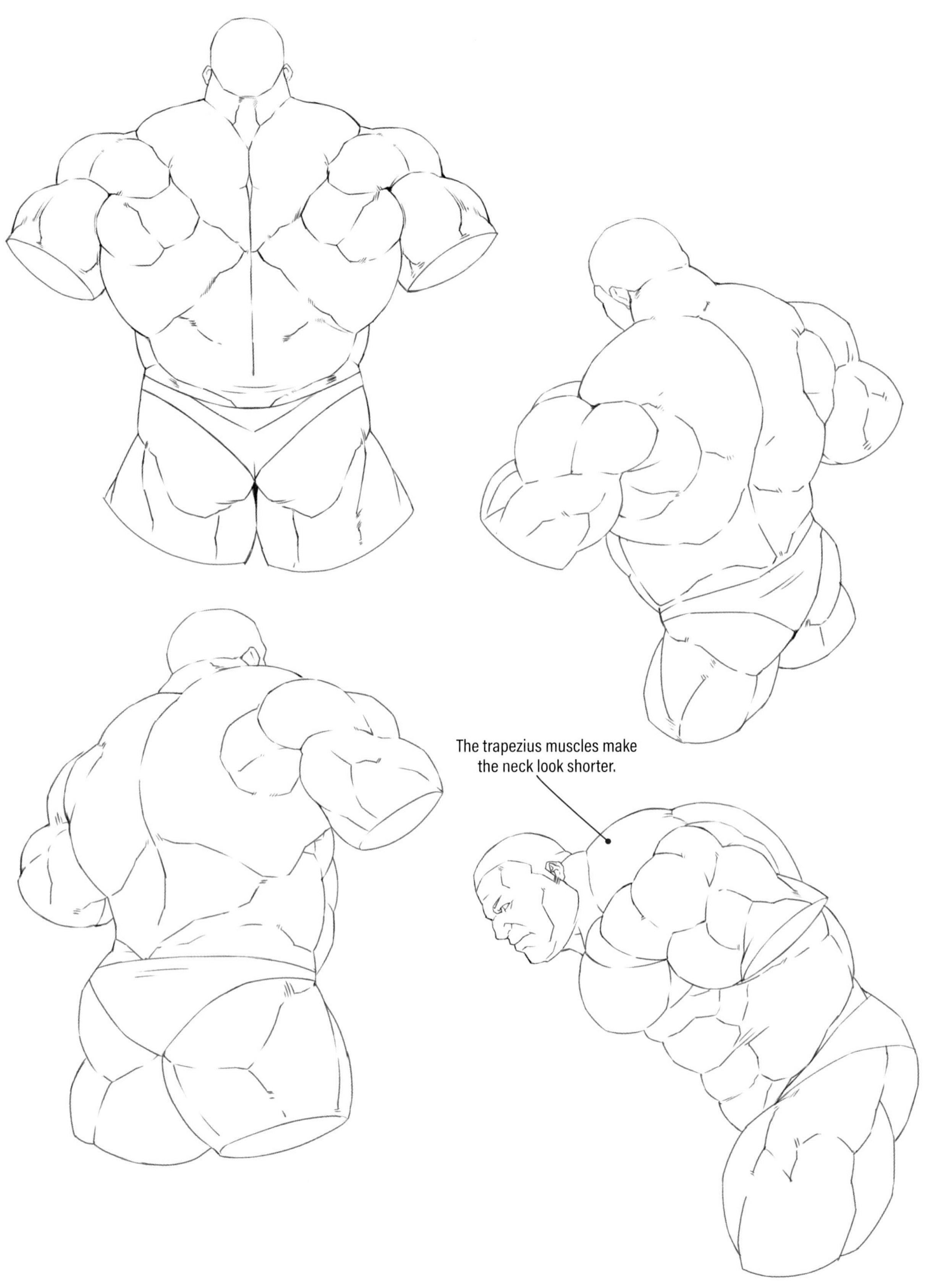
The trapezius muscles make
the neck look shorter.

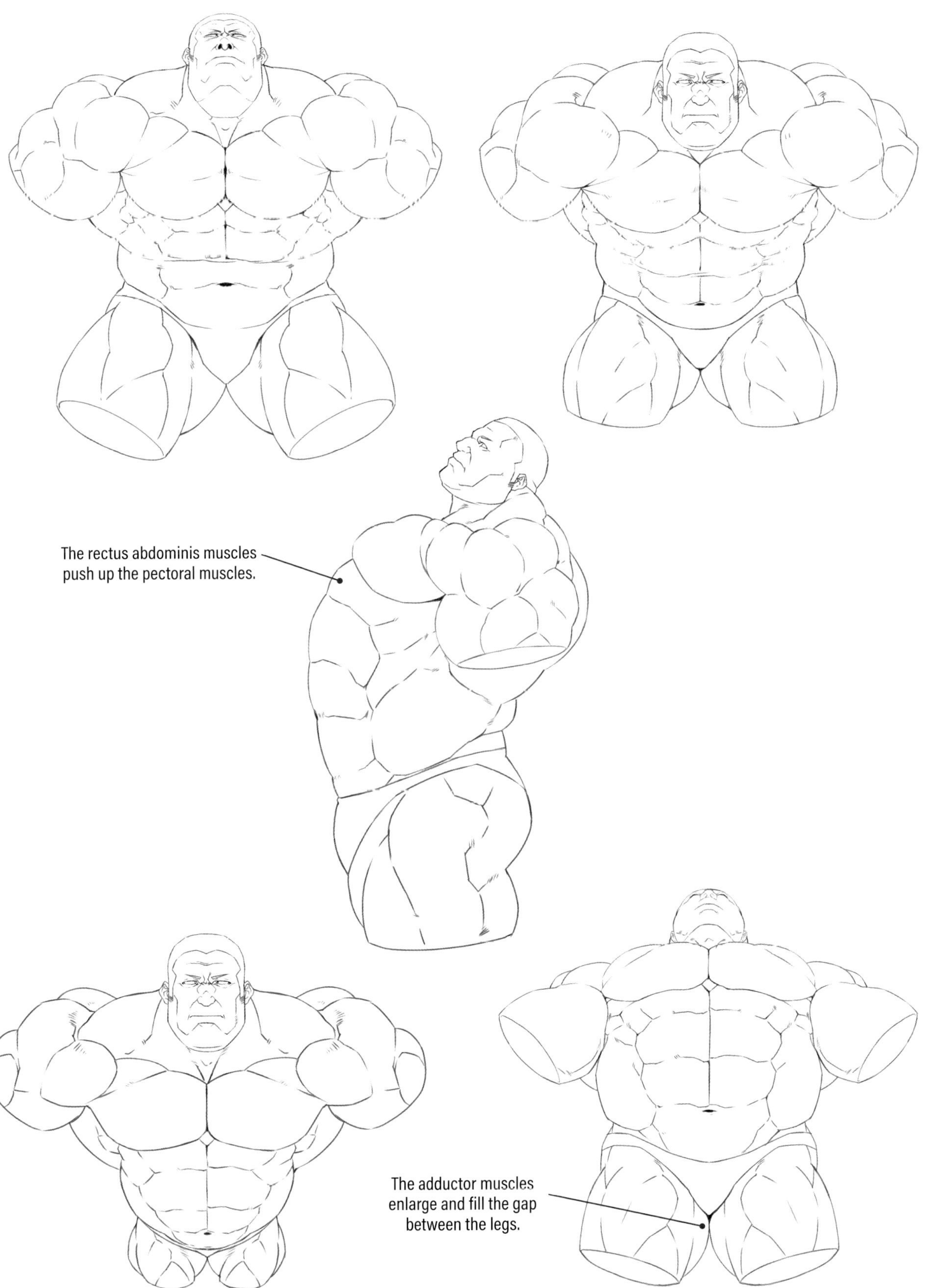
The rectus abdominis muscles push up the pectoral muscles.
The adductor muscles enlarge and fill the gap between the legs.

Arm Muscles

Front View
Side View
Forearm wider than the fist
Back
Wavy, raised muscles
Inner Side
Supinated
Bulging deltoid muscle
Pronated
Extended
Raised Elbow

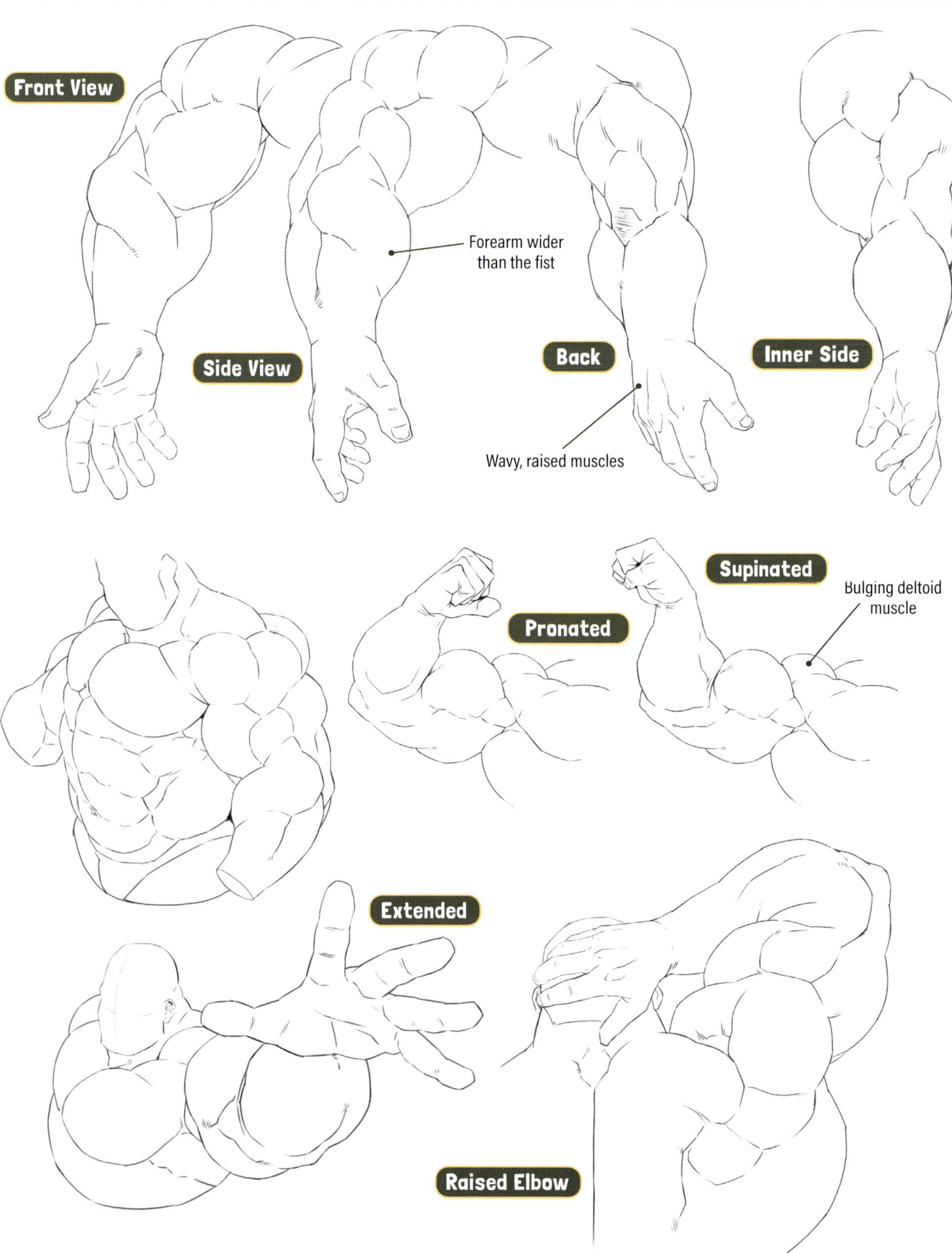

Leg Muscles

Enlarged calf
muscles visible
from the front
Side
Back
Calf muscles thicker
than the bones
Inner side
Front
Muscles drawn as
tapered rectangular
blocks
Squatting
Rolling
Low Angle
Raised Leg

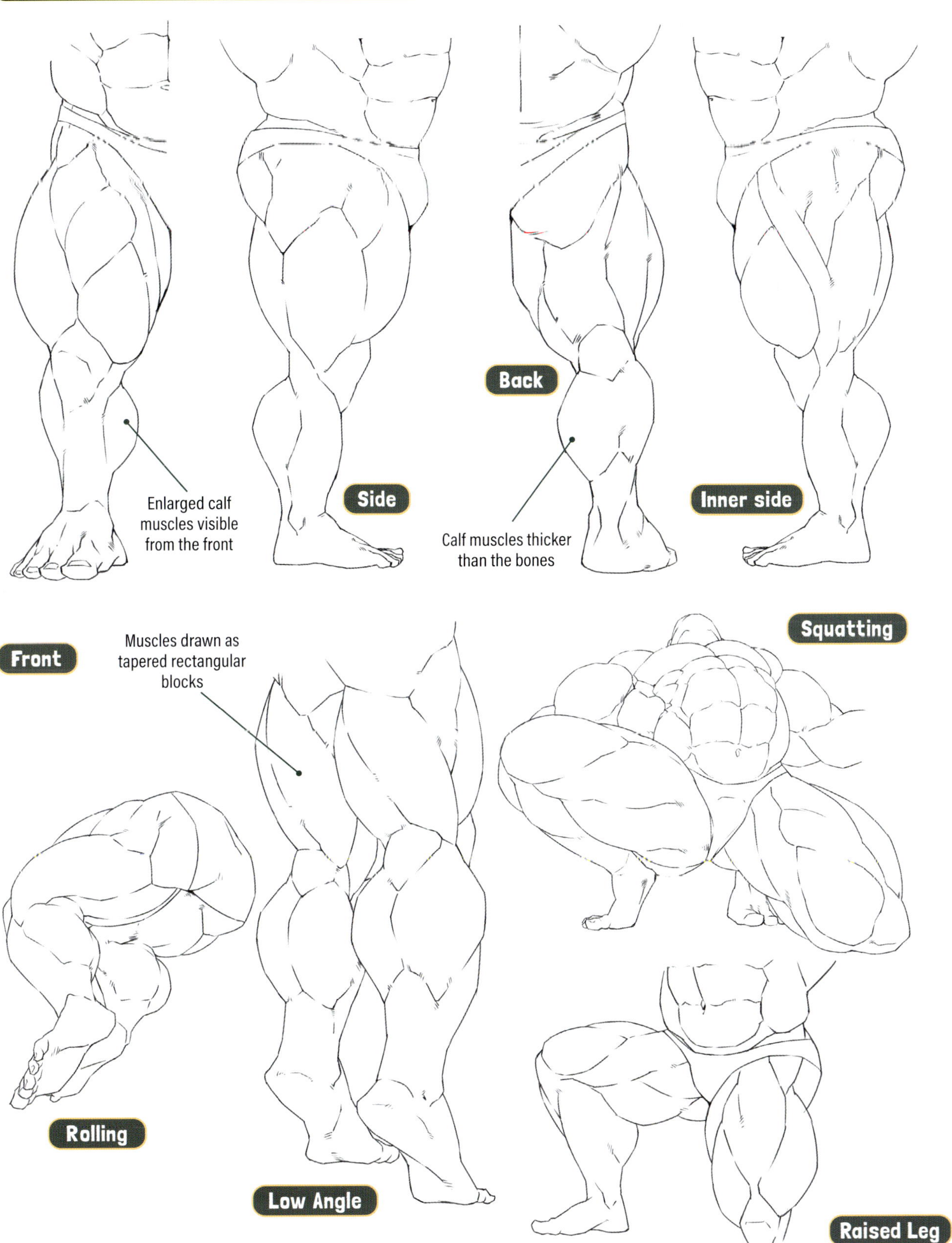

Character Movement and Muscle Properties

Pose and Muscle Coordination

When a person moves their body, muscles move along with it. When muscles are connected to parts with a wide range of motion like arms or legs, pay attention to how the muscles change shape along with the movement of those parts. The pectoral muscles are especially easy to see, as they stretch and contract significantly, as shown in the drawings below. The pectoral muscles are connected from the center of the chest to the humerus bones of the upper arms, so when you stretch upward, they are pulled along with the arms and change into a longer shape. Even very strong muscles are not rigid. They have an elastic quality that repeatedly tightens and relaxes with movement. Remember that expressing strong, dynamic muscles starts with expressing suppleness.

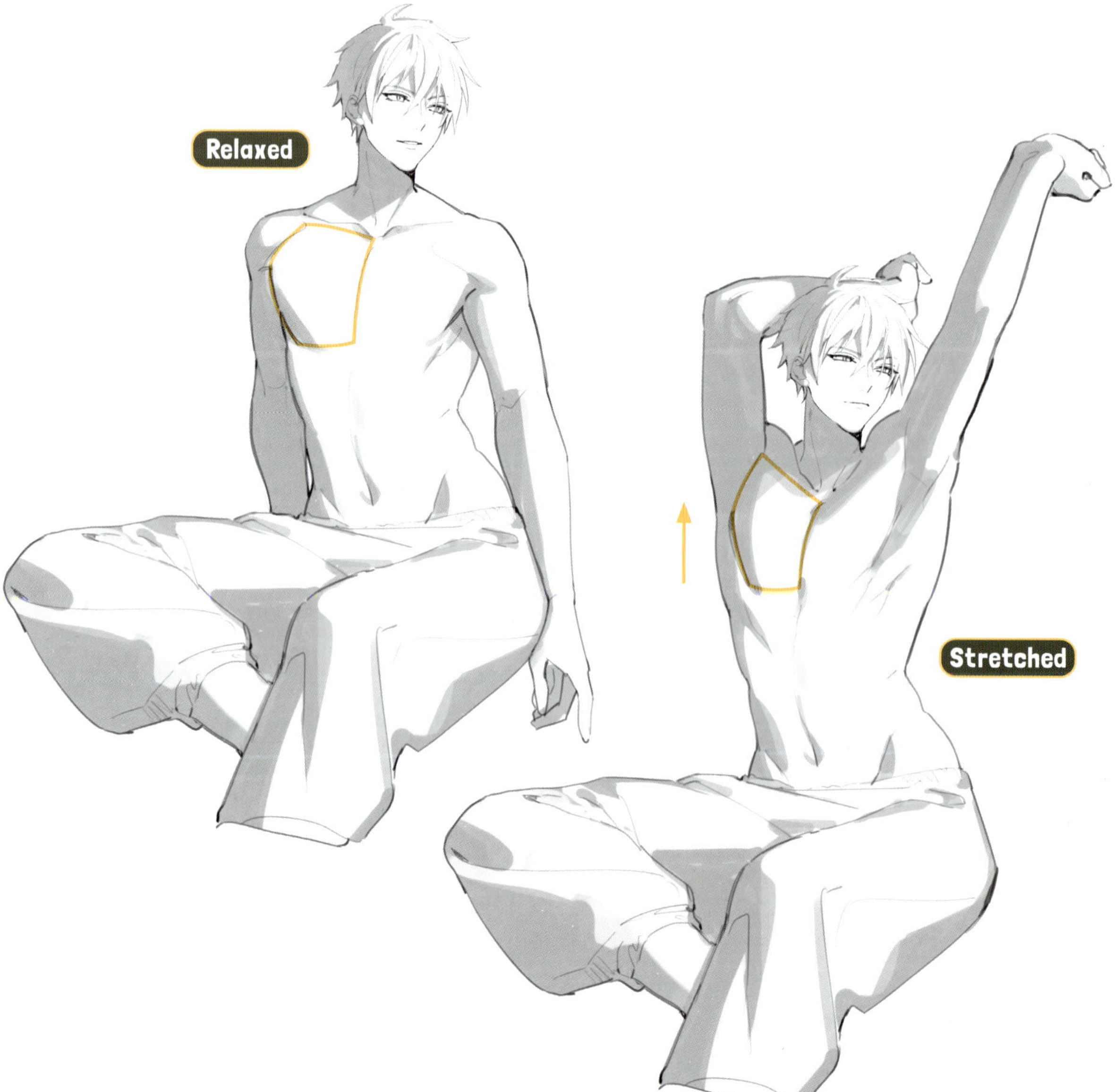

Relaxed

Stretched

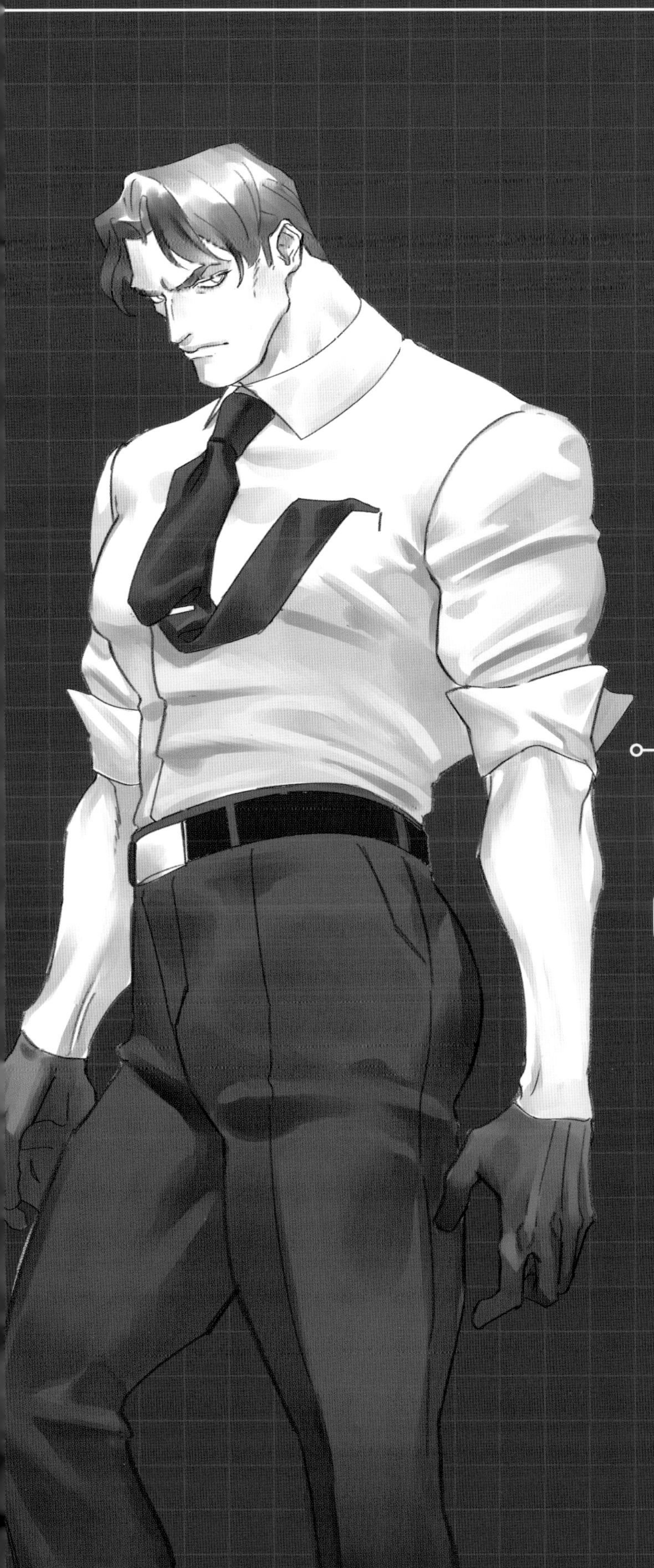

CHAPTER 3

Differentiating Characters

Differentiating Characters

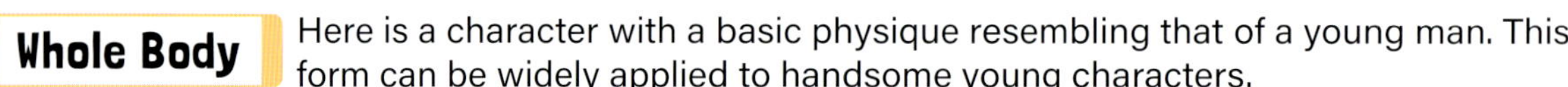

Whole Body Here is a character with a basic physique resembling that of a young man. This form can be widely applied to handsome young characters.

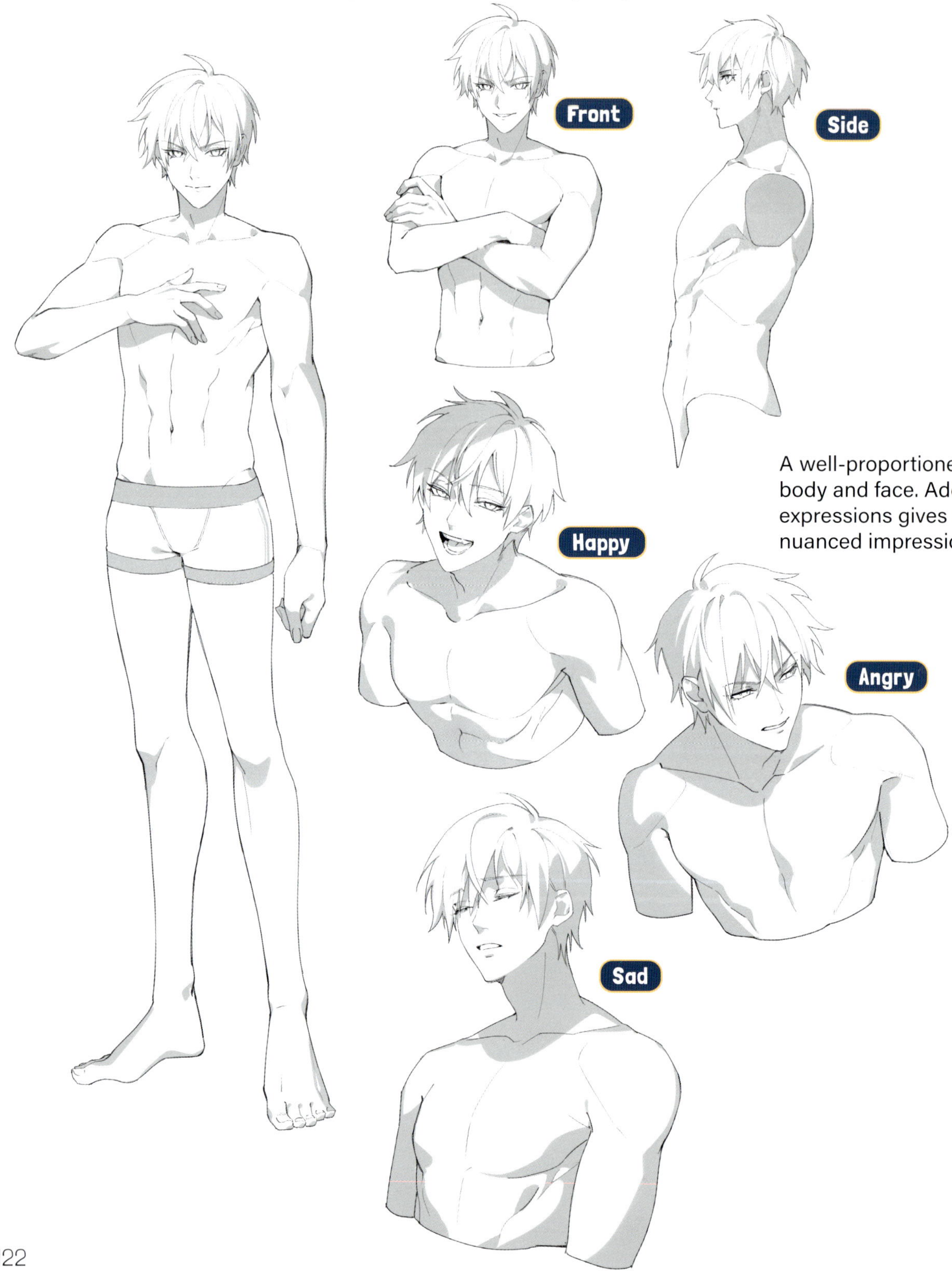

Front

Side

A well-proportioned body and face. Adding expressions gives a nuanced impression.

Happy

Angry

Sad

Lean Body Type

Distinguishing Features

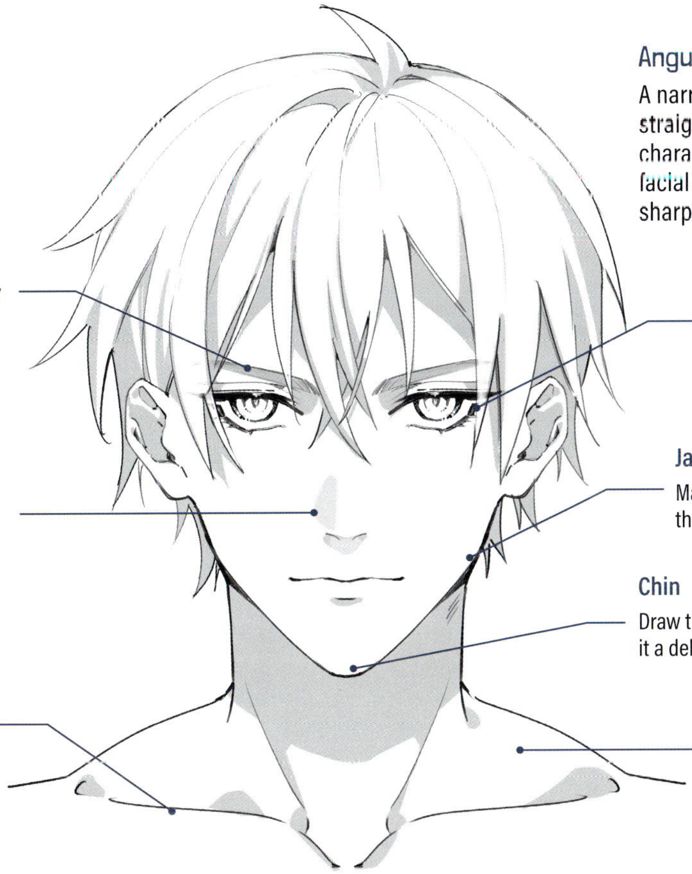

Angular Facial Features

A narrow jaw, large eyes, and a straight nose. When drawing a character with well-proportioned facial features, use overall sharpened features.

Eyebrows

Make the eyebrows thin. Slightly curve them toward the outside of the face.

Eyes

Draw large pupils. Clearly depict the eyelashes and the outline of the eyes.

Nose Bridge

Draw triangular shadows beside and under the nose to express a thin nose.

Jaw Angle

Make it softly angular below the ears.

Chin

Draw the chin narrow to give it a delicate impression.

Collarbones

Prominent collarbones give a sensual impression.

Trapezius Muscles

Draw a gently raised area to express the body's three-dimensionality.

Lean Body Type

Facial Variations

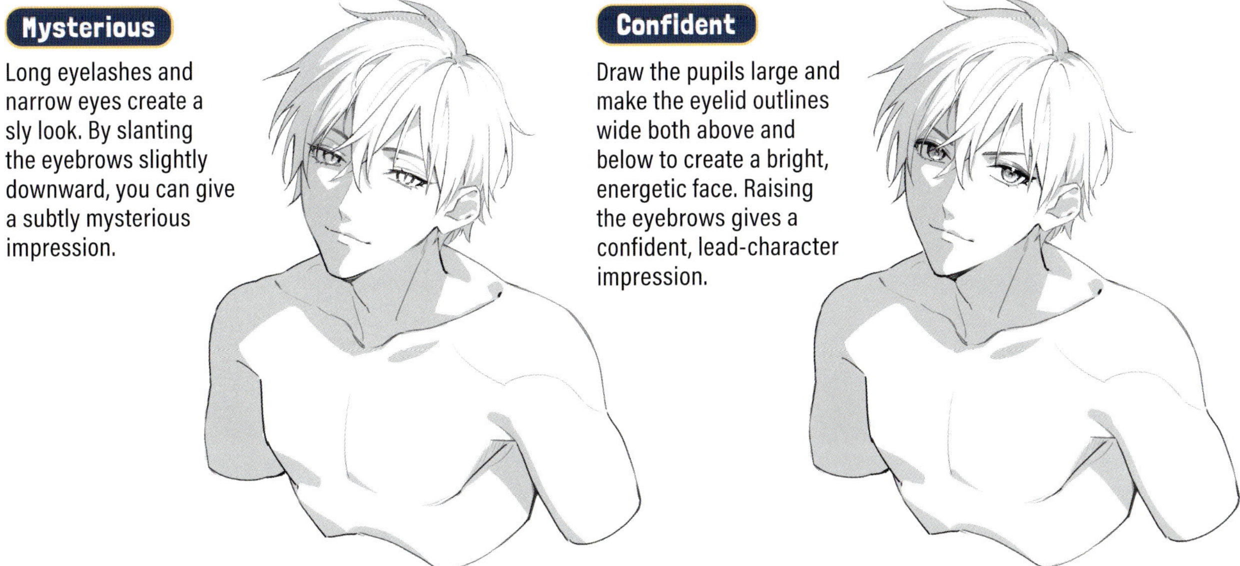

Mysterious

Long eyelashes and narrow eyes create a sly look. By slanting the eyebrows slightly downward, you can give a subtly mysterious impression.

Confident

Draw the pupils large and make the eyelid outlines wide both above and below to create a bright, energetic face. Raising the eyebrows gives a confident, lead-character impression.

Wearing Formal Clothes

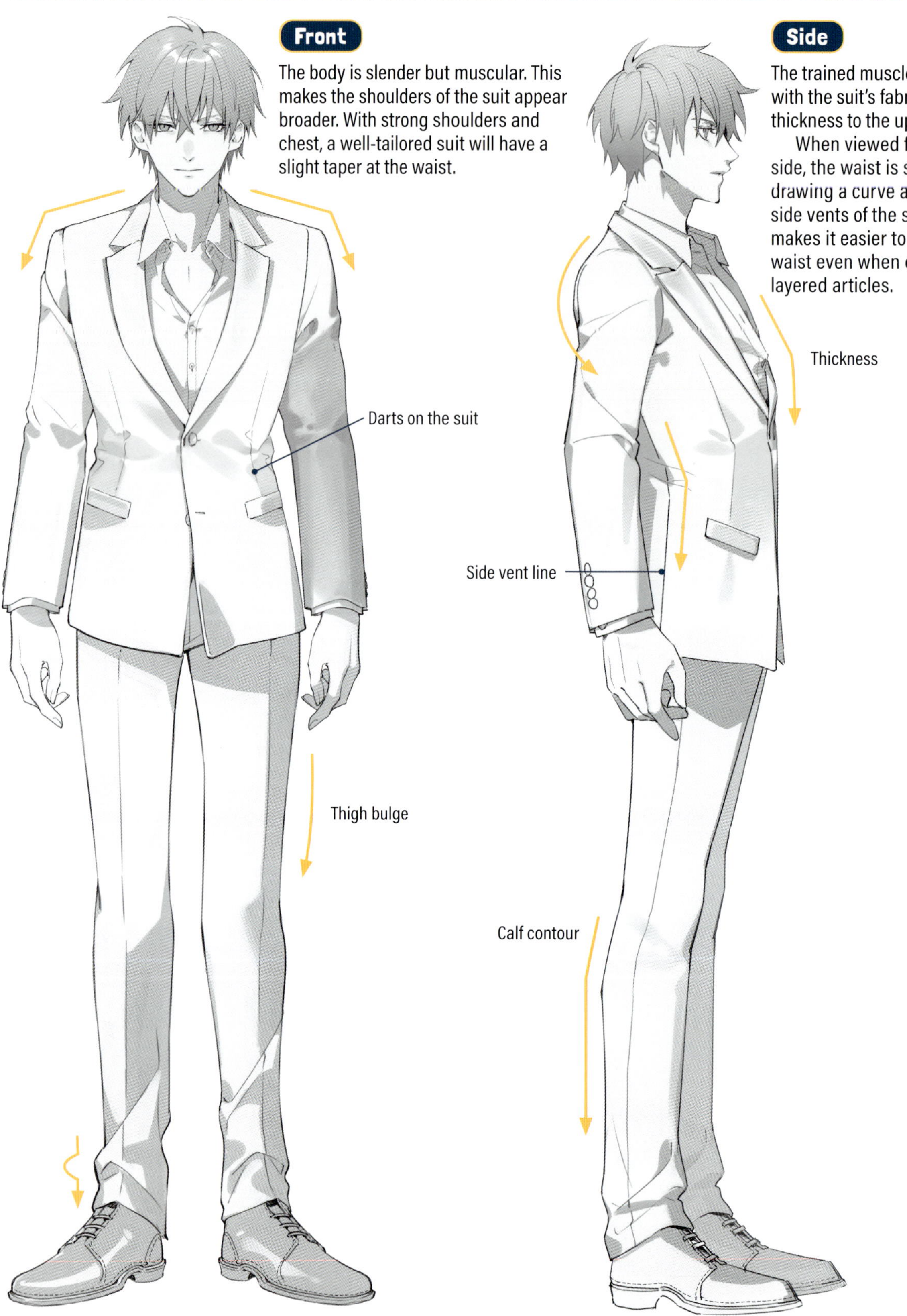

Front

The body is slender but muscular. This makes the shoulders of the suit appear broader. With strong shoulders and chest, a well-tailored suit will have a slight taper at the waist.

Side

The trained muscles, combined with the suit's fabric, add thickness to the upper body.

When viewed from the side, the waist is shown by drawing a curve along the side vents of the suit. This makes it easier to express the waist even when clothed with layered articles.

Illustrator Insights

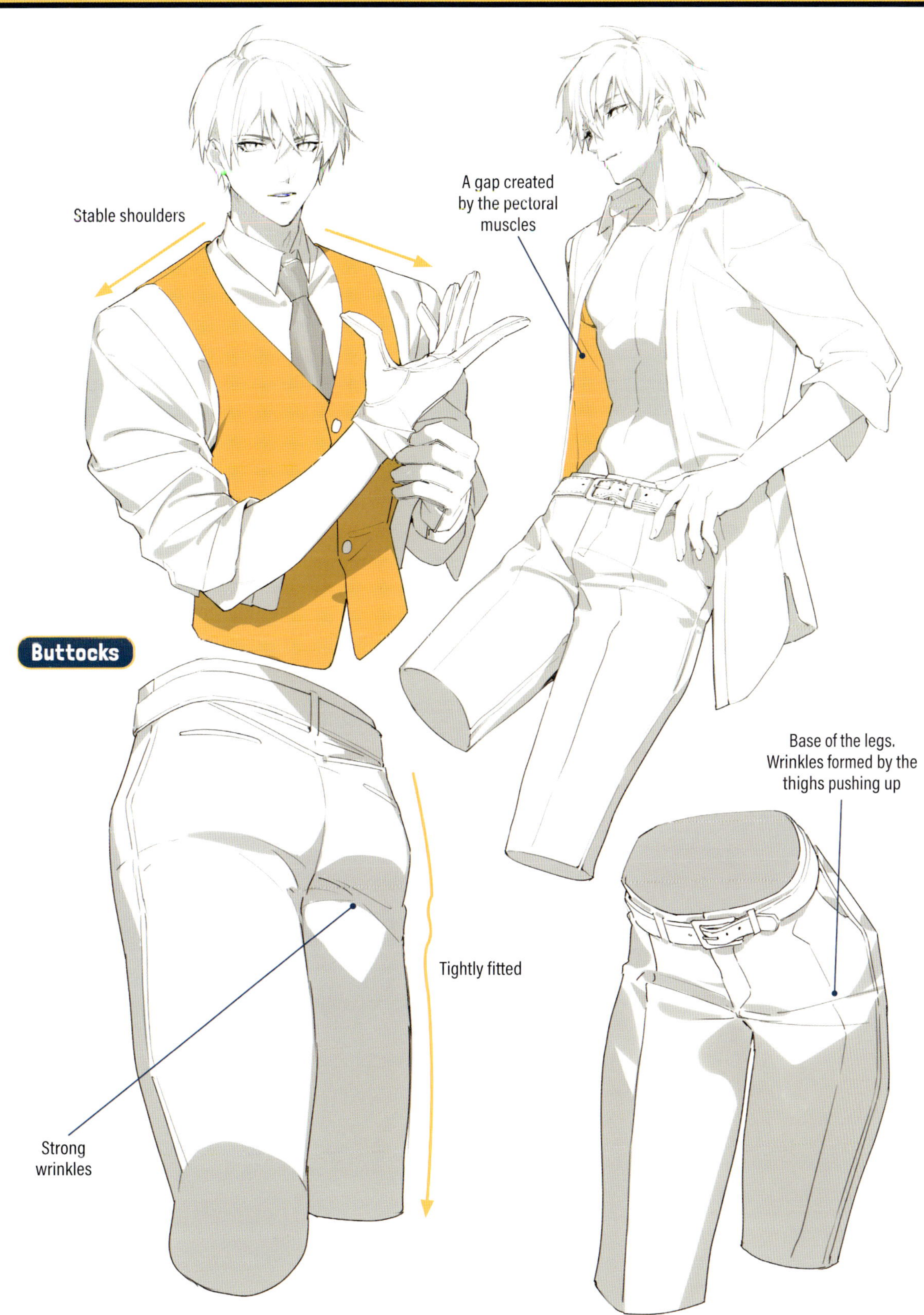

Differentiating Characters

Whole Body

A character with deep facial features and mature charm. This lends an air of experience. This appealing look is suitable for various characters, from dependable adults to masterminds.

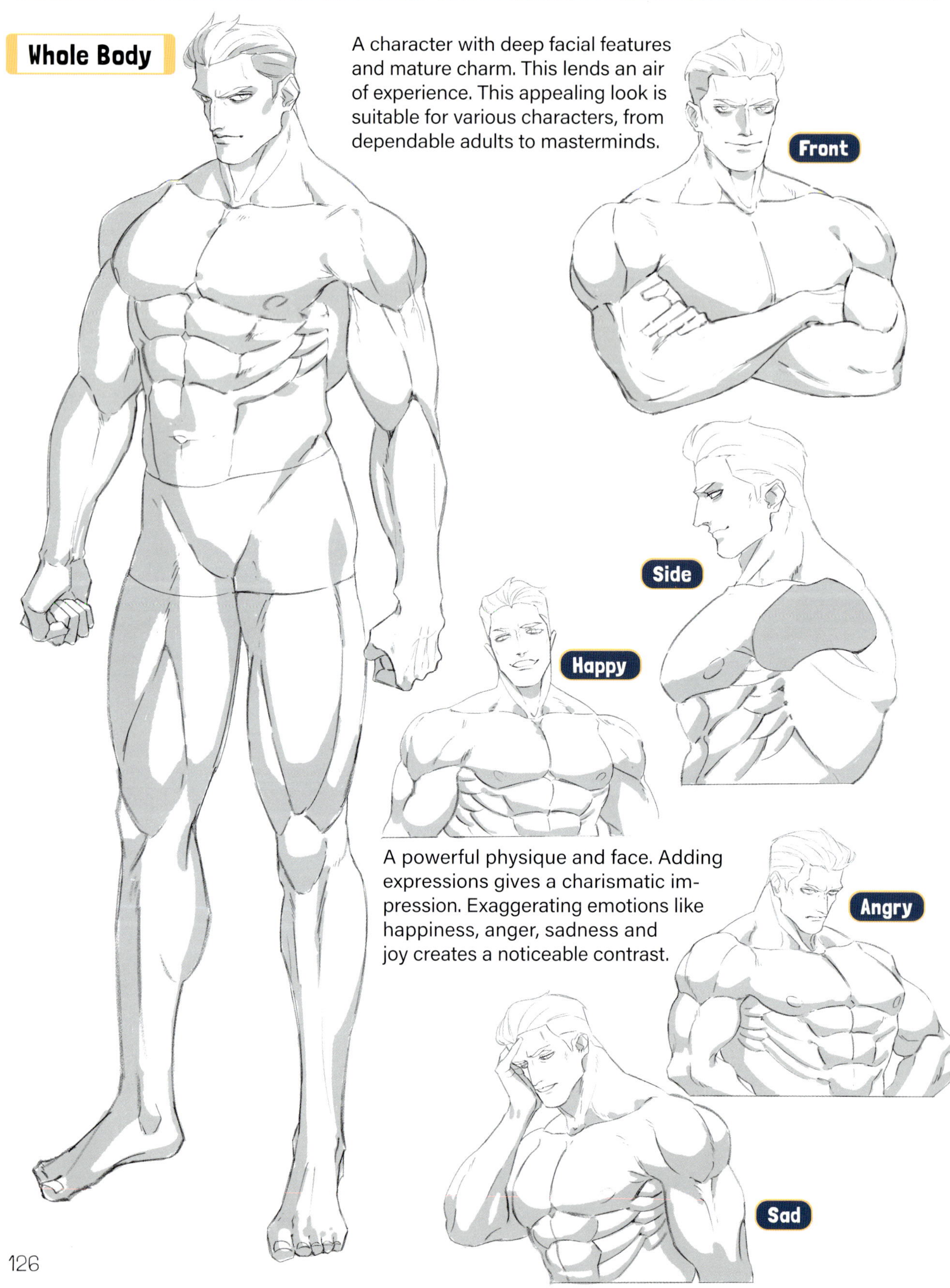

A powerful physique and face. Adding expressions gives a charismatic impression. Exaggerating emotions like happiness, anger, sadness and joy creates a noticeable contrast.

Distinguishing Features

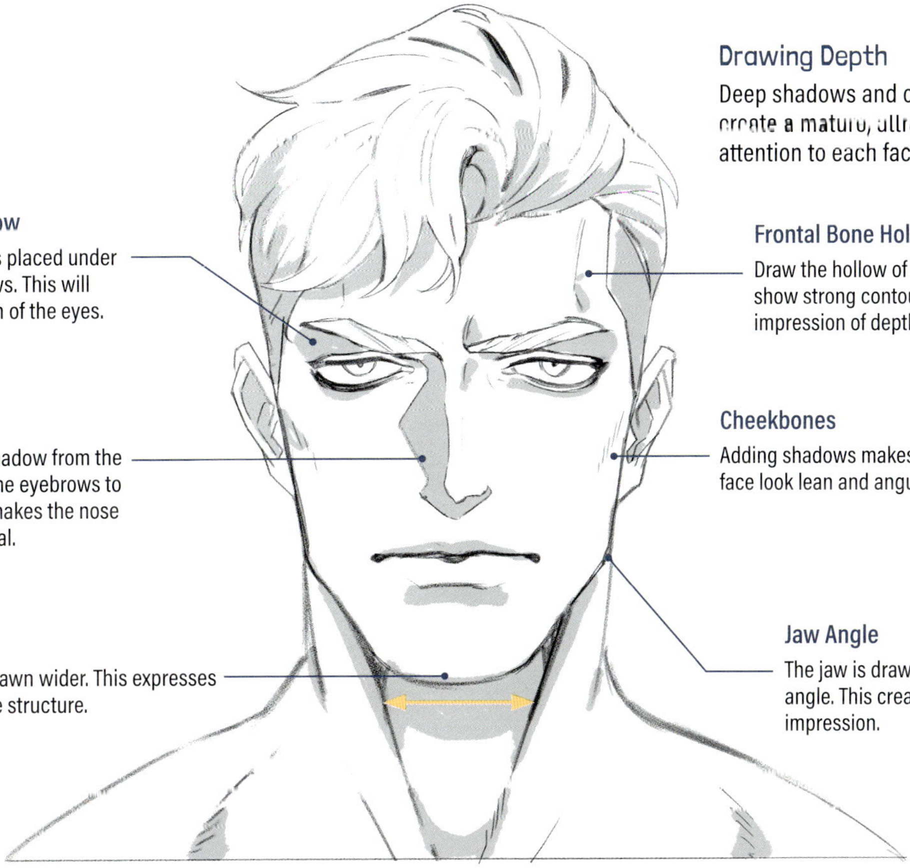

Drawing Depth

Deep shadows and contours on the face create a mature, attractive look. Pay attention to each facial feature.

Eyebrow Shadow

A large shadow is placed under the thick eyebrows. This will express the depth of the eyes.

Frontal Bone Hollow

Draw the hollow of the frontal bone to show strong contours. This creates the impression of depth.

Nose Bridge

Adding a large shadow from the space between the eyebrows to below the nose makes the nose appear substantial.

Cheekbones

Adding shadows makes the face look lean and angular.

Chin

The chin is drawn wider. This expresses a strong bone structure.

Jaw Angle

The jaw is drawn with a strong angle. This creates a masculine impression.

Facial Variations

Stern

The facial bones, like the space between the eyebrows and cheekbones, are detailed. Increasing the details, like stubble, adds depth and gives the face a mature, rugged look.

Gentle

The nose and contours are rounded, and the details are intentionally reduced. This brings out a youthful impression. The gentle face can create a contrast with the muscular physique, which is also appealing.

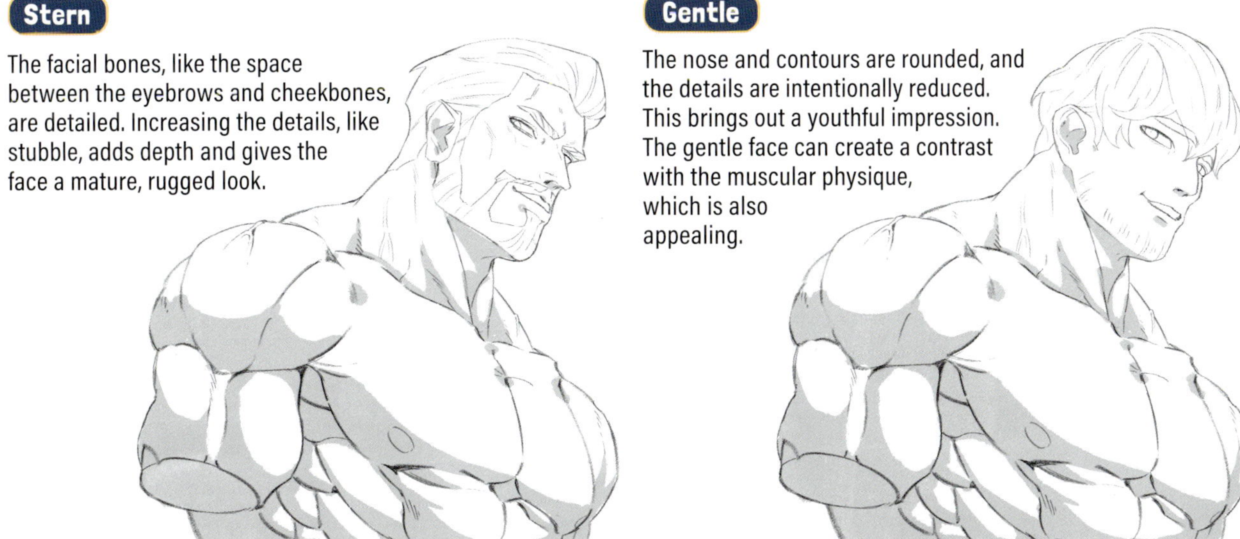

Wearing Formal Clothes

Front

A three-piece suit that makes a muscular physique look attractive. The chest is depicted as a flat surface. Adding a large shadow below the chest strongly emphasizes the three-dimensionality of the muscles.

Side

Adding movement, the tight shirt hints at the muscles underneath. The contours of the thigh and arm muscles are visible from the side.

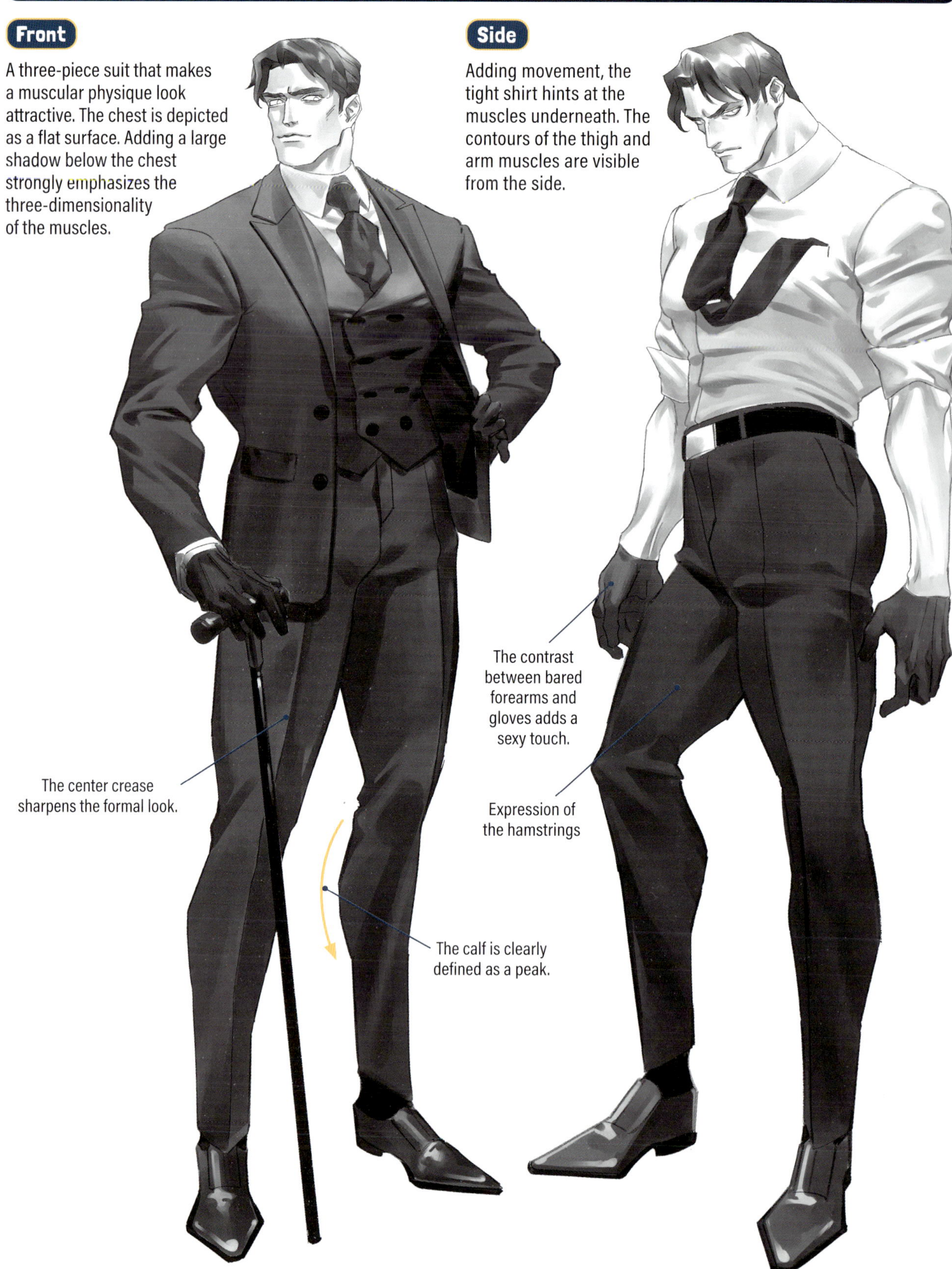

Illustrator Insights

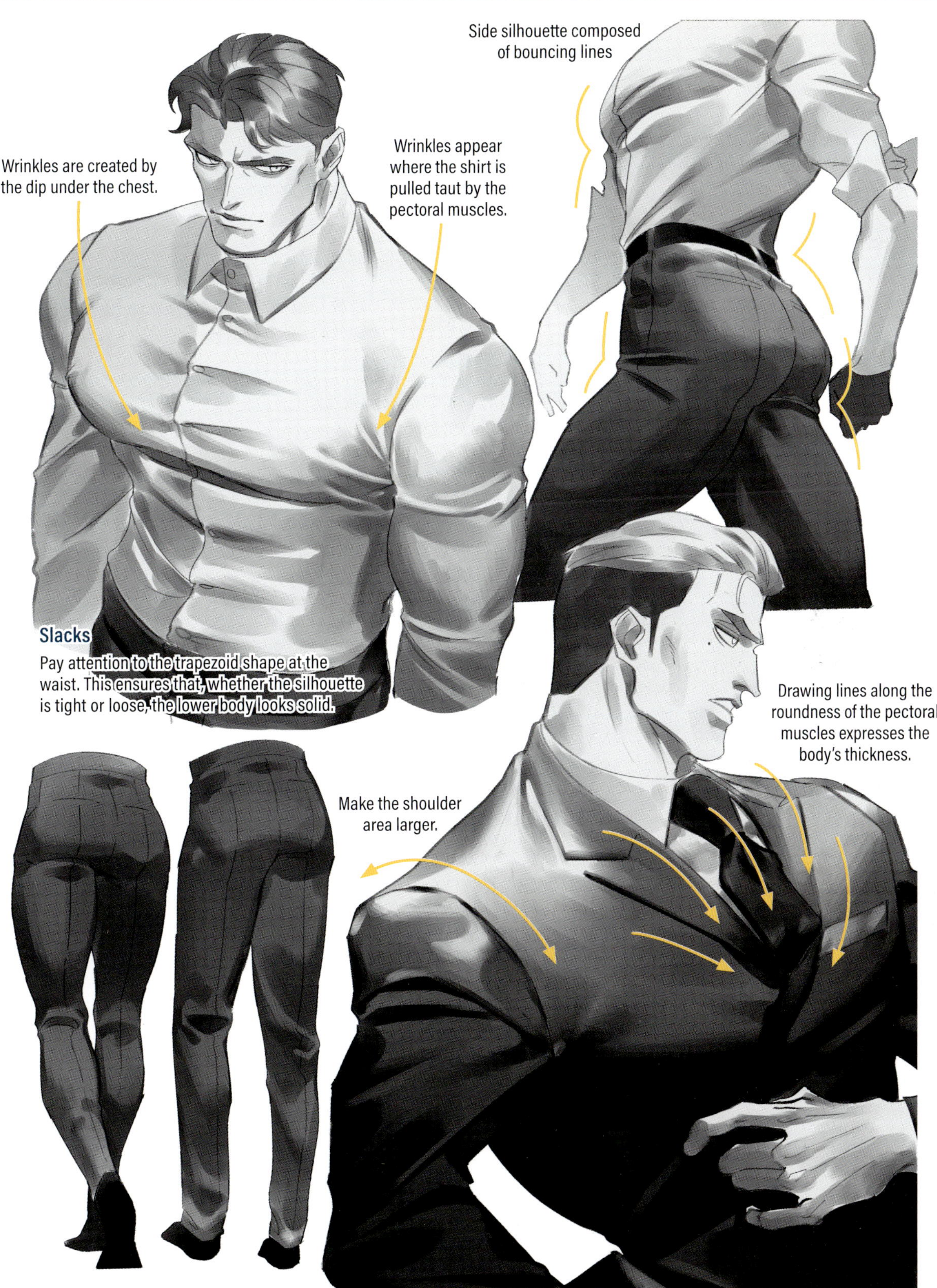

Slacks

Pay attention to the trapezoid shape at the waist. This ensures that, whether the silhouette is tight or loose, the lower body looks solid.

Differentiating Characters

A super muscular character with a strong impression of power. This large build suggests a character involved in combat, or one with a bold personality.

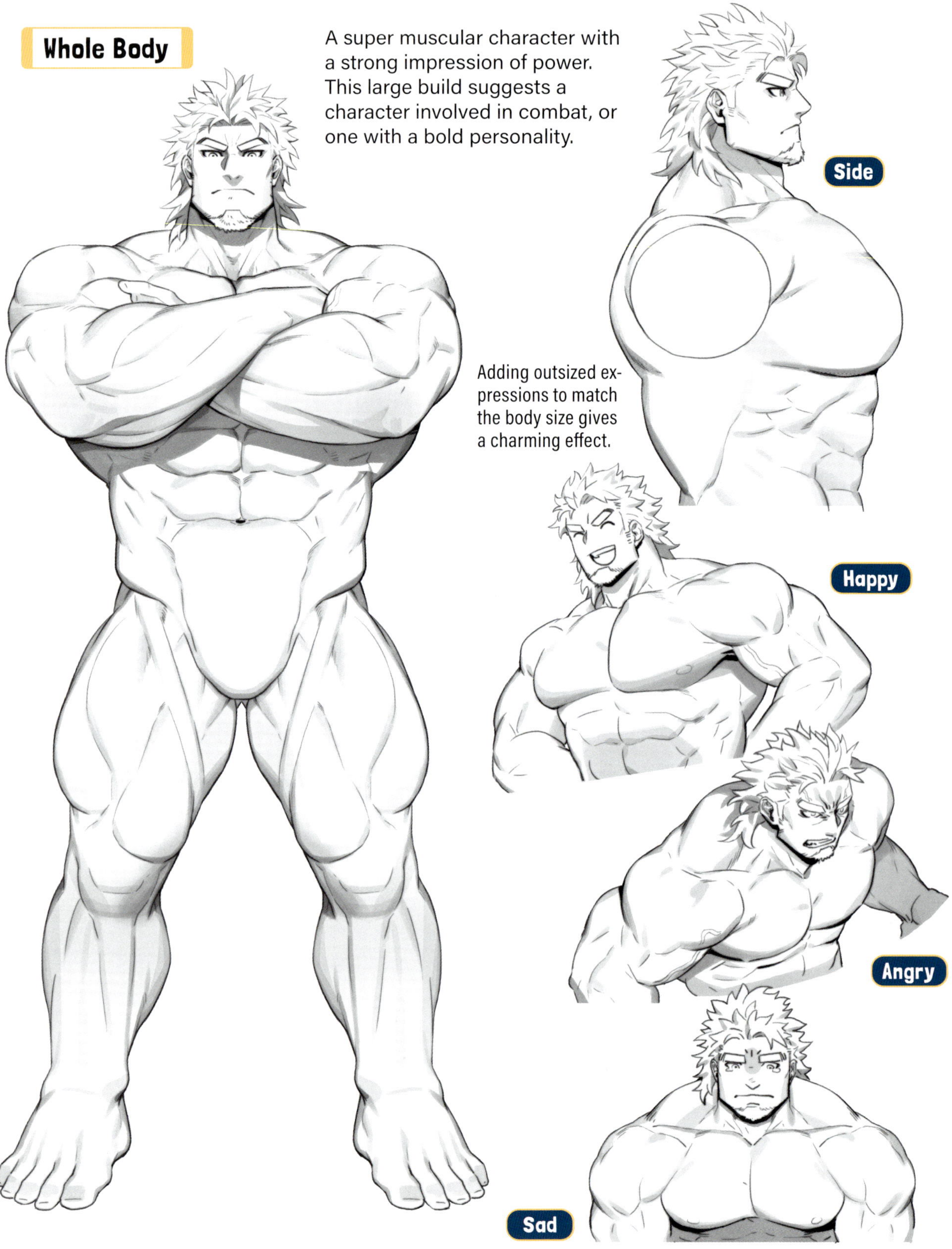

Distinguishing Features

Combining Large Features

A bold, yet dependable-looking face. The overall outline is close to that of a square. The key is to make features like the eyebrows, nose, jaw and mouth larger.

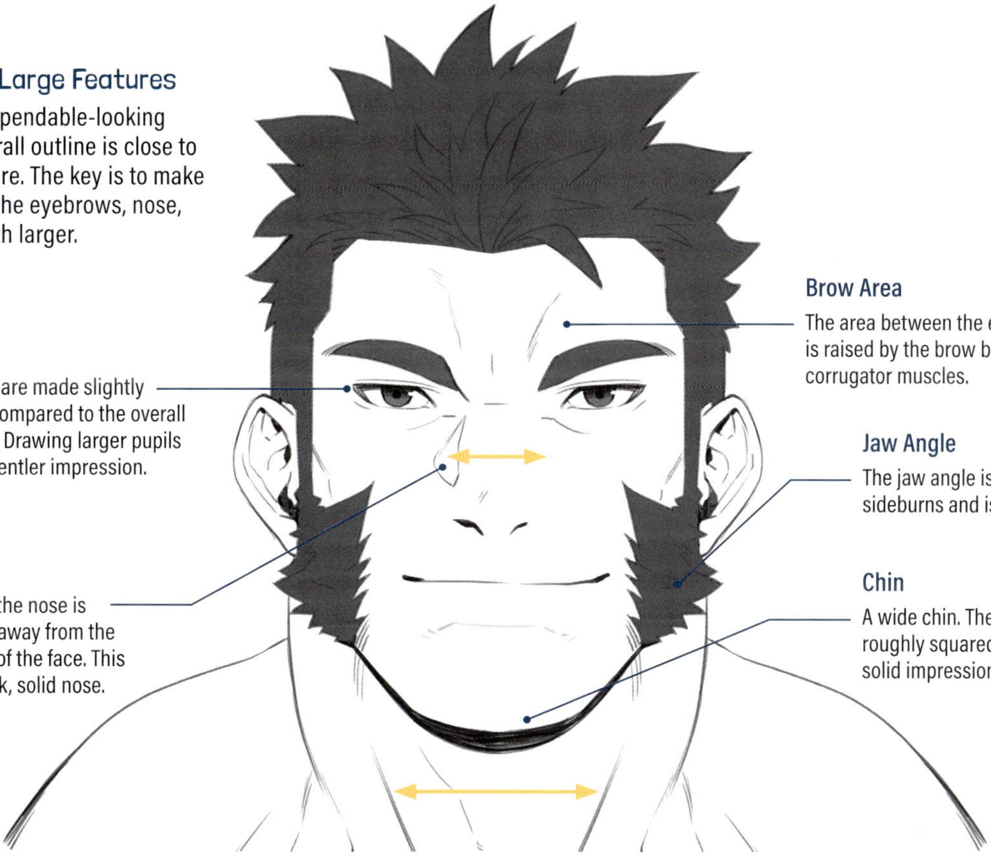

Eyes

The eyes are made slightly smaller compared to the overall face size. Drawing larger pupils gives a gentler impression.

Nose

The shadow of the nose is placed slightly away from the vertical center of the face. This indicates a thick, solid nose.

Brow Area

The area between the eyebrows is raised by the brow bone and corrugator muscles.

Jaw Angle

The jaw angle is covered by sideburns and is angular.

Chin

A wide chin. The jawline is roughly squared, giving a solid impression.

Heavyweight Bodybuilder Body Type

Facial Variations

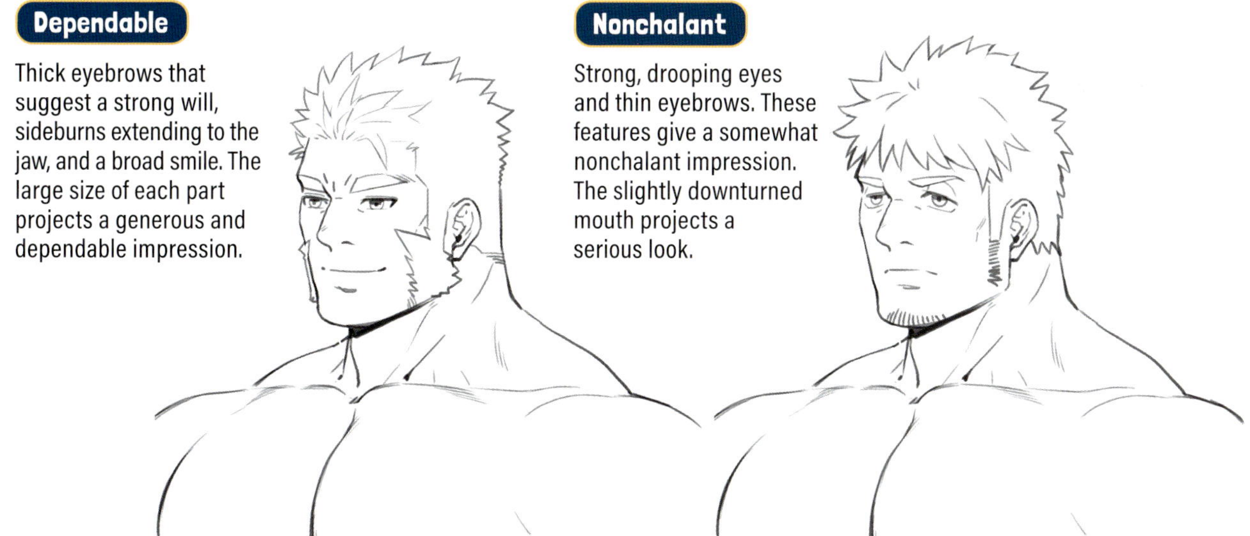

Dependable

Thick eyebrows that suggest a strong will, sideburns extending to the jaw, and a broad smile. The large size of each part projects a generous and dependable impression.

Nonchalant

Strong, drooping eyes and thin eyebrows. These features give a somewhat nonchalant impression. The slightly downturned mouth projects a serious look.

Wearing Formal Clothes

Front

A suit for a super muscular physique is much larger in every dimension. An average size wouldn't fit. Be bold and size up each piece of clothing.

Side

The shirt is tight around the shoulders and chest. The contours of each muscle stand out. Even areas where the fabric would normally lift are drawn snugly to enhance the cool look.

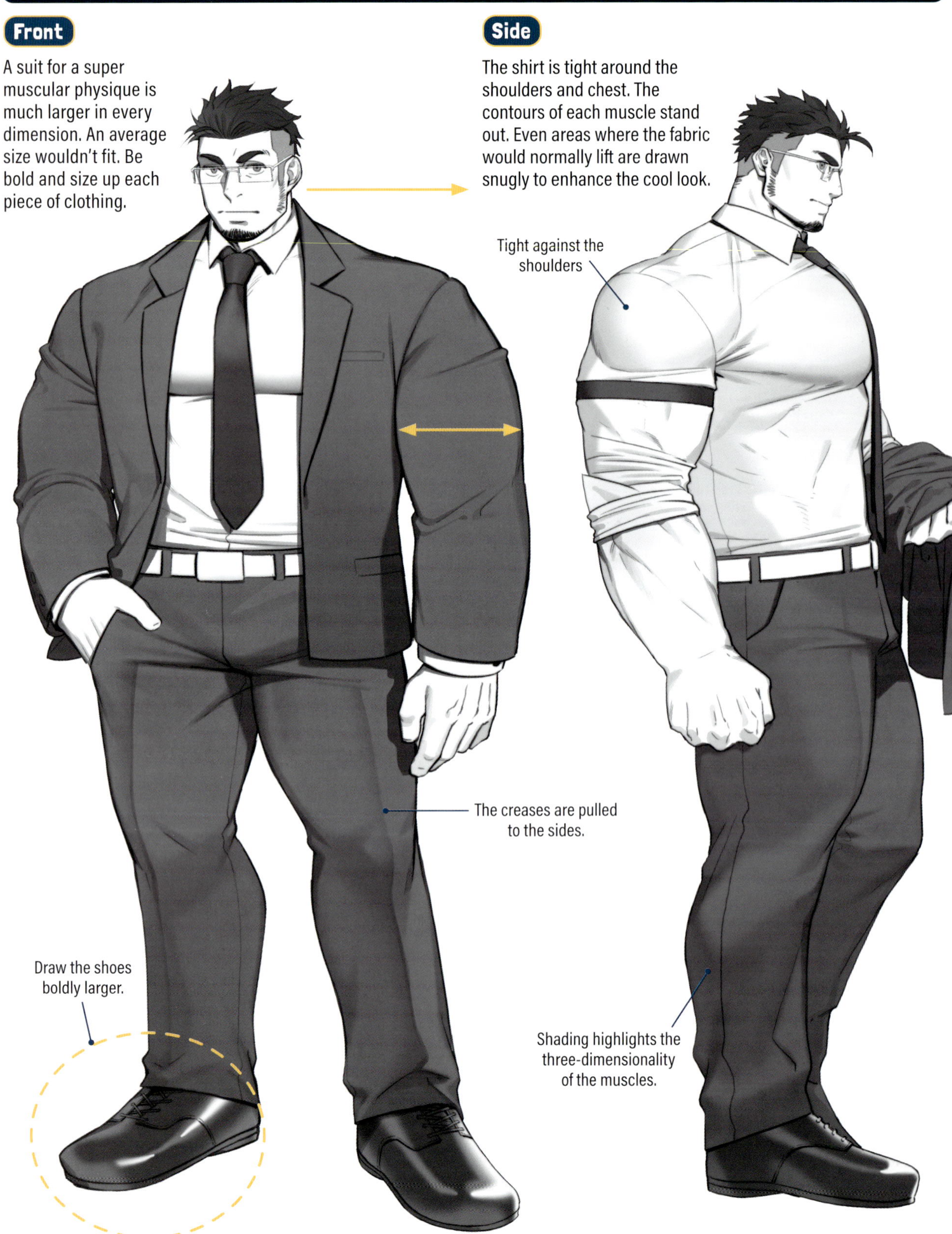

Illustrator Insights

The upper body forms an inverted triangle visible through the shirt. The broad back looks cool.

The muscular physique can't be fully concealed. The tight shirt shows it off.

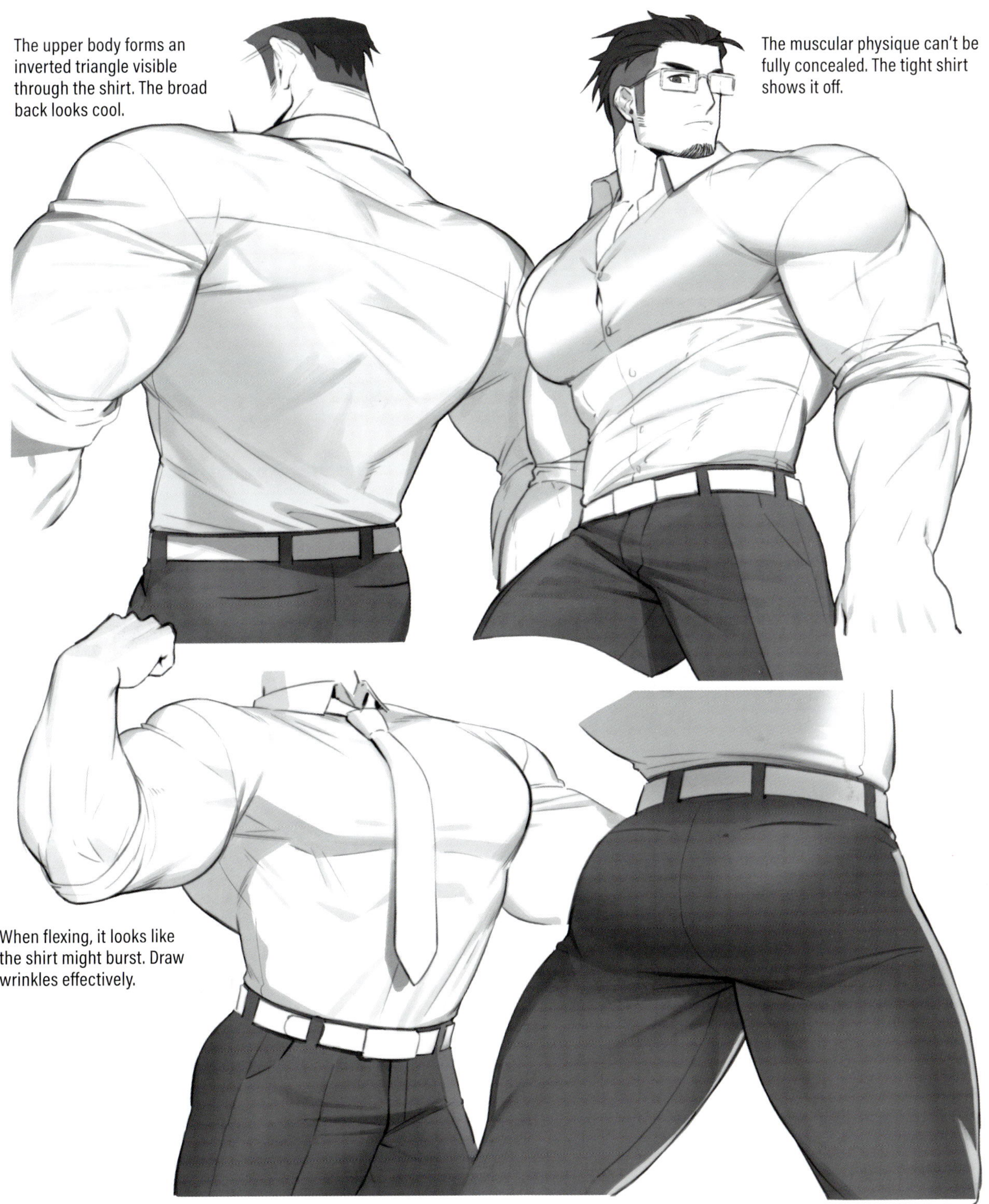

When flexing, it looks like the shirt might burst. Draw wrinkles effectively.

Thick legs make the pants tight. Draw the characteristic sheen of the taut fabric of the slacks in this situation.

Differentiating Characters

Whole Body

A cartoonish and uniquely monstrous physique. This character demands a strong personality. For this example, I chose to add an aged look with a bearded face, creating a contrast with the body shape and portraying an older, but still powerful, character.

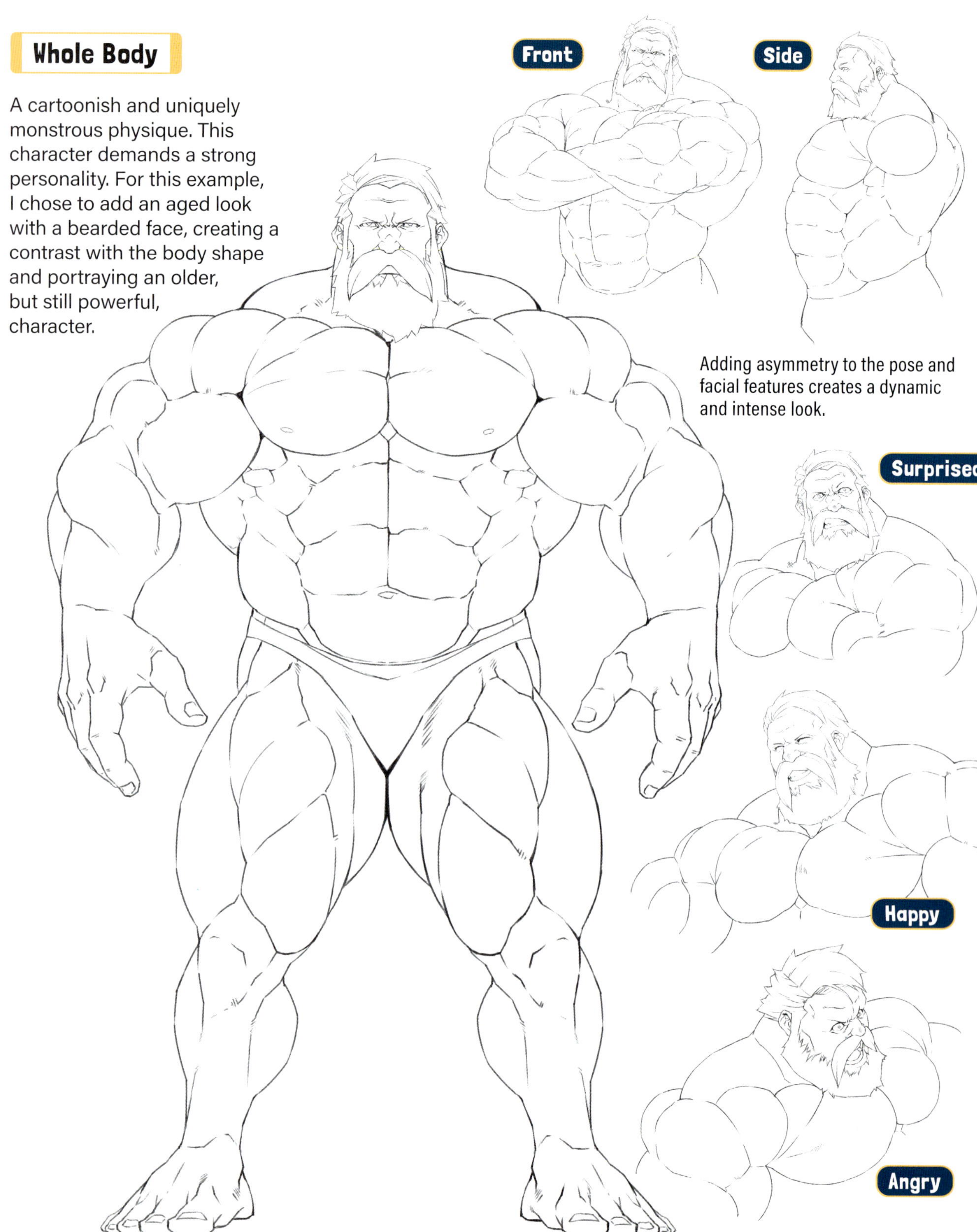

Adding asymmetry to the pose and facial features creates a dynamic and intense look.

Distinguishing Features

Strongly Defined Parts

Because the body makes a strong impact, the face is made up of strongly defined parts to match. This includes deep wrinkles on the forehead, prominent contours and a striking beard. Various elements are combined to enhance the effect.

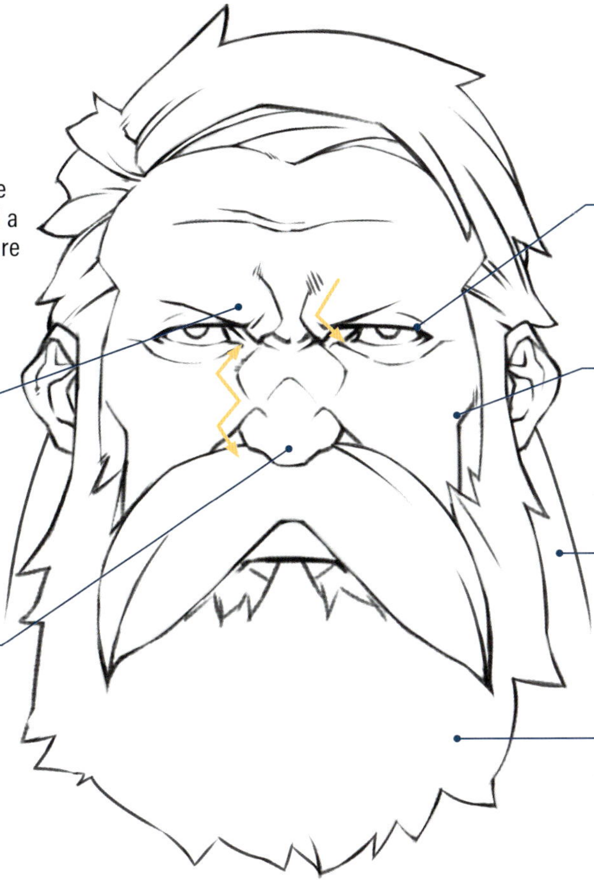

Brow Area

Deeply etched wrinkles between the eyebrows in a V-shape give a stern impression.

Nose

The area around the nose is drawn with zigzag lines. The deep-set eye area, nostrils and mouth wrinkles all connect.

Eyes

Eyes are deeply wrinkled, with drooping upper and lower eyelids.

Cheekbones

Sunken cheeks due to age reveal a strong bone structure.

Neck

The muscles of the neck and shoulders are so developed that the neck muscles are visible from below the ears, even from the front.

Beard

A shaggy beard conveys a strong character that matches the powerful physique.

Facial Variations

Ogre

An ogre with a body beyond human proportions. It has distinct features like horns and fangs. Other characteristics, like larger ears and thicker lips, are also slightly exaggerated to emphasize the character's unique traits.

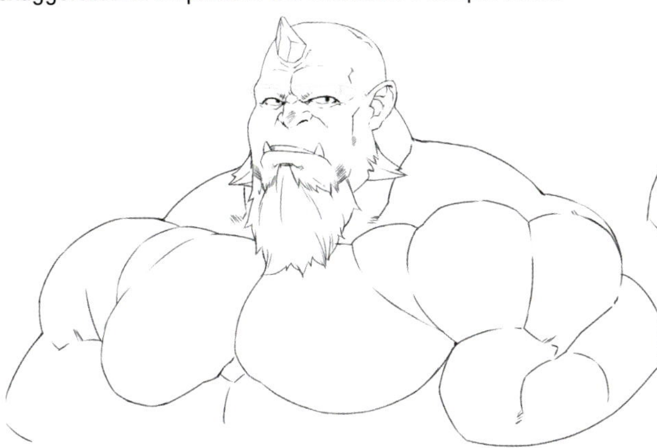

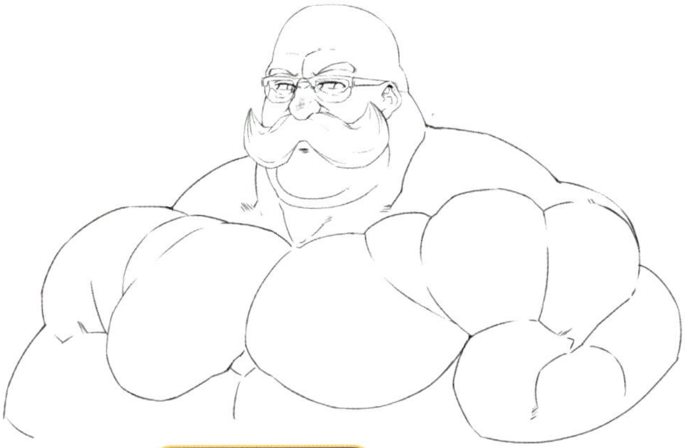

Senior Citizen

A beefy old character with a large, bulbous nose. Additionally, a double chin creates a soft outline, giving a gentle impression.

Wearing Formal Clothes

To maintain the monster-physique's uniqueness in a suit, various adjustments are necessary. Here, the suit is drawn to look very tight, with the exaggerated contours of the muscles showing through. This helps keep the character's distinctive look and prevents the overall impression from becoming flat.

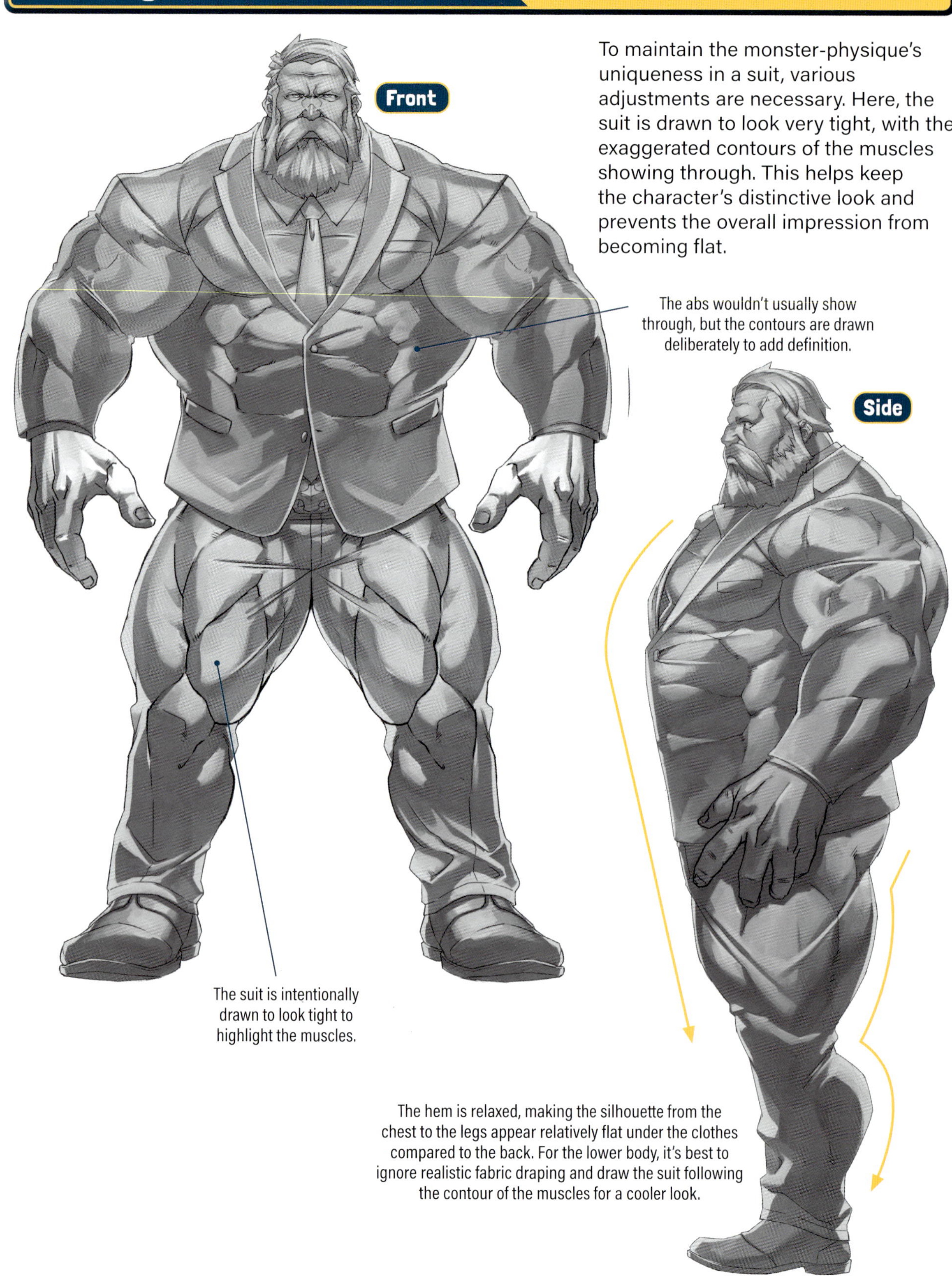

Illustrator Insights

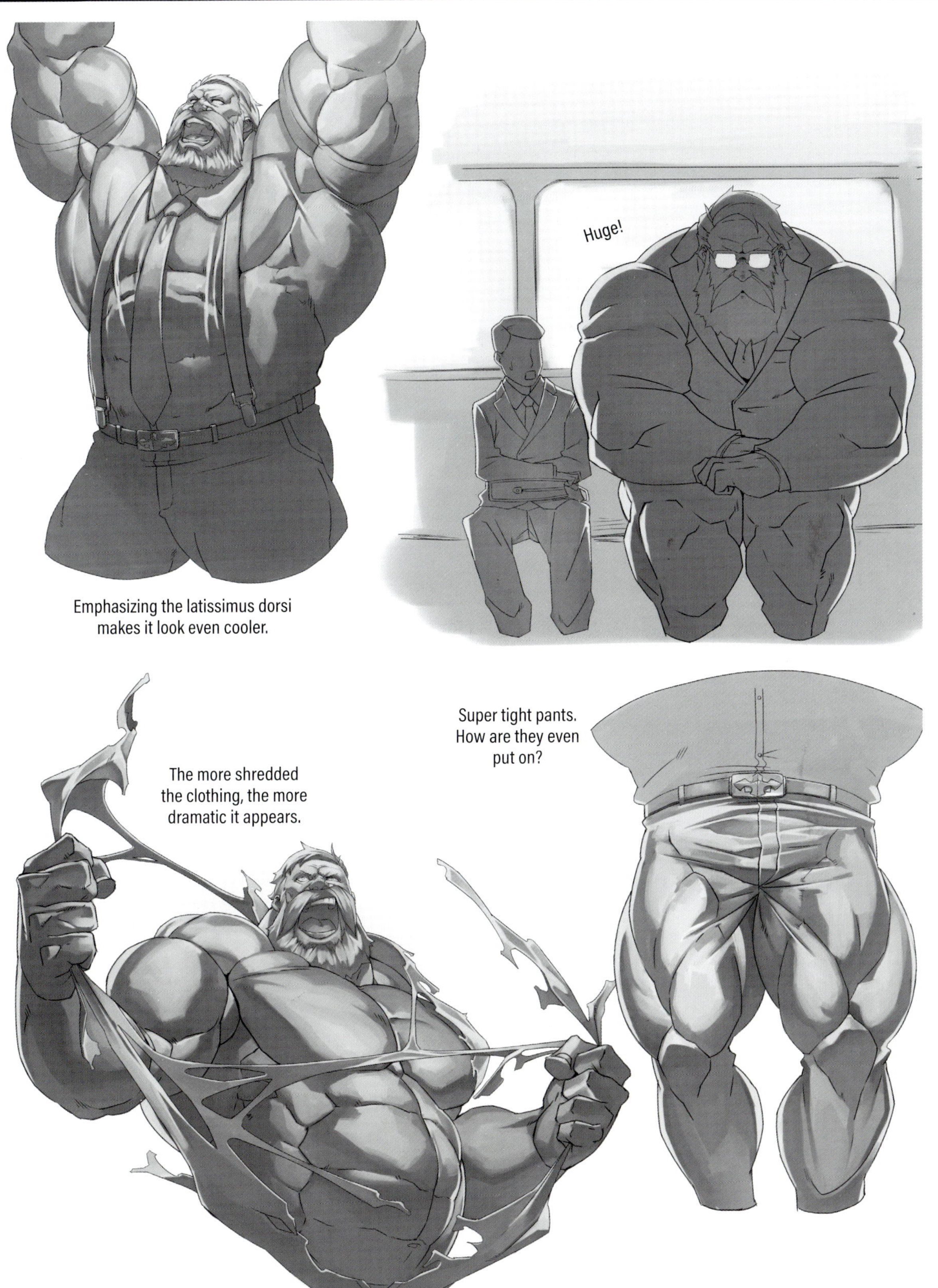

Emphasizing the latissimus dorsi makes it look even cooler.

KiKi (キキ)

Since 2017, I have been working as a freelance illustrator, mainly creating illustrations for social games and merchandise.

TwitterID: @udon_118
Pixiv URL: www.pixiv.net/users/3299532

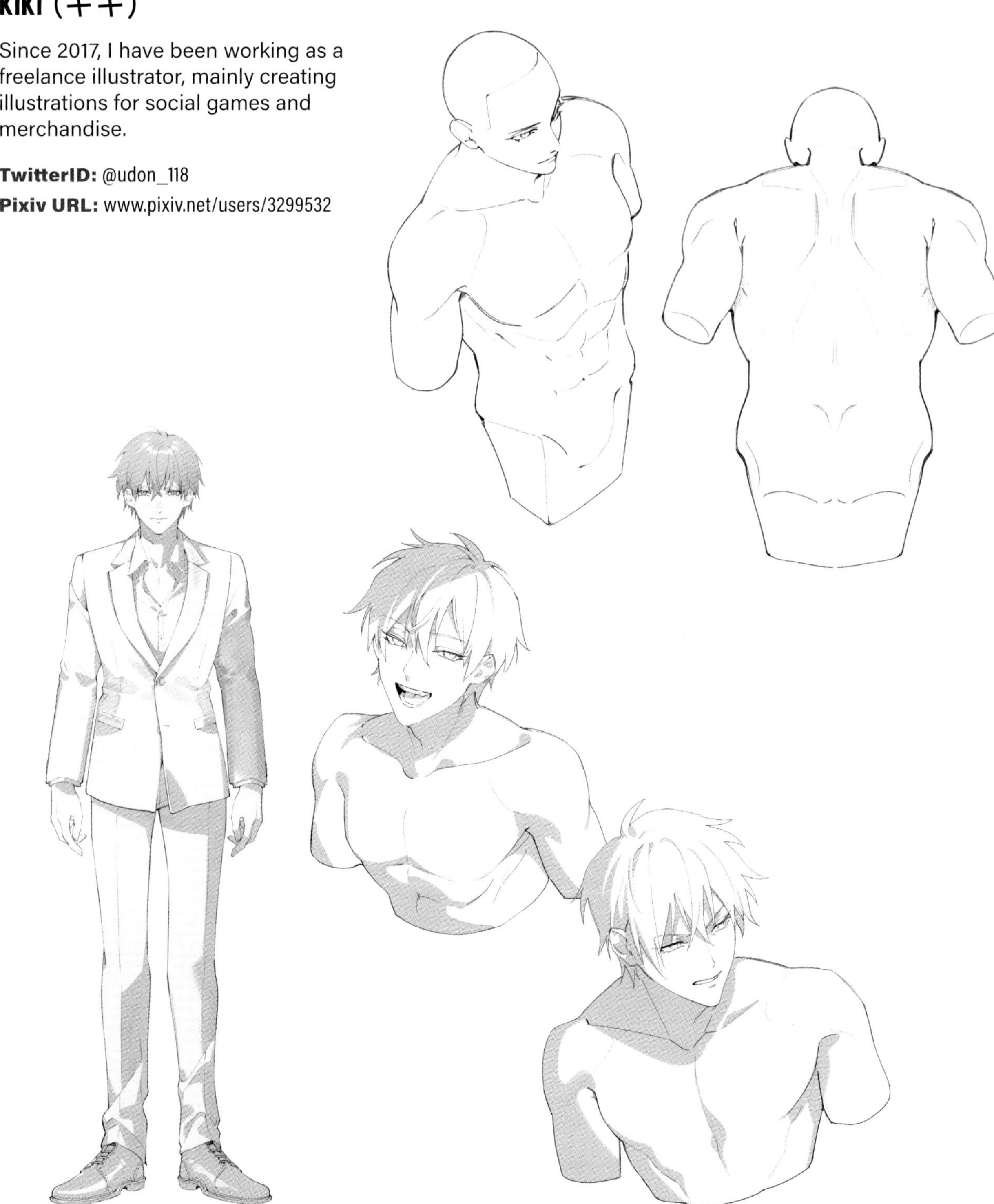

Kishi Ueno (上野 綺士)

I am an illustrator and manga artist. I loves suits, middle-aged men, muscles and penguins. I'm currently promoting my anthropomorphic penguin manga *Penguin Gentleman* (KADOKAWA). I also work on character design and illustration projects. It was fun drawing lots of muscles for this book!

TwitterID: @reisei_zero

Website: nostar-nolife.tumblr.com

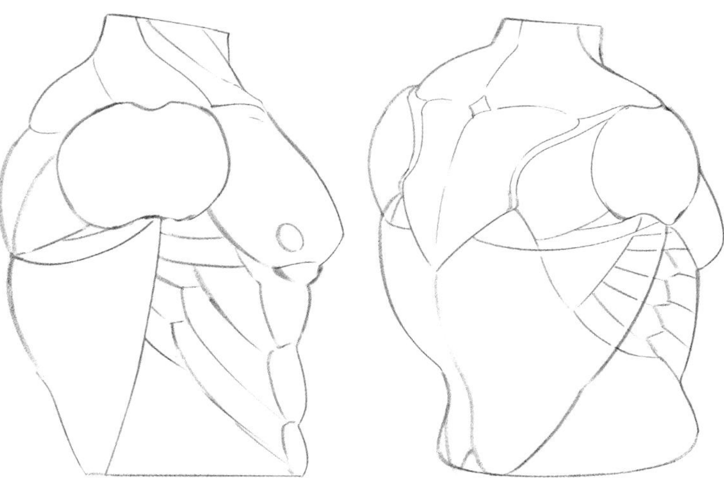

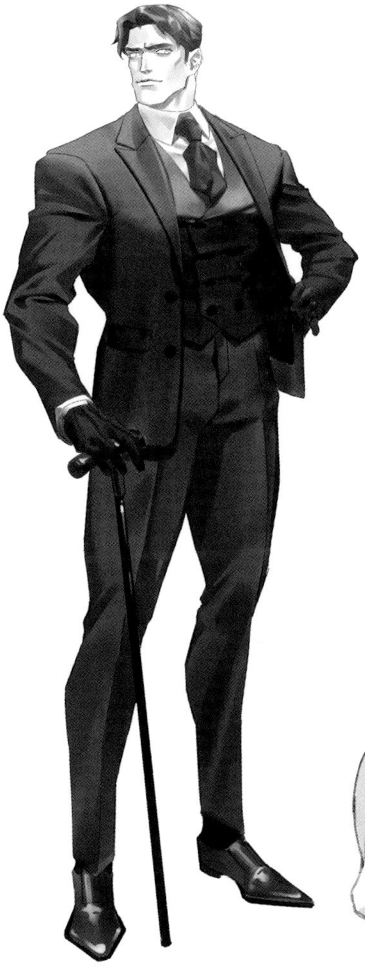

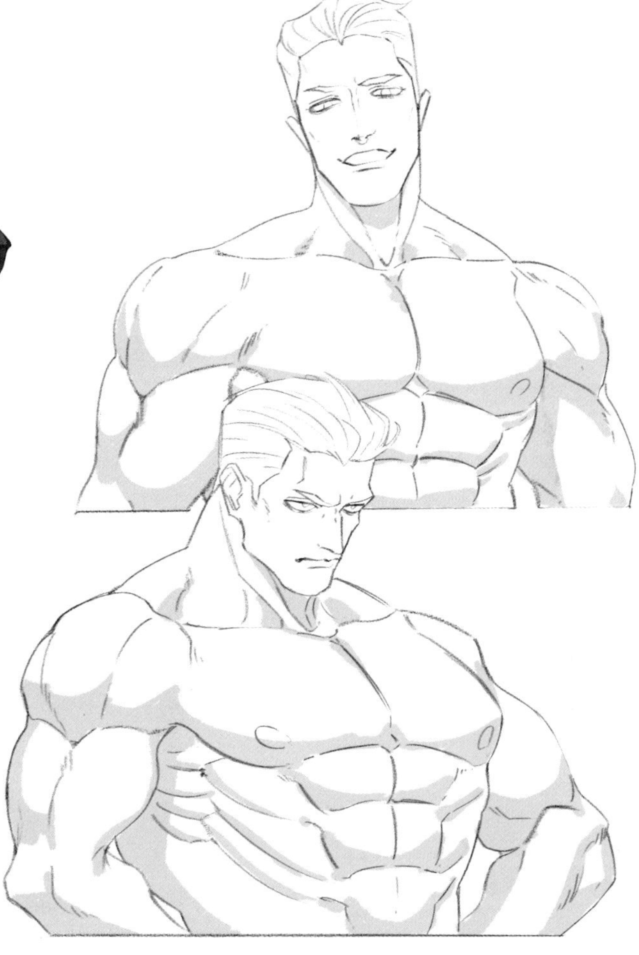

GomTang（ゴムタン）

I am an illustrator who deeply loves beards and muscles. Primarily, I design characters, and in recent years, I have worked on character designs for smartphone game apps.

TwitterID: @GomTang_P

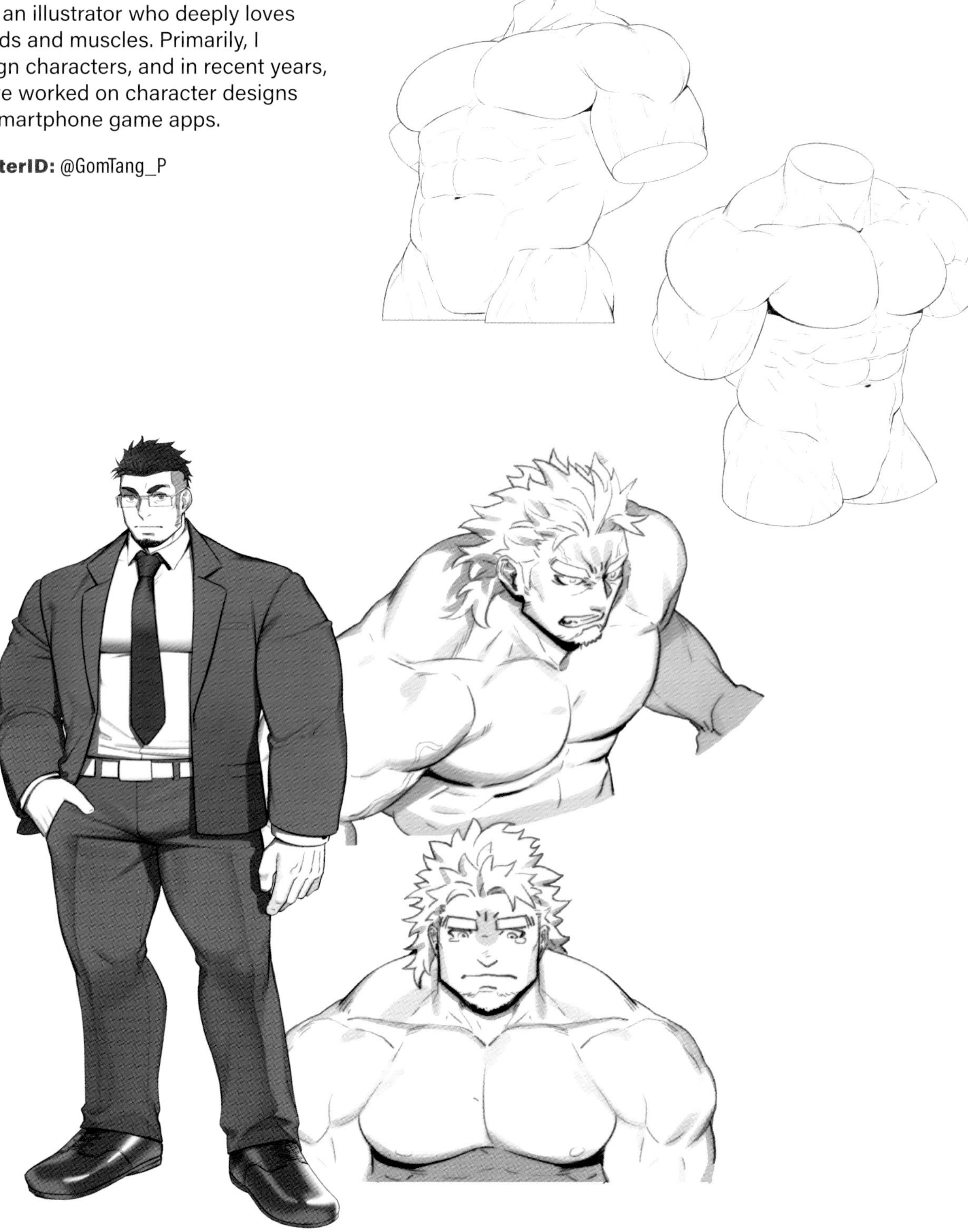

Syu Itadori (虎杖 鷲)

I draw intense, muscle-focused illustrations. But I'm not very muscular myself! Nice to meet you!

TwitterID: @Itadori_syu
Pixiv URL: www.pixiv.net/users/4246970
Website: higumaita.jimdofree.com

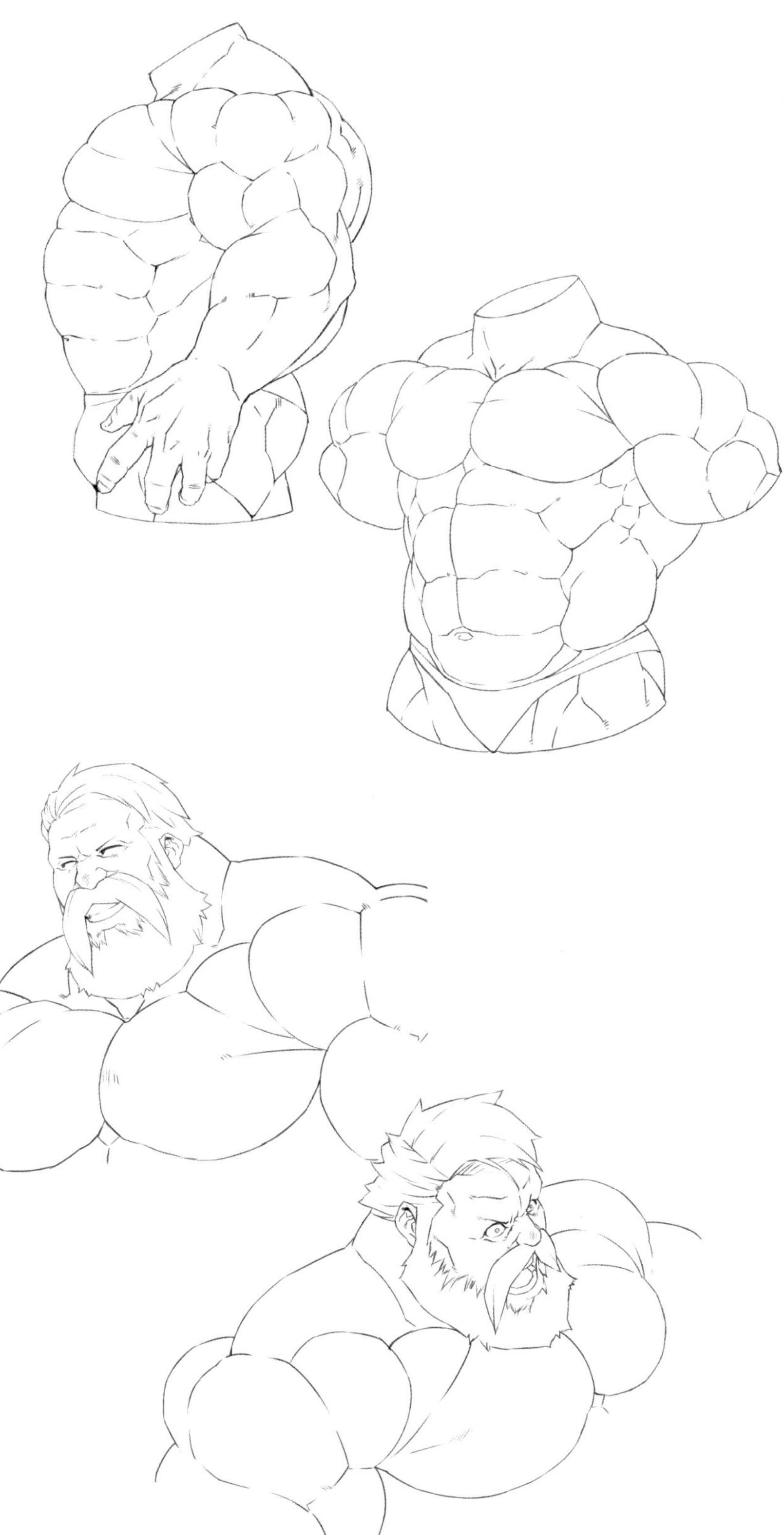

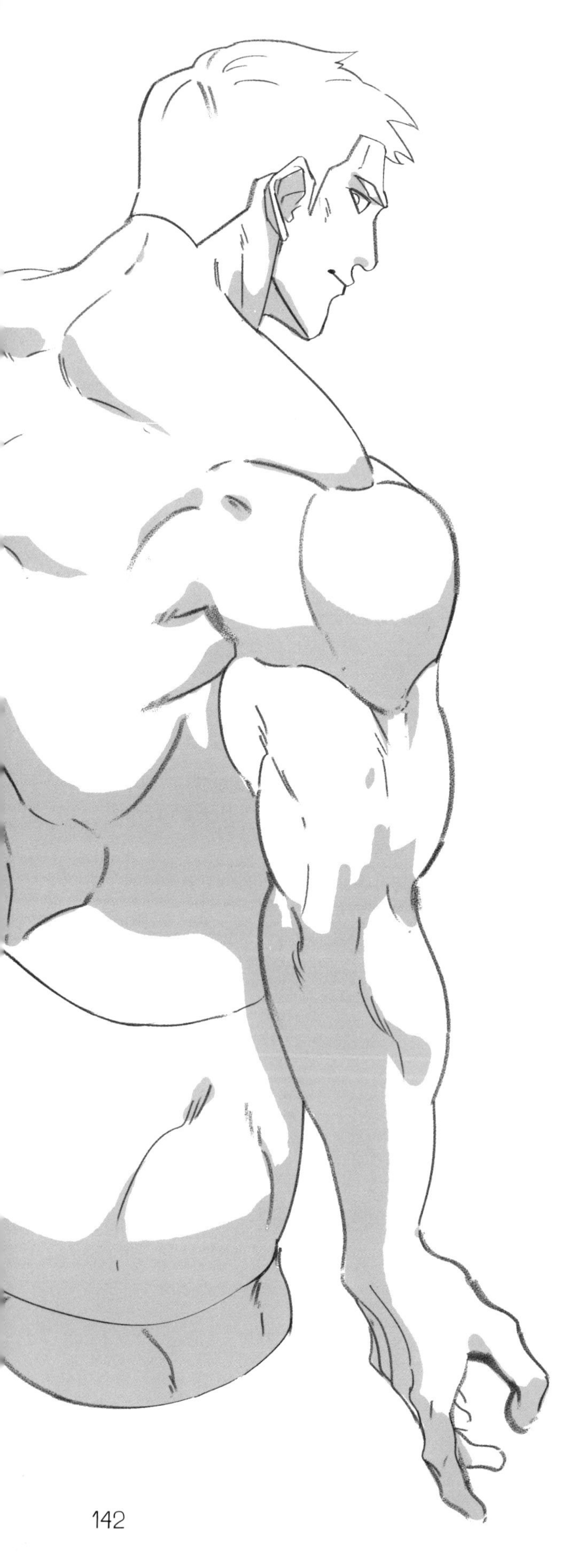

References

- *Anatomy For Sculptors, Japanese Edition* by Uldis Zarins, Sandis Kondrats (Born Digital) (ISBN: 978-4-8624-6360-9)
- *Sokka's Art Anatomy Notes* by Sok Jonghyun (Ohmsha) (ISBN: 978-4-2745-0715-1)
- *Drawing the Ultimate Muscular Body* (Morpho Anatomy Drawing Mini Series) by Michel Lauricella (Graphic-Sha) (ISBN: 978-4-7661-3493-3)
- *Quick and Useful! How to Draw Muscles* by Jun Sekizaki (Ichijinsha) (ISBN: 978-4-7580-1420-5)
- *Learn Structure and Movement to Improve Your Skills! How to Draw Muscles: Basic Lessons* (Super Drawing Series) by Kazuo Yorikane (Genkosha) (ISBN: 978-4-7683-0707-6)
- *Art Anatomy Taught Through Sketches* by Kota Kato (Genkosha) (ISBN: 978-4-7683-1410-4)

"Books to Span the East and West"

Tuttle Publishing was founded in 1832 in the small New England town of Rutland, Vermont [USA]. Our core values remain as strong today as they were then—to publish best-in-class books which bring people together one page at a time. In 1948, we established a publishing outpost in Japan—and Tuttle is now a leader in publishing English-language books about the arts, languages and cultures of Asia. The world has become a much smaller place today and Asia's economic and cultural influence has grown. Yet the need for meaningful dialogue and information about this diverse region has never been greater. Over the past seven decades, Tuttle has published thousands of books on subjects ranging from martial arts and paper crafts to language learning and literature—and our talented authors, illustrators, designers and photographers have won many prestigious awards. We welcome you to explore the wealth of information available on Asia at **www.tuttlepublishing.com**.

Published by Tuttle Publishing, an imprint of Periplus Editions (HK) Ltd.

www.tuttlepublishing.com

ISBN 978-0-8048-5826-7

Tsuyoi Kinniku no Kakikata

29 28 27 26 25
10 9 8 7 6 5 4 3 2 1

Printed in China 2506EP

Distributed by:

North America, Latin America & Europe
Tuttle Publishing
364 Innovation Drive
North Clarendon
VT 05759-9436 U.S.A.
Tel: (802) 773-8930; Fax: (802) 773-6993
info@tuttlepublishing.com; www.tuttlepublishing.com

Japan
Tuttle Publishing
Yaekari Building 3rd Floor
5-4-12 Osaki Shinagawa-ku
Tokyo 141 0032
Tel: (81) 3 5437-0171; Fax: (81) 3 5437-0755
sales@tuttle.co.jp; www.tuttle.co.jp

Asia Pacific
Berkeley Books Pte. Ltd.
3 Kallang Sector, #04-01
Singapore 349278
Tel: (65) 6741-2178; Fax: (65) 6741-2179
inquiries@periplus.com.sg; www.tuttlepublishing.com

GPSR representative
Matt Parsons
matt.parsons@upi2mbooks.hr
UPI-2M PLUS d.o.o., Medulićeva 20
10000 Zagreb, Croatia

Check Out Some Other Manga Drawing Guides Available from Tuttle Publishing

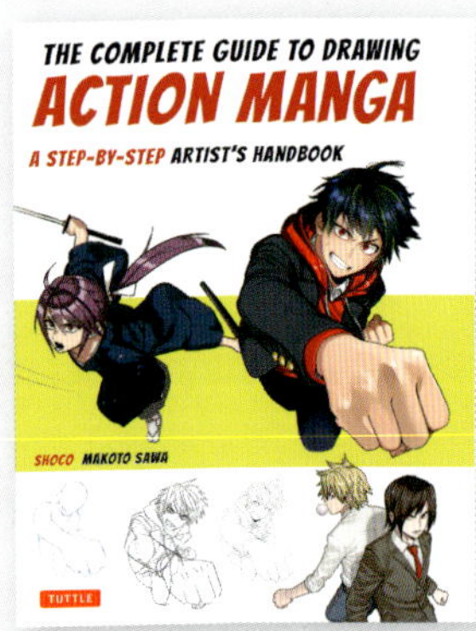

ISBN: 978-4-8053-1525-5

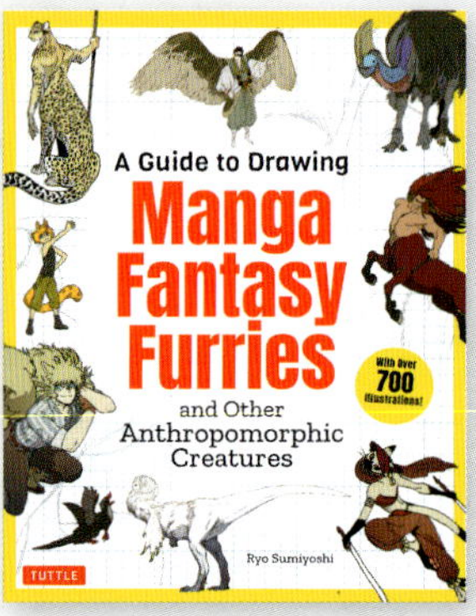

ISBN: 978-4-8053-1734-1

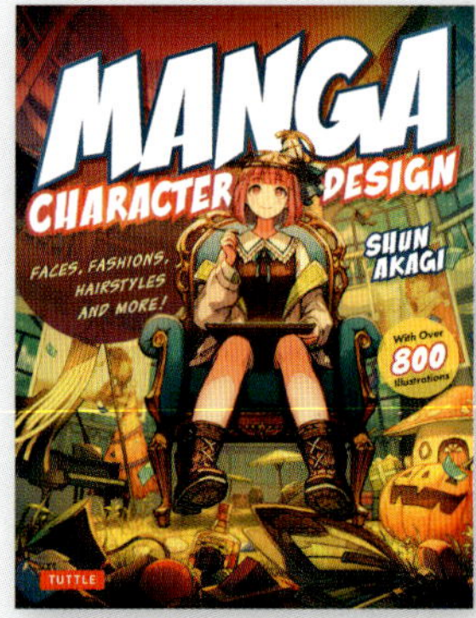

ISBN: 978-4-8053-1802-7

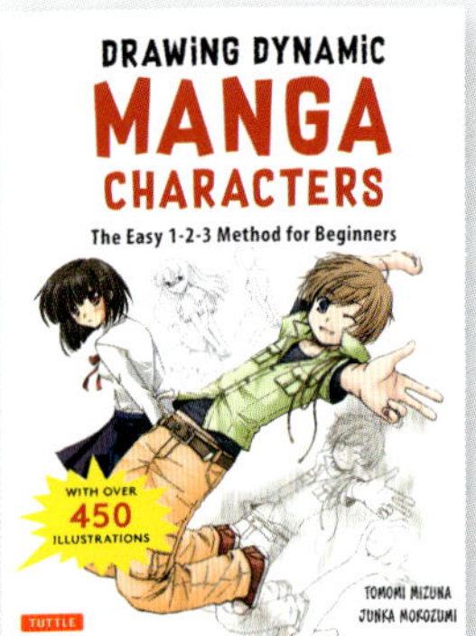

ISBN: 978-4-8053-1571-2

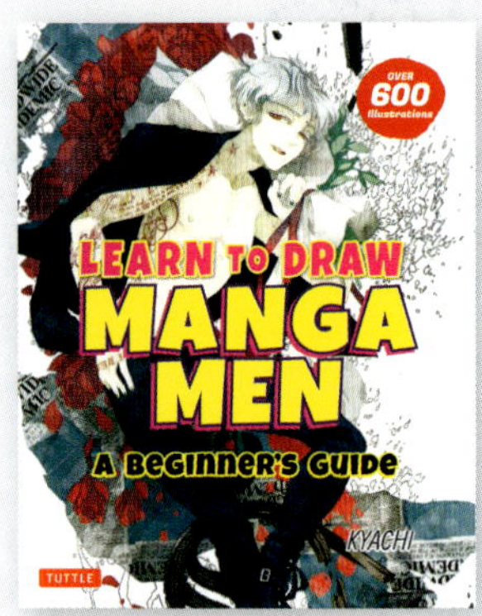

ISBN: 978-4-8053-1609-2

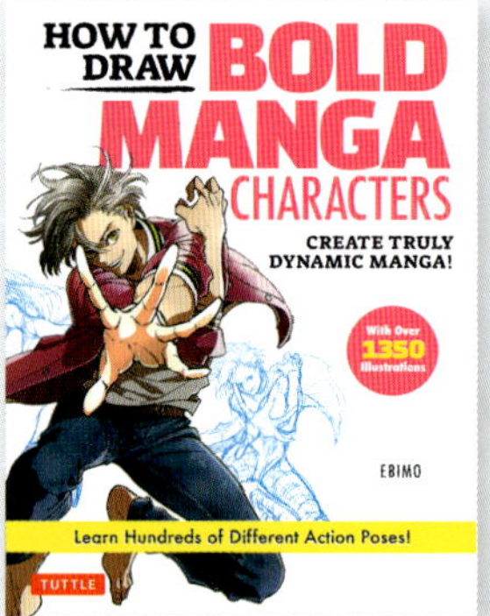

ISBN: 978-4-8053-1675-7

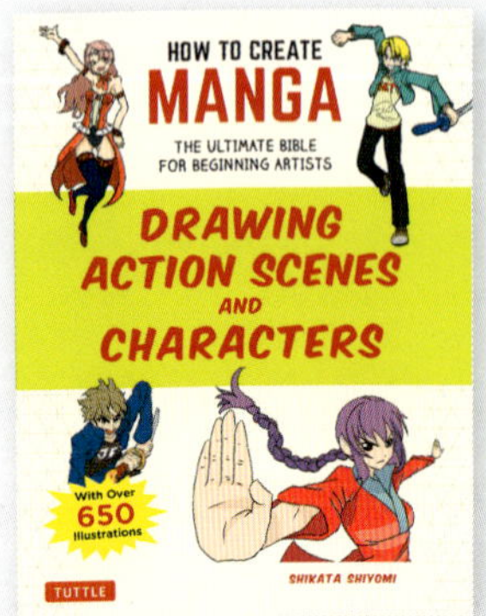

ISBN: 978-4-8053-1564-4

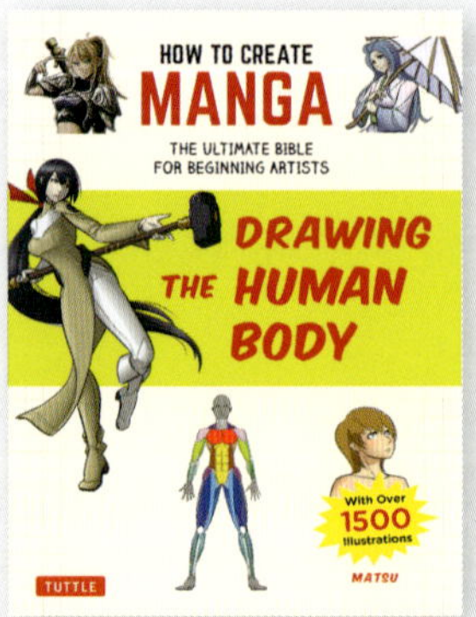

ISBN: 978-4-8053-1561-3

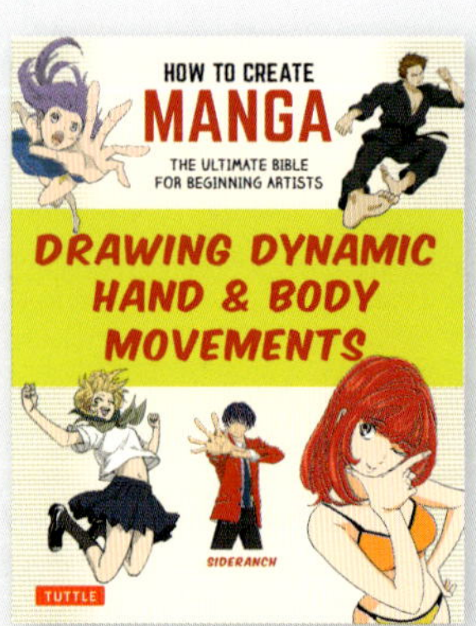

ISBN: 978-4-8053-1863-8